Ethology

D0234285

Professor Robert A. Hindé was educated at
Oundle School, St John's College, Cambridge,
and the Edward Grey Institute of Field
Ornithology, Oxford. He served as a pilot in RAF
Coastal Command during the Second World
War. He has been a member of the Cambridge
University Department of Zoology since 1950,
first as Curator of the Madingley Ornithological
Field Station (subsequently the Sub-Department
of Animal Behaviour) and more recently as
Honorary Director of the Medical Research
Council Unit on the Development and Integration
of Behaviour. He is a Fellow of St John's College,
Cambridge. His research has been concerned with
various aspects of behaviour and endocrinology
of birds, with the social development of monkeys,
and with social behaviour and interpersonal re-
lationships in man. He was appointed a Royal
Society Research Professor in 1963. He is a
Fellow of the Royal Society, a Foreign Honorary
Member of the American Academy of Arts and
Sciences, an Honorary Foreign Associate of the
National Academy of Sciences, and an Honorary
Fellow of the American Ornithologists' Union
and of the British Psychological Society. He holds
honorary doctorates at the Université Libre
(Brussels) and Nanterre (Paris). He is the author
of *Animal Behaviour*, *Biological Bases of Human
Social Behaviour*, and *Towards Understanding
Relationships*, as well as of numerous scientific
papers.

Masterguides

Ethology, Robert A. Hinde
Religion, Leszek Kolakowski
Social Anthropology, Edmund Leach

Forthcoming titles

Sociology, Daniel Bell
Developmental Psychology, Jerome Bruner
Law, Ronald Dworkin
Macroeconomics, Wynne Godley
Sociolinguistics, Dell Hymes
Language and Poetry, Roman Jakobson
Music, Joseph Kerman
Cognitive Psychology, George Miller
Linguistic Philosophy, John Searle
Moral Philosophy, Bernard Williams

Ethology

Its nature and relations with other sciences

Robert A. Hinde

Fontana Paperbacks

First published by Fontana Paperbacks 1982
Copyright © Robert A. Hinde 1982

Set in Lasercomp Times

A hardback edition is available from Oxford
University Press.

Made and printed in Great Britain by
William Collins Sons & Co. Ltd, Glasgow

TO W. H. THORPE

with gratitude and respect
in his eightieth year.

Contents

Acknowledgements

This book arose from an invitation to give the Niko Tinbergen Lecture to the Association for the Study of Animal Behaviour: I am grateful to that Association for their agreement to its publication in an extended form. Much of the writing was done whilst I held an appointment as Hitchcock Professor in the University of California. My thanks are due to Professors S. Glickman and P. Licht, Chairmen of the Psychology and Zoology Departments at Berkeley, for their wonderful hospitality. In addition my work has been supported by the Royal Society, the Medical Research Council and the Grant Foundation.

I am grateful to a number of colleagues for critical comments on this manuscript. Nick Davies and Joan Stevenson-Hinde read the whole, and I am especially grateful to them for their help. I am also indebted to Pat Bateson, Napoleon Chagnon, Gabriel Horn, Nick Humphrey, John Hutchison, Elizabeth Lack, Peter Marler, Fernando Nottebohm, Steven Schulman and Richard Wrangham for their comments on particular sections.

12 *Acknowledgements*

Grateful acknowledgement is made to Priscilla Barrett for drawing figures 1, 3, 11, 12a, 17, 18, 19 and 22.

For kind permission to reproduce the following figures, the author is grateful to the authors and publishers.

Fig. 4, G. Baerends and J. Kruijt in *Constraints on Learning*, eds. R. Hinde and J. Stevenson-Hinde (Academic Press, 1973).

Fig. 5, N. Miller in *Psychology: a Study of a Science*, ed. S. Koch (McGraw Hill, 1959).

Fig. 6, N. Tinbergen in *The Study of Instinct* (Oxford University Press, 1951).

Fig. 7, G. Baerends *et al.* in *Behaviour*, *8* (Brill, Leiden, 1955).

Fig. 8, D. McFarland and R. Sibly in *Anim. Behav.*, *20* (Ballière Tindall, 1972).

Fig. 9, D. McFarland and R. Sibly in *Phil. Trans. Roy. Soc.*, *27* (Royal Society, 1975).

Fig. 10, D. McFarland in *Adv. Study Behav.*, *5* (Academic Press, 1974).

Fig. 12, T. Halliday in *Anim. Behav.*, *24* (Ballière Tindall, 1976).

Fig. 13, G. Baerends in *Anim. Behav.*, *24* (Ballière Tindall, 1976).

Fig. 15, W. Thorpe in *Bird Song* (Cambridge University Press, 1961).

Fig. 16, Y. Spencer-Booth and R. Hinde in *J. Child Psychol. & Psychiat.*, *7* (Pergamon Press, 1967).

Fig. 20, K. Lorenz in *Journal für Ornithologie* (Friedländer, 1941).

Fig. 21, D. Lack in *Darwin's Finches* (Cambridge University Press, 1947).

Fig. 23, E. Steel in *Anim. Behav.*, *27* (Ballière Tindall, 1979).

Fig. 24a, P. Slater in *Sex Hormones and Behaviour* (Edward Arnold, 1978).

Fig. 25, F. Nottebohm in *J. exp. Zool.*, *177* (Wistar Institute, 1971).

Fig. 26, P. Bateson in *Biochem. Soc. Trans.*, *2*.

Fig. 27, P. Bateson in *Constraints and Learning*, eds. R. Hinde and J. Stevenson-Hinde (Academic Press, 1973).

Figs. 29 and 30, J. van Hooff in *Non-verbal Communication*, ed. R. Hinde (Cambridge University Press, 1972).

Preface

Ethology is an approach to the study of animal behaviour which, though having roots in the work of the nineteenth- and early twentieth-century naturalists (Thorpe, 1979), has developed rapidly during the last three decades. My principal aim here is to convey its flavour by indicating the sort of problems with which ethologists are concerned and the ways in which they tackle them.

In pursuing this aim I have not tried to convey an impression of the diversity of animal behaviour, and must leave to the non-ethological reader's imagination the excitement, the spirit of adventure and the humility felt by every investigator confronted with that diversity. Nor have I tried to review or synthesize the considerable body of knowledge about animal behaviour now available. Rather I have focused on specific examples, hoping that those already involved in the field will be able to transpose the issues I raise into the contexts of their own problems, while non-ethologists will be able to survey the area without the need to acquire too great a factual background. My choice of examples has inevitably been a personal one, and I would not expect all ethologists to select similarly.

I have sought first to convey the nature of 'core' ethology, and to describe some of the ways in which it is currently being developed. However I have also devoted considerable space to the overlap zones between ethology and other sciences. I have felt justified in the latter course in part because surveys of ethology already exist;* in part because I

* See e.g., Tinbergen (1951), Lorenz (Collected papers, 1970) and Thorpe (1963) for the earlier work; Manning (1979) for an excellent introductory survey; and Hinde (1970) for a now somewhat dated

believe these overlap zones contain some of the more important growing points of ethology, but principally because they illustrate special characteristics of ethology, and perhaps throw light on the development of science in general. This last issue requires a digression.

Most universities are organized into departments defined by the areas of knowledge with which they are concerned – psychology, biology, biochemistry, and so on. Within those departments the corridors may have even more specific labels – developmental psychology or entomology, for instance. This is functional: each area of science can develop its own tools, its own techniques, even its own rules of evidence to suit the nature and complexity of its subject matter. And such a system permits those who work on related problems and speak similar scientific languages to interact with each other. They may develop a sense of common purpose, and a camaraderie, that are conducive to good research. However, the camaraderie, the sense of belonging to an in-group, may be associated with a feeling of superiority over or antipathy to those in the next corridor or department: psychologists may label the physiologists reductionists, and the physiologists may see the psychologists as woolly. Competition between departments for resources can exacerbate such attitudes.

At the same time, however, some of the most interesting developments take place at the boundaries between disciplines. If I may revive a simile I have used previously in another context, one can picture science as like an *Amoeba*, its pseudopodia* representing the disciplines, growing by engulfing areas of ignorance. Sometimes the items most readily engulfed are those already between two pseudopodia – the interdisciplinary areas. And as it grows and engulfs new

---

synthesis of ethology and comparative psychology. See also Alcock (1975) and Eibl Eibesfeldt (1975) for different viewpoints.
* Although technical terms have for the most part been avoided, in many cases this would have involved circumlocutions which would not have contributed to clarity. A brief glossary is provided (p. 277).

items, the shape and structure of the *Amoeba* changes –
pseudopodia coalesce and new ones bud out. Attempts to
recognize or promote such changes in the shape and structure
of science are sometimes codified by new labels – 'developmental biology' or 'psycholinguistics'. But the interdisciplinary areas, though of great potential growth, often face
special problems – problems of communication between
scientists, of reconciling standards, of fashioning mutually
useful tools, and even of obtaining a share of the funds
traditionally divided up amongst the parent disciplines.

The early ethologists, notably Niko Tinbergen and
Konrad Lorenz, were not carving out a new set of problems,
but pioneering a new approach to old ones – problems that
were already being studied in established disciplines.
Perhaps for that reason there are still very few departments
of ethology, and most ethologists work within traditional
departments. The majority are in departments of biology,
but there are now ethological groups within departments of
psychology, veterinary studies, physiology, psychiatry and
several others. In these groups exciting developments are
taking place. The opening up of new problems, and of new
approaches to old ones, the clash of convergent theoretical
perspectives, lead to progress in research.

These interdisciplinary endeavours are in fact the fruition
or continuation of a trend present in ethology for three
decades. In *The Study of Instinct*, published in 1951 but
written some years earlier, Niko Tinbergen stressed the close
relations which ethology had and must have with other
branches of science. At that time he mentioned specifically
psychology, physiology, ecology, sociology, taxonomy and
evolution. A few years later, when trying to write a survey of
ethology for a volume concerned with 'General systematic
formulations' in psychology (Hinde, 1959), I felt that these
relations with other disciplines were among the most
important aspects of ethology. It seemed that the vitality of
ethology depended not so much on attempts to build a self-
contained system of the type then fashionable in psychology,
but on 'attempts to establish bridgeheads for liaison both

with workers in peripheral fields and also with investigators of the same phenomena at a different level, such as physiologists and biochemists'. I continued, 'Its success must be judged by the extent to which those bridgeheads are secured.'

I have taken the unseemly course of quoting my own words to expose, and in order that I might have a chance now to reject, the naive and militaristic metaphor I then used. Apparently I saw ethologists as an in-group storming the bastions of the established disciplines. We shall see in later chapters that aggressive overtures are common on inter-disciplinary boundaries, and I erred in that way myself. In the long run, of course, liaison must depend not on a territorial invasion, as I implied, but on a mutual welcome for those who cross no-man's-land.

But before focusing on these overlap zones with other disciplines, it is proper to examine the central core. No interdisciplinary achievements would have been possible were it not for the methods, concepts and principles derived from the classic ethological studies of animal behaviour for its own sake – studies of jackdaws and greylag geese, of sticklebacks and herring gulls, of fiddler crabs and honey bees and a host of other species. Such studies must be continuously pursued, both for their own intrinsic value and because they may provide the bases for further inter-disciplinary liaisons in the decades ahead.

PART I

Core Ethology

1. The Nature of Ethology

(i) Ethology's biological roots: the four whys

Scientists of a number of types are interested in behaviour – psychologists, psychiatrists, sociologists, veterinarians, physiologists and representatives of a number of other disciplines. What, it may be asked, is special about the ethological approach? The answer cannot be given in a neat definition, for ethologists are not differentiated from other students of behaviour by the subject matter they study or by the particular problems they tackle. Rather ethologists are united through the sharing of a number of orienting attitudes. In this section we shall discuss those attitudes in some detail, using them to convey the flavour of ethological work.

A basic issue is that the early ethologists were biologists. They were thus aware of the diversity of animal species, and of the even greater diversity of their behaviour. This has influenced the methods they use, the questions they ask, and the descriptive and explanatory concepts they employ.

For example, ethologists follow a biological tradition in attempting to start their analyses from a secure base of description. And as biologists thinking in terms of evolution through natural selection, they are aware that an understanding of the diversity in the animal kingdom requires that the behaviour of each species be seen in relation to the environmental context to which it has been adapted. Though only a small proportion of ethologists work in a natural situation, nearly all attempt to relate their research to the environment to which the species they are studying was adapted.

Beyond that, the diversity of phenomena to be explained means that detailed analytical study is possible in only a tiny proportion of instances. Nevertheless the ethologist must seek for principles with at least some degree of generality. The range of validity of any principle is likely to be inversely related to the precision with which it is stated. But how can that range be assessed? One answer is to pursue analytical study of one type of behaviour in one situation in one species, and to assess the range of validity of the conclusions from more superficial study of other behaviour, situations and species. Ethologists adopt both approaches.

Species diversity is important in yet another way. Just as there are many different ways to build a bridge, so have animals solved the problems to which they are exposed in different ways (Pantin, 1950). A number of ethological concepts refer, like 'bridge', to the solution of a problem, but not to a particular means to that end. In this they resemble terms like 'leg' or 'eye': there is no suggestion that the legs of caterpillars and cows, or the eyes of ants and antelopes, involve similar structures. Across a range of species such functional labels permit generalizations about the relations between different kinds of behaviour, but not about the precise nature of the machinery on which they depend. But in particular cases they can pave the way for detailed examinations of mechanisms. The necessity for the investigator to be conscious of where he is on this continuum between 'software' and 'hardware' explanations will be apparent.

But perhaps the most important consequence of ethology's biological heritage concerns the sorts of questions in which ethologists are interested. Most non-ethological students of behaviour are concerned either with its immediate causes, or with its development. Ethologists admit two further problems – that of the function of behaviour, 'What is it for?', and that of its evolution, 'How did this behaviour evolve?' (see Huxley, 1942; Tinbergen, 1963).

Consider a simple example. Suppose you were asked,

'Why does your thumb move in a different way from the other fingers?' You might give an answer in terms of the anatomy of the hand – the differences in skeletal structure and muscle attachments between the thumb and the other fingers: that would be an answer concerned with the immediate causation of thumb movement. You might give an answer in terms of the hand's embryology, describing how, as the finger rudiments developed, one came to have a different structure from the others. Or you might give a functional answer – an opposable thumb makes it easier for us to pick things up, climb trees, and so on. Or finally you might say that we are descended from monkey-like creatures, and monkeys have opposable thumbs, so of course we do too. This would be an answer in terms of evolutionary origin. All of these answers would be correct: no one would be complete.

In the same way, ethologists are interested in questions of all four types about behaviour. Indeed they believe that, although logically distinct and independent, questions concerning immediate causation, development, function and evolution are sometimes inter-fertile.

(ii) Aspects of chaffinch behaviour

To illustrate how these four whys of causation, development, function and evolution arise from observations of animals in their natural surroundings, we may consider research on a particular species, the Chaffinch (*Fringilla coelebs*). Although some of this work is now thirty years old, it illustrates the manner in which descriptive field studies throw up problems for analysis both at the behavioural and at more detailed levels.

Chaffinches are small sexually dimorphic song-birds, common in Western Europe. Marler (1956a) studied them in a wood and the surrounding fields near Cambridge. Part of his work involved establishing the basic natural history of the species. During the winter chaffinches feed and roost in flocks, but in early spring the males confine their activities to a particular area, defending it from other males. The fighting is at first centred on certain perches which the males use as song posts. The male's song attracts females. When a female first arrives in a male's territory she may be threatened, but the male soon switches to courtship. After some days or weeks the female starts to build a nest, in which about five eggs are laid. These are incubated by the female, though the male may give some assistance in feeding the young. In late summer the birds undergo a moult, during which they behave very cryptically, before joining the winter flocks.

Marler provided a detailed description of the various activities involved, including both maintenance activities (feeding, preening etc.) and the social behaviour involved in flocking, territorial defence and reproduction. Special attention was paid to the displays used in social communication, for when one studies a new species, these are often extraordinarily difficult to understand. The behaviour of a male chaffinch facing obliquely towards a female, his body horizontal and tilted so as to direct the white wing patch to the female, is at first incomprehensible. But, in keeping with work on other species, Marler showed that such displays can be understood on the assumption that (a) the displaying bird is ambivalent and (b) the display has the effect of influencing the behaviour of the other individual. For example, a 'head forward' threat is used in encounters over food in the winter. Some of the components of this display, such as the sleeking of the head feathers and slight raising of the wings, are linked with a tendency to attack the rival; others, such as the sleeking of the body feathers and the flexing of the legs, with a tendency to flee.

The courtship postures are even more complex (fig. 1). Early in the season the male is dominant to the female, and the obliquely oriented 'crouched lopsided' posture differs only slightly from the 'head-forward' threat posture. At this time the female often adopts a fluffed submissive posture. As time goes on the male ceases to be dominant, and the female may exploit this by attacking him. When the time for copulation approaches the female begins to adopt a crouched soliciting posture, and the male approaches intermittently in a hesitant fashion, his body upright, edging towards her and then moving away until finally he flies up and on to her back. Many copulation attempts are unsuccessful, usually because the male flees at the last moment and/or the female attacks him.

This sequence can be understood in terms of a gradual change in the nature of the male's ambivalence. At first he has tendencies to attack and flee from the female, with the former predominating, and only a small tendency to behave sexually. As the latter increases, his tendency to behave aggressively diminishes relative to his tendency to flee from the female, so that just before copulation the main conflict is between tendencies to flee from and behave sexually with the female. Interestingly, after dismounting the male often gives the alarm call usually evoked by an avian predator (see also Hinde, 1953a). This postulation of conflicting 'tendencies' to explain complex behaviour shown during threat and courtship is based on purely observational evidence: we shall discuss the nature of that evidence later (pp. 67–9). First, however, we may sketch some of the ways in which the analysis of chaffinch behaviour has been pursued experimentally.

If the displays used in threat and courtship do in fact function in communication between individuals, we may ask just which characters are important. Two aspects of the visual stimuli used in social behaviour were investigated experimentally. One was the 'soliciting' posture that the female adopts just before copulation. If males are confined individually in largish aviaries in the spring, and a female stuffed in the soliciting posture is placed inside, nearly half the males will mount the female almost immediately. If the female is in the normal perched posture, none do (Hinde, 1959b). Thus the adoption of this posture by the female is likely to elicit a particular response from the male.

The second issue is the colour difference between the sexes – males have pink breasts and females brownish-olive ones.

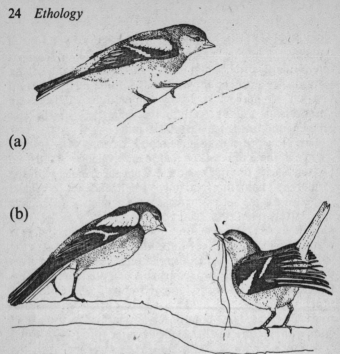

(a)

(b)

fig. 1. The courtship of the chaffinch.

a.   The male's courtship posture. The male is lateral to the female,
     and the white wing flash is directed towards her.
b.   The male's approach to the female. The female, carrying nest
     material, is soliciting with moderate intensity. The male walks
     hesitantly towards her, with wing flashes exposed.

This, coupled with the fact that males are dominant to
females in winter fighting, suggested to Marler (1955) that
the pink breast might be a threatening stimulus to other
individuals. He tested this by colouring the breasts of caged
females pink, and found that such females usually dominated normally coloured ones, and sometimes even dominated males. Thus a bird with a pink breast apparently elicits
avoidance by other individuals more readily than a bird with
a brownish-olive one.

(c)

c. Copulation.

However, Marler (1956b) also showed that the male breast colour elicits attack. Working with small groups of captive birds, he placed two food sources in each aviary. By varying the distance between the food sources, he was able to determine the distance at which one feeding bird would tolerate another on 50 per cent of occasions. This distance was about 7 cm for females, and 21–25 cm for males. In mixed flocks, males allowed females to come closer than males before attacking them. However, females with dyed breast feathers were treated as though they were males. Such disguised females attacked normal males and females as naturally coloured females would do, but responded to another dyed female as though it was a male. Thus the data indicate that the male breast colour may elicit both attack and withdrawal from other individuals: we find here a basis for the ambivalence postulated to underlie threat postures from observational evidence (see above). This finding raises many interesting issues, to some of which we shall return (p. 219) and some of which are still unresolved.

Turning to a different problem, we have seen that the behaviour of the chaffinch changes with the season. In particular, territorial and reproductive behaviour increase in the spring: the bases of this change require investigation. In many vertebrates, male sexual behaviour depends largely on male sex hormones (androgens). Evidence that this is true also for chaffinches has been obtained by injecting male chaffinches with a particular sex hormone – testosterone propionate. Treated males responded more aggressively to a live male introduced into the aviary, showed more sexual behaviour to a live female or to a female stuffed in the soliciting posture, and were more likely to sing, than were untreated males. While such experiments strongly suggested that sex hormones are important in the induction of male sexual behaviour, they also indicated that the particular hormone preparation used was by itself not fully adequate: males in normal spring condition showed even more marked sexual behaviour to a female stuffed in the soliciting posture, and were more likely to sing, than testosterone treated birds.

But given that reproductive behaviour depends on sex hormones we must ask whether the seasonal changes in behaviour are due to seasonal changes in the secretion of hormones, or to changes in their effectiveness, or both. Much evidence from other species, including seasonal changes in the size of the hormone-secreting gonads, show that the former is important. Some support in the case of the chaffinch came from the demonstration that the male's beak colour, which changes from dull pink to blue in the breeding season, could be similarly changed by testosterone. With modern techniques it would be possible to show that the concentrations of circulating hormones do in fact change seasonally. This still leaves open the possibility of changes in responsiveness to hormones, an issue to be discussed later (p. 167).

The next question concerns what external factors determine the seasonal changes in hormone concentration. In line with work on other temperate zone species (Murton and Westwood, 1977) it was not difficult to show that changes in daylength were important. If males were confined in artificially lit cages, and the light was gradually increased, the males' beaks gradually turned blue, and some males started to sing. This is in accord with work on other species showing that the length of the day affects a part of the brain, the hypothalamus, which in turn causes the pituitary gland to secrete hormones, gonadotrophins, which in turn cause the gonads to increase in size and secrete sex hormones.

But once again, we must make reservations. First, longer daylengths may not be essential for reproductive development: some birds will start to sing if kept with only one or two hours' light a day if the treatment is continued for long enough (Hinde, 1959c). Second, longer daylengths may not be the only external variable that facilitates reproductive development: other environmental factors, such as temperature (Murton and Westwood, l.c.) may also be important. And third, longer daylengths may affect reproductive behaviour not only by increasing the levels of sex hormones: this will be discussed in chapter 8 (p. 167).

In addition to the specific stimuli which elicit particular responses or groups of responses, as discussed above, there are also environmental factors that affect the probability of reproductive behaviour in a more general way. In nature, the likelihood that a male chaffinch will sing and court females is much greater if he owns a territory. In captivity, males are more likely to sing if confined in a large cage than if in a small one, and are unlikely to sing if another more dominant individual is in the cage with them or even in an adjacent one.

Not all changes in responsiveness can be ascribed to changes in hormone secretion. For example early in the reproductive season, and to a lesser extent throughout its course, male chaffinches show short-term fluctuations in the probability that they will show reproductive behaviour. For a while they will sing from conspicuous song posts and attack any other male who encroaches on their territory, but a few minutes later they may feed alongside other birds in a flock. Such short-term changes in behaviour imply short-term changes in internal state – changes that are unlikely to be due to short-term changes in hormone concentration. They may be described as changes in 'mood'.

Some such changes can be ascribed to the consequences of showing particular types of behaviour. Thus if a male chaffinch mounts a dummy female in the soliciting posture, and the dummy is presented again on a later occasion, he is more likely to mount again the longer the interval between the presentations. The data indicate that recovery is virtually complete after about thirty minutes.

However, experiences with a particular stimulus object may also have longer-term consequences. Captive male chaffinches normally never mate with male dummies or with females stuffed in the normal perched position. But if such dummies are presented to a male who has had considerable experience of mounting soliciting female dummies presented in exactly the same way, they may be mounted and may even elicit ejaculation (Hinde, 1959c).

Another response of the chaffinch has been used for a more detailed study of such changes in responsiveness. When a chaffinch encounters a predator, such as an owl, it may sit and call vigorously, flicking its wings and tail as it does so. This 'mobbing' behaviour wanes with time. The calls can easily be counted, and experimental study of the course of this waning indicates that it is considerably more complex than appears at first sight. There is first a short 'warming-up' period, during which the response increases in strength. The response then wanes, but analysis indicates that the observed waning depends on interactions between a number of different internal processes, some tending to produce an increase in response strength and others a decrease, and producing effects which may be permanent or which may decay in periods ranging from fractions of a second to hours (Hinde, 1970).

So far we have been concerned with the immediate causation of behaviour. But field observation of the chaffinch poses also questions about behavioural development. The behaviour of the nestlings is quite different from that of the fledglings, and their behaviour differs in many ways from that of adults: how do these changes come about? Individuals differ in the songs that they sing: is this a consequence of learning? In what ways does an individual's experience affect its capacity and propensity to show the display movements characteristic of the species, and to respond appropriately to those of others? We shall see later (chapter 3) that problems of considerable complexity arise: the common sense view that some patterns of behaviour are 'instinctive' and independent of experience, whilst others are learned, can be highly misleading.

The data also present problems of function and evolution. What good does it do the male chaffinch to expend so much energy in defending a territory? Why does the chaffinch breed later than most of the blackbirds and earlier than the flycatchers breeding in the same area? Might it not do better to lay more than five eggs? Why do chaffinches divide up their time between the activities in their repertoire in just the way that they do? In seeking answers to such questions, ethologists are fortunate in having the integrating theory of evolution by natural selection. This prompts them to ask whether the behaviour they observe is such as to maximize the individual's chances of survival and reproduction. The vigour of territorial defence, variation in the number of eggs laid, even the fine details of alternations between activities make sense when seen as contributing to reproductive success (chapters 4 and 7).

Finally, if aspects of behaviour have become adapted in evolution to functional ends, what was the course of that evolution? Since the fossil record tells us rather little about the evolution of behaviour, many of the questions here are permanently unanswerable. However comparisons between the behaviour of living species permit some progress. We shall see later that it is possible to make reasonable hypotheses about, for instance, how the chaffinch's display movements evolved, and to use data about its behaviour to assess its evolutionary relationships to other apparently similar species (chapter 5).

The chaffinch is but one of many species whose behaviour is now known in some detail, and the behaviour of every species similarly poses questions of causation, development, function and evolution. The issues mentioned so far are, I hope, representative of those studied by ethologists, but the survey is far from complete. Some problems that arise when such issues are pursued are discussed in chapters 2–6. First, however, it is necessary to consider briefly the basic tasks of describing and classifying behaviour.

(iii) Description and classification

Ethologists regard a descriptive base as essential for tackling all the problems with which they are concerned. The tradition had its roots in the field studies of such men as Fabre, Selous, Eliot Howard, J. S. Huxley, Makkink and Vervey in the first three decades of this century, though the tone for post-1945 studies was perhaps most clearly set by the work of Tinbergen (1939), Lorenz (1935) and Nice (1943). Lorenz and Tinbergen contrasted their approach with that of contemporary experimental psychologists, who tended 'to concentrate on a few phenomena observed in a handful of species which were kept in impoverished environments, to formulate theories claimed to be general, and to proceed deductively by testing these theories experimentally' (Tinbergen, 1963, p. 411).

The problems of describing behaviour are considerable. Behaviour involves a continuous stream of events, and it is necessary to cut it up into chunks one can handle, to discard some items or aspects and to focus on others. Such selection is likely to be influenced by the problems to be tackled, and by preconceptions about the answers. Ethologists endeavour constantly to ensure that the selection is appropriate, and that initial biases will not affect the conclusions.

Two methods of description are available. 'Physical description' involves reference ultimately to the strength, duration and patterning of muscular contractions, though it is usually limited to patterns of limb or body movement. Terms such as 'soliciting posture' or 'cry' are shorthand terms for such descriptions. 'Descriptions by consequence' do not refer to particular patterns of movement but cover all patterns that lead, or could lead, to the result specified: 'Approaching the nest', or 'Hiding from the hawk' are examples.

Description by consequence often calls attention to important features of the behaviour that might be missed in physical description – for instance responsiveness to particular stimuli is implied by 'seeking for food'. But it also has dangers: it may be difficult to be sure whether a rat in a maze is approaching the goal box or escaping from the alley, and which description is chosen may affect the subsequent analysis.

Often the earlier phases of a behaviour sequence are characterized not by the movements shown, but by responsiveness to stimuli, and are thus more suitable for description by consequence. They are followed by phases in which particular types of behaviour occur, which are more susceptible to physical description. Thus a bird may hop from branch to branch, selectively responsive to caterpillars. In this phase the motor pattern, hopping, is one found in many other activities, but the behaviour is characterized by the selectivity in responsiveness. When a caterpillar is seen, a new movement appears, seizing. This also may be common to some other activities, such as picking up nest material. However, it provides stimuli for further more or less stereotyped activities, such as beating the caterpillar against the branch, or swallowing it. It is sometimes convenient to label the early phases as 'appetitive behaviour' and the later ones as 'consummatory' responses (Sherrington, 1906), but the distinction is by no means an absolute one (Hinde, 1953b).

Having described behaviour in a manner which permits

the grouping of instances as examples of the 'same' type of behaviour – for instance all 'soliciting postures' or all 'foraging', it is usually convenient to classify the types of behaviour. The four sorts of criteria most commonly used correspond to the ethologists' four 'whys'. Thus we may group together types of behaviour on the grounds that they share causal factors (e.g., all activities influenced by male sex hormone); that they were acquired in the same way (e.g., learned behaviour); that they lead to the same consequence (e.g., all activities involved in nest-building); or that they had similar evolutionary origins (e.g., all activities that are derived from 'intention movements', see p. 67). These systems of classification must not be confused. Often activities that have related consequences also share causal factors, but this is by no means always the case, and we must be clear whether we mean a causal or functional category when we use terms like 'sexual' or 'aggressive' behaviour.

It will be apparent that good descriptive work is not easy. Yet just as biology depends on the work of taxonomists and systematists, so does ethology depend on a taxonomy and systematics of behaviour.

2 The Study of Immediate Causation

(i) Levels of analysis

The question 'What causes the animal to behave in this way?' can be answered at a number of levels. For many purposes the behavioural level of analysis is adequate. If you observe a number of people queuing outside the closed door of a restaurant, peering in eagerly through the chinks in the shutters, clasping their stomachs and drooling at the lips, you might explain their behaviour by saying they were hungry. There are actually two stages involved here – you observe that several different types of behaviour are associated together, and you explain their occurrence by postulating an internal state, hunger. Your explanation would become even more probable if you were to learn that they had just got off a bus which had been marooned in a snow drift without supplies for two days. Although usually more sophisticated than this, many scientific explanations of behaviour remain at this level – a level that is adequate so long as, for instance, prediction and understanding are the main aims.

Such explanations can be regarded as 'software' explanations. They specify the relations between stimulus and response, between antecedent conditions and motivational states, between motivational states and behaviour, and between different sorts of behaviour, without specifying the hardware – the neural and other mechanisms on which those relations depend. Of course any particular item of behaviour may be influenced by many external stimuli, and by diverse and unrelated aspects of the individual's motivational state. Furthermore, external stimuli may affect the internal state (the smells coming through the restaurant door may increase the travellers' hunger) and the internal state may affect the effectiveness of stimuli (they were susceptible to the smells because they were hungry). Thus interactions of many sorts are possible, and no behaviour has a single cause – there is always a nexus of causality to be unravelled. In higher organisms that nexus may include internal representations of possible consequences of the behaviour (e.g., its goal), mechanisms to monitor the discrepancy between the present situation and that goal, and even mechanisms to monitor the effectiveness of that monitoring.

Whilst 'software' explanations serve for many purposes, many ethologists hope that they will pave the way for more detailed analysis of the mechanisms underlying the behaviour. To continue our example, one might investigate the physiological concomitants of the postulated state of hunger. For instance, do the erstwhile bus passengers have empty stomachs? What are their blood sugar levels? One might even ask what parts of the brain are especially important for the behaviour that they show. Further still, one might attempt to explore in detail the properties of the sense organs, of the muscles and salivary glands, and of the nervous mechanisms that relate them. In this way causal analysis, starting at the behavioural level, and depending initially only on correlational evidence, might lead gradually to understanding of the mechanisms involved at finer and finer levels of analysis.

Ethologists are generally concerned primarily with the behavioural level of analysis, and with the initial steps beyond it. Work beyond that level would usually be regarded as physiology, though we shall see in later chapters that its success may depend on ethological groundwork and/or collaboration. Most classical ethological studies of causation concern either the stimuli that elicit the behaviour, the nature of the behaviour itself, or the relation between stimulus and response. We may now consider these in turn.

(ii) Analyses of stimulus situations

All perception is selective. We notice some things in our environment, and fail to notice others. This fact is exploited by caricaturists, whose art depends in part on exaggeration of those features on which recognition depends. Selectivity in perception has been demonstrated repeatedly in animals: some aspects of the situation upon which a response, group of responses or propensity to respond depends are more important than others. For example, while the mobbing response made by chaffinches to owls is affected by a number of features of owls, the eyes and speckled colour pattern are of paramount importance: models having owl-like eyes but lacking virtually all other features of owls will nevertheless elicit the response (fig. 2). Comparable selectivity in responsiveness has been demonstrated in numerous other studies (e.g., Tinbergen, 1948): stimulus characters having special effectiveness are referred to as 'sign stimuli'.

Selective responsiveness to stimulation has been investigated especially in the context of studies of social communication. Two cases, the pink breast of the male and the soliciting posture of the female chaffinch, have already been mentioned. As a more classic example, Tinbergen (e.g., 1948) assessed the significance of the red belly that male three-spined sticklebacks (*Gasterosteus aculeatus*) develop in the breeding season. Quite crude models of a stickleback were effective in eliciting antagonistic behaviour from a territory-owning male, provided that they had a red belly: models lacking that character, though otherwise closely resembling sticklebacks, were relatively ineffective. The red belly is in fact displayed in a threat posture made to rival males. This and other comparative evidence strongly suggest that the red belly was evolved in relation to its signal function.

Such sign stimuli are known as 'social releasers'. While the concept of 'sign stimulus' implies selective responsiveness by

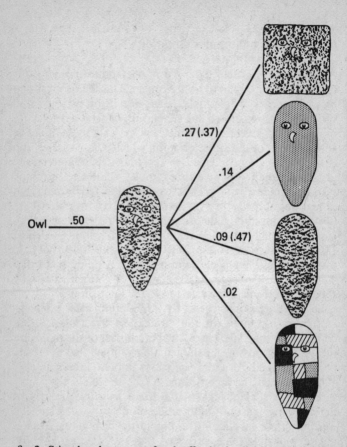

fig. 2. Stimulus characters of owls effective in eliciting the mobbing call from chaffinches. Data from experiments in which a stuffed owl and the central model, or the central model and one of those to the right, were tested in eight counter-balanced presentations repeated with at least four wild-caught individuals. Each figure represents the median ratio between the number of calls elicited by the model to its right and the number elicited by the model to its left. Figures in brackets are for tests with four or more hand-reared individuals who had never seen owls.

the respondent (and as used by ethologists has usually implied selectivity common to all individuals of the species [see below]), 'social releaser' implies the evolution of especially effective stimulus features, involving movements or structures or both, in the signaller. Since owls often avoid small birds that mob them, it is not reasonable to suppose that their large eyes were evolved to elicit mobbing, but it is likely that the stickleback's red belly was evolved to make threat more effective. The evolution of social releasers is referred to as 'ritualization' – an issue we shall return to later.

As another example, Baerends and Kruijt (1973) studied the egg-rolling response shown by herring gulls when they perceive an egg on the nest rim – a response usually functional in retrieving displaced eggs (fig. 3). By experimenting with models, Baerends was able to compare the effectiveness of different stimulus characters. In each experiment two eggs were placed on the nest rim, and the experimenter recorded which was rolled in first. Baerends and Kruijt found the larger models were preferred to smaller ones, speckled to plain, green to a variety of other colours, but shape made rather little difference.

fig. 3. Herring gull rolling an egg back into its nest.

Many sign stimuli involve relational properties: thus a
model stickleback with a red belly is most effective if held
with the belly down. As another example, a fish, the zebra
danio (*Brachydanio rerio*) reacts to an approaching predator
when the rate of change of the angle it subtends exceeds a
threshold level (Dill, 1974).

When a response depends on a number of sign stimuli,
their effects may summate (Seitz, 1940–1). Baerends and
Kruijt (1973) were able to demonstrate this in their egg-
rolling experiments by making use of the fact that many
individual gulls tend to respond preferentially to one of two
eggs on the nest rim by virtue of its relative position. By
playing off larger size against the position preference, they
showed that any pair of eggs with a certain ratio between
their maximal areas (projected on to a flat surface) were
equally effective in reversing the preference, no matter what
their actual sizes. They could thus arrange a series of eggs,
similar in all respects except size, along a scale of increasing
effectiveness. They were then able to compare the effect of
changing one character (e.g., shape, colour, speckling) with
that of changing size. As shown in fig. 4, the change
produced by altering one stimulus character is independent
of size – in other words, the characters summate. With other
responses, however, the effect of adding a particular stimulus
element may depend on those already present.

These experiments also demonstrate the phenomenon of
supernormal stimuli. The most effective colour, green is
preferred to the natural colour, and larger than normal eggs
are preferred to normal ones: it is thus possible to make a
model that is more effective than life – in fact, a caricature.

In the cases cited so far, the responses have been
characteristic of the species, and occur in mature individuals
on the first occasion they are exposed to the stimulus.
However, comparable selectivity is well known from
conditioning experiments in the laboratory (e.g.,
Sutherland, 1969) as well as from caricatures. Selectivity
may or may not depend on experience. However, a relatively
extreme dependence of the response on one or a very few

stimulus features seems to be more characteristic of responsiveness general to all individuals of a species, and ethologists used to emphasize a distinction between species-characteristic behaviour, which depended on sign stimuli, and learned responses, which depend on diverse features of the appropriate object. This fits, for example, with data on species recognition in sexually dimorphic species. In many cichlid fish and ducks the males are conspicuously coloured and the females are more cryptic. There is evidence that mature females respond appropriately to the species-characteristic colour patterns of the males even if they have never seen a male before, but the males must learn the subtler characteristics of the less distinctive female colour pattern (Baerends and Baerends van Roon, 1950; Schutz, 1965).

But the distinction between responses elicited by a few sign stimuli and those dependent on many stimulus characters is one only of degree: in both cases some aspects of the total stimulus array are more important than others. Indeed some species-characteristic responses depend on quite a number of stimulus characters. For instance the laughing gull chick obtains regurgitated food from the parent by pecking at the latter's beak. The most effective stimulus is an oblong rod, about 9 mm in width, held vertically, and moved horizontally about eighty times a minute. It must contrast with and be darker than its background; if coloured, red and blue are more effective than intermediate wavelengths. The object should be held at eye level, and be visible to both eyes (Hailman, 1967).

To explain selectivity in responsiveness, ethologists proposed a 'releasing mechanism' in the responding individual, selectively responsive to particular stimulus features. Experimental psychologists used a related but independent concept in speaking of 'analysers' or 'filtering' (Sutherland, 1959; Barlow, 1961; Baerends and Kruijt, 1973). Of course such concepts are 'software' specifications of the job done: the actual mechanisms vary from case to case.

However an initial classification of the mechanisms

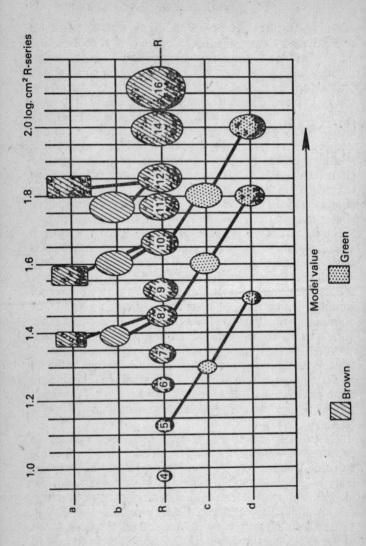

fig. 4. The value of various dummy eggs in releasing the egg rolling response of the herring gull. The code numbers 4 to 16 stand for 4/8 to 16/8 of the linear dimensions of the normal egg size (i.e., 8 indicates the size of a normal egg). Eggs differing in shape (line a), speckling (line b), colour (line d), or colour and speckling (line c) from the normal were 'titrated' against the reference series (line R) to determine the size on the reference series having similar effectiveness. Thick lines connect eggs of equal effectiveness. The maximal projection surfaces of the eggs of the reference series have been plotted along the logarithmic scale of the abscissa. (Re-drawn from Baerends and Kruijt, 1973.)

involved is possible. In some cases the special effectiveness of a stimulus character may apply to a wide range of responses, and even to almost all the behaviour of which the species is capable. For example the effectiveness of sounds increases with their loudness, and that of visual stimuli with their contrast, in many contexts. In such cases selectivity can be ascribed to the mechanisms of sensation or perception. In many of the cases cited above, however, selectivity is specific to one or a few responses. Thus an incubating herring gull responds more strongly to eggs that are green than to eggs of other colours, red eggs being relatively weak stimuli, but a gull cannibalizing other birds' eggs prefers red, green eggs being relatively ineffective. Responsiveness that is specific to a particular response cannot depend on the general mechanisms of sensation and perception, and the ethologist must turn to the physiologist to identify the mechanisms involved. Thus selectivity in responsiveness implies filtering involving sensitivity to some stimulus modalities and not others, then preferential responsiveness to particular parameters of stimulation valid for all responses, and then selectivity more or less specific to a particular response.

The concept of releasing mechanism, though diffuse in terms of its neurophysiological implications, poses further questions as to the precise range of responses influenced by the stimuli that are effective. Thus in the gull's differential responsiveness to colours there is evidence for two 'filters', one giving preferential responsiveness to green, the colour for which the bird's eye is maximally sensitive, and the other to blue and red. The former operates for retrieving eggs and attending the nest, the latter for removing broken egg shells from the nest, robbing eggs of other gulls and for the juvenile begging response (Baerends and Kruijt, 1973).

Another example concerns the mobbing behaviour of the pied flycatcher. This can be elicited by either shrikes or owls, and the effective stimulus characters differ. Curio (1975), on the basis of extensive field experiments with models, produced compelling evidence that two independent releasing mechanisms feed into a common response mechanism. For example, the sign stimuli appropriate for each predator summate among themselves, but not with those appropriate for the other, and habituation of response to one does not affect the response to the other.

Most ethological studies of sign stimuli have involved the use of models, the effectiveness of two or more models differing in one character being compared. Naturally the technique differs according to the stimulus modality concerned and the nature of the response, but the principle is the same. In order to ensure that the results have generality, it is usual to make the comparison in a number of individuals. Of course this method gives information only about stimulus characters that are effective for all the individuals tested. As mentioned above, selectivity in the responsiveness of individuals may be idiosyncratic, but this will not be detected in such experiments.

While the general method of comparing two objects differing in one stimulus character sounds simple, there are other snags. For instance the motivation of the subjects must be in the right range: one food item might be preferred to another by a moderately hungry animal, but both would be ignored by a satiated one and both would be consumed immediately by a ravenous one. Again, if the two models are presented simultaneously, there is a danger that the response elicited by one will be directed on to the other; and if the models are presented in succession, the effects of one presentation on the next can give difficulties. The experimenter must also be aware that relational properties may be important, and that the effect of one stimulus character may depend on the presence of others. Indeed there is a basic logical difficulty: often what is meant by 'a character' is no more than what an experimenter chooses to vary, and there is always the possibility that the animal abstracts from reality differently.

Thus the concepts of 'sign stimulus' and 'social releaser', though basic to many ethological endeavours, are slippery at the edges. The selectivity in responsiveness that they imply may be due to a number of different mechanisms. And since all responsiveness is selective, it is not possible to specify precisely which effective stimulus characters are to be regarded as sign stimuli. If one introduces a developmental criterion, and limits the concept of sign stimulus to characters that are responded to independently of experience, then it must be recognized that the mechanisms of selection may be similar in responses both to sign stimuli and to other stimulus characters. But such difficulties with the concept of sign stimulus do not make it any the less useful. Faced with the diversity of nature, the ethologist does not expect to find hard and fast categories equally suitable in all cases. Concepts like sign stimulus that call attention to a phenomenon have an important role to play even if their validity is greater in some contexts than others.

(iii) Studies of modal or fixed action patterns

A generalization crucial for the development of modern ethology is that every species has a repertoire of more or less stereotyped movements. These movements are as much characteristic of the species as structural features. The displays of chaffinches (fig. 1), an infant's cry, and the human smile are all examples. Such species-characteristic relatively stereotyped movements are often termed 'fixed action patterns' (Lorenz 1937; Lorenz and Tinbergen, 1939;

Tinbergen, 1942). Although sometimes variable in intensity, and forming intermediates with other patterns, fixed action patterns are nearly always recognizable by their form.

Fixed action patterns are important to ethologists because they are readily identifiable units which break up the stream of behaviour (cf. p. 30). They have been especially valuable in comparative studies, since they can be treated like morphological characters and the small differences between related species can be used to establish hypotheses about their evolution (see pp. 122–7). While they are important in most aspects of the behaviour of most species, those used for locomotion and social communication have been studied most thoroughly. Yet, as with sign stimuli, a generally useful definition is not easy to find.

In the first place, 'fixed' is a relative term. In a stimulating review Barlow (1977) pointed out that close measurement reveals some variability in even the most apparently stereotyped movements, and suggested that the term be replaced by 'modal action pattern'. He proposed a definition which stressed that an MAP would be recognizable (and describable at least in statistical terms), indivisible into smaller units, and characteristic of all members of the group.

However, the classic fixed action patterns studied by the early ethologists also had other interesting properties. For instance, their stereotypy had led Lorenz and Tinbergen to suggest that external stimuli, though usually important in triggering the movement, played no part in controlling their form. They therefore distinguished between the invariant 'Erbkoordination', and the orientation component whereby it is directed with respect to the environment. Orientation may be determined by aspects of the stimulus situation different from those that elicit the Erbkoordination. Thus a goose, like a gull (see fig. 3), will retrieve an egg which has rolled out of its nest by putting its beak beyond it and then moving its beak towards its breast. The wobbling movements of the egg are compensated by side to side movements of the bill. The Erbkoordination, consisting of the movement of the beak to the breast, is elicited by visual and tactile stimuli from the egg and, once elicited, continues to completion even if the egg is suddenly taken away. The side-to-side orientation movements depend on stimuli on the side of the beak and disappear as soon as the egg is removed.

But attempts to delimit a category of stereotyped movements on the basis that, once elicited, their form is not influenced by external stimuli run into a number of difficulties. Many species-characteristic movements are oriented and elicited by the same stimuli: it is thus impossible to separate the Erbkoordination from the orientation component. In such cases (e.g., the threat and courtship postures of the male chaffinch) the form of the movement is sufficiently constant for it to be recognized on every occasion, and yet the precise pattern of muscular contractions varies enormously as the animal orients the movement with respect to the rival or mate. In any case the form of many movements is affected by feedback from sense organs stimulated in the early phases of the movement: it would be arbitrary to divide them according to whether that stimulation came from inside or outside the body. And attempts to distinguish the products of central patterning, proprioceptive feedback and exteroceptive feedback have revealed unexpected complexities even in relatively simple locomotory movements like walking in Amphibians (Gray and Lissmann, 1946) and the flying of insects. When a sequence of different action patterns, such as those involved in the grooming behaviour of mice, are studied, interactions occur not only between feedback and the central control of the movements themselves, but also between feedback and the central control of *groups* of movements (Fentress and Stillwell, 1973; Northup, 1977).

Other authors state as a matter of definition that the form of an FAP is not determined by experience (e.g., Eibl Eibesfeldt, 1975). Quite apart from the conceptual difficulties with such a view which will become apparent later (pp. 85–94), this would involve dividing a category of actions which was defined phenomenologically (by stereotypy) or causally (independence of external stimuli once released) by a third quite different sort of criterion, the role of experience in its development. Furthermore, movements that have been idiosyncratically acquired can become not only as stereotyped, but also as independent of environmental stimuli as the classic fixed action patterns (Fentress, 1976). These, however, would be excluded by such a criterion – as well as by Barlow's requirement that an MAP should be widely distributed throughout an interbreeding population.

It will be apparent that the category 'fixed' or 'modal action pattern' is not easy to define satisfactorily. Dewsbury (1978) has listed eleven characters which have been used by one author or another and he argues that the term should be either dropped or redefined – perhaps by a 'polythetic' definition, that is, one that depends on many characters none of which is *a priori* more important than the others.

But this difficulty of definition has done little to reduce the usefulness of the concept. Species do have characteristic movement patterns, and a concept which calls attention to the phenomenon has proved its value. The problem of definition becomes acute, of course, when generalizations about fixed action patterns go beyond the issue of relative stereotypy. For that reason it is perhaps best to disregard other properties of fixed or modal action patterns for purposes of definition, specifying the presence or absence of the other properties in each case.

(iv) The problem of motivation: the behavioural level of analysis

A given stimulus does not always evoke the same response. If the external situation is constant, alterations in the responsiveness of an organism must be ascribed to changes in its internal state. The nature of such changes poses the problem of motivation.

By convention 'motivational' changes are those that are temporary and reversible: more permanent changes are ascribed to learning or ageing. It is also usual to exclude changes in behaviour due to changes in the sense organs or effectors. It will be apparent that there is a certain arbitrariness in the limits of 'the problem of motivation', but this is as it should be. The ethologist starts with a group of phenomena labelled loosely as 'motivational', and attempts to analyse the processes involved.

As we have seen, the first stage in such an analysis, a stage which in itself can bring considerable understanding, may not involve any attempt to investigate the nature of the internal processes which underlie the changes in behaviour, but merely to label them. It involves a search for 'causal factors' which may be either events in the real world, or postulated variables which relate such events to behaviour or the behavioural events to each other. Thus both food (external stimulus) and degree of hunger (postulated state) are causal factors for eating behaviour.

The problem of motivation embraces searches for factors that operate over a number of different time scales. Thus we may wish to explain the gradual changes in the overall daily frequencies of the male chaffinch's various activities as the season advances, or the moment to moment changes as he courts a female (see pp. 22–9). Clearly both the explanatory concepts used and the methods of analysis must be adjusted to the sorts of problems that are being tackled.

Of all the factors that affect the behaviour of an animal, it is now usual to assume that each affects some types of behaviour and not others. The alternative extreme view that all causal factors contribute to a general motivational state which influences the intensity of all types of behaviour has been found less useful than formerly seemed likely (e.g., Bolles, 1967; Hinde, 1970). Nevertheless the issue is not quite settled. Whilst the behaviour shown at any one time may be related to the animal's state of 'arousal', which may vary from unconsciousness through sleep and alertness to panic (Moruzzi, 1958; Andrew, 1974), it seems more profitable to regard 'arousal' as having a permissive role on behaviour rather than as determining its intensity. Furthermore sleep may properly be regarded as an activity in its own right. However, the occurrence of items of behaviour seems occasionally to be due to factors normally irrelevant to them. Whilst some of these are understandable as displacement activities (discussed on pp. 66–7), others are still difficult to account for: thus sexual behaviour may be augmented by painful or alerting stimuli (see also Fentress, 1976).

We customarily explain changes in behaviour in terms of postulated internal states. We say a man drinks because he is thirsty, eats because he is hungry, ogles because he is randy, explores because he is curious. Now if we merely observe that an animal ignores water at one time and drinks at another, it does not add anything to say that it is 'thirsty', because our only criterion for saying it is thirsty is that it drinks water. But if we note not only that it drinks water if water is offered, but also that it goes and looks in places where it has found water previously, is ready to drink adulterated water that it would normally reject, and so on, application of the word thirsty implies that these several changes in behaviour can be explained in terms of a common factor. And if in addition we find that we can make the animal behave thus by treating it in a number of different ways – for instance, by depriving it of water, giving it dry food, or injecting it with strong salt solution, postulating the 'intervening variable' of thirst will have even more explanatory value.

However, there are two restrictions on this procedure. First, the economy provided by a thirst variable depends on the number of treatments and types of behaviour being considered: if there were only two of each, four relations between treatments and behaviour would have to be established whether or not a thirst variable was postulated (cf. fig. 5). Second, the usefulness of postulating a unitary variable supposedly antecedent to several measures of behaviour depends in part on the extent to which the latter are correlated with each other: it is much greater if a given treatment, which is more effective than another as assessed by one type of behaviour, is also more effective as assessed by

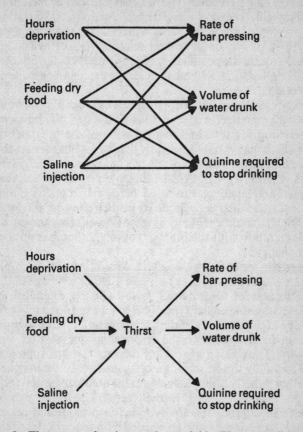

fig. 5. The nature of an intervening variable. The upper diagram shows the nine possible relationships between three possible treatments administered to rats (independent variables) and three possible ways of measuring the consequences of those treatments (dependent variables). The lower diagram shows how this is reduced to six if an intervening variable can be interposed. (From Miller, N. E. in *Psychology: A Study of a Science, Vol. 2.* Copyright © 1959 McGraw-Hill Book Company and used with their permission.)

another. Any particular type of behaviour can be measured in many different ways – its latency, frequency, and duration for example. Lack of rank order correlation between measures of one or of several related types of behaviour would require the postulation of more intervening variables for its explanation, and thus reduce the explanatory value of any one.*

Identification of the various aspects or types of behaviour that 'go together', and can thus be related to the same intervening variable, and identification of the 'treatments' that affect that variable, are only first steps, but they set the stage for further analysis of the mechanisms involved. Here it is useful to distinguish three types of procedure: behavioural analysis, discussed here, and modelling and physiological analysis, discussed in the following sections. Although the success of any of these depends to some extent on integration with the others, that integration has not yet been achieved.

Further behavioural analysis can bring considerable progress. For example, we may ask whether a change in the effectiveness of an external factor (e.g., a stimulus) in influencing a particular type of behaviour is due merely to a change in the efficiency of the sense organs, or is due to some change more specific to the response in question (cf. pp. 39–40). Thus rats, when they become adult, approach preferentially the odour of an oestrous female: we may ask whether puberty brings a change in the ability to perceive the odour, or a change in its attractiveness. The former can be assessed from the rats' ability to learn to go to that odour rather than another when rewarded with food for doing so; the latter by simple choice tests. In practice puberty involves an increase in the attractiveness of female odour (Le Magnen, 1952). There are in fact a number of studies which show that particular changes in behaviour can be related not to the

* Houston and McFarland (1976) point out that behavioural measures may not provide estimates of the postulated factor on an interval scale, so that a low product-moment correlation may be irrelevant. Hinde (1970) overlooked this point.

sensory input to the brain, but to the responsiveness of particular brain mechanisms to that input (e.g., MacDonnell and Flynn, 1966). Again, having found that food deprivation increases aggressive behaviour, we might ask in more detail about the behavioural mechanisms involved. Is a hungry individual more prone to seek out others to fight, or is he more likely to attack individuals whom he encounters, or is he merely more active and thus more likely to encounter others? In caged chaffinches the latter seems to be the case (Marler, 1956b).

We must study not only what initiates particular activities or internal states, but also the several ways in which they are brought to an end. In the first place external stimuli, which we have so far regarded as eliciting responses, may equally well terminate them. For example during the breeding season the male three-spined stickleback guards a territory and builds a nest therein (fig. 6). If an egg-laden female enters his territory he responds selectively to her swollen belly and courts her. If she lays eggs in his nest he swims over them and ejaculates his sperm – and then turns on the female and chases her away. One might think that it was the act of ejaculation which caused the change in his behaviour to the female, but in practice it is the smell of fresh eggs in the nest. This stimulus causes a switch in his internal state from 'sex' to 'territorial defence' (Sevenster-Bol, 1962). Such stimuli, perceived as a consequence of a behavioural sequence and bringing it to an end, are called 'consummatory' stimuli.

Often we can regard an animal's behaviour as being directed towards the achievement of a rather precisely defined consummatory situation and maintaining it over a period which may or may not be defined by its own activity. An obvious example is an incubating female bird. Baerends and colleagues (in Baerends and Drent, 1970) showed that the maintenance of incubation by herring gulls depends on adequate stimulation from the eggs: bouts are more likely to be interrupted by resettling on the eggs, nest building or preening if the tactile or thermal feedback obtained from the eggs is inadequate.

A case that has been investigated in some detail is the 'creeping through' of the male three-spined stickleback. From time to time the male of this species 'creeps through' the nest he has built, a behaviour which may be functional in maintaining a tunnel through the nest. Later the spawning female will pass through this tunnel to lay her eggs, and he will follow her to fertilize them (fig. 6). While the male is waiting for a female, creeping through occurs fairly regularly. If the duration of the act of creeping through is artificially shortened by shortening the nest or making a hole in the roof, the interval before the next creeping through is shortened. On subsequent visits he may compensate by staying in the nest for longer, and he is likely to rebuild the nest to the previous length. If the nest is artificially lengthened, the male breaks through the roof or side when creeping through has lasted the usual time: keeping the male in the nest for longer does not result in an extension of the subsequent inter-creeping through interval. In other words the male behaves as though there was a required duration of creeping through: once it is achieved he stops creeping through and will not creep through again for a standard time ('T Hart, 1978).

Stimuli perceived as the result of an activity may not only have immediate consequences on its continuation or repetition, but also longer-term effects mediated by a change in internal state. Thus the conclusion of nest-building behaviour by canaries (Hinde and Steel, 1966), or the switch-over from one phase of nest-digging to another by a digger wasp (Brockmann, 1980), is mediated by stimuli received as a result of the previous activity. Again, in mammals ingestion of food has a whole series of consequences, including perception of the taste of the food, the filling of the stomach, the change in blood composition and an increase in fat reserves. These all affect future eating behaviour, though in different ways and with different time courses. Some have a positive effect, as in 'whetting the appetite', whilst others contribute to satiation. And the effects of eating which affect eating behaviour in the short run may be quite different

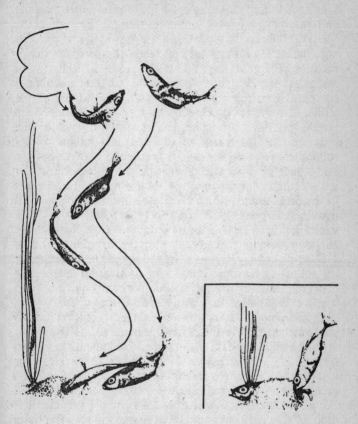

fig. 6. The courtship of the three-spined stickleback. In the main diagram, the male is shown on the left, and the female on the right. The male's initial zig-zag dance is elicited by the swollen belly and by the body posture of the female. He then leads her to the nest and she follows. At the nest he shows her the nest entrance. Then (inset) she enters and lays her eggs when he stimulates the base of her tail. (From Tinbergen, 1951.)

from those that affect food preferences in the long run.

Of course activities may cease for reasons other than the perception of goal or consummatory stimuli. Sometimes the eliciting stimulus disappears: after a 'hawk' alarm, crouching chaffinches resume feeding when the predator disappears. In other cases responding seems to result in changes in responsiveness even though there is no obvious consequence comparable to the ingestion of food. The waning of the mobbing response of chaffinches to owls, mentioned on p. 28, provides an example. In general it is a safe presumption that every response to a stimulus affects subsequent responsiveness to that stimulus in diverse ways. Sometimes positive effects are the more important: for instance in a wide range of species locomotory movements have consequences which facilitate continued locomotion (Davis and Ayers, 1972; see also Hogan and Bols, 1980), whilst in others, such as the owl-mobbing case, the negative effects predominate, at any rate after the first minute or two.

Such effects may have a rather widespread importance, for the following reason. Analyses of motivation are usually concerned initially with behaviour like eating and drinking, where it is possible to identify extra-neural changes (e.g., changes in blood sugar) which bear at least some relation to the tendency to show the behaviour in question. However it is not possible to relate the moment-to-moment changes in behaviour – the structure of the bouts of pecking, for instance – to changes in extra-neural factors. Similarly, many species show reproductive behaviour only if blood hormone concentration is above a certain level, but it is unlikely that moment-to-moment changes in sexual activity depend on hormonal fluctuations: positive and negative consequences of sexual performance which may not be mediated hormonally clearly do play a role. And fluctuations in the tendencies to show some types of behaviour, such as the human activities of reading or playing the piano, are not known to be related to any extra-neural factors. But although we understand very little about the control of such activities, it may well be that no new principles will be required. Given that the organism is active, what it does may be determined by mutually inhibitory and facilitatory effects between the various possible activities, and the strengths of these may depend in part on effects consequent upon the performance of each of them. We shall return to this issue shortly.

(v) Motivation: modelling

The second way of tackling the problems of motivation is closely related to the last, but lays emphasis on mathematical modelling of behaviour. This leads to more accurate descriptions of the relations between causal factors and behaviour, or between different types of behaviour, and may require less detail about how those causal factors actually produce their effects. Such an approach may utilize the classical control theory principles of negative and positive feedback, and of feed forward: in the former the consequences of behaviour reduce the propensity to continue behaviour, as when the ingestion of food leads to cessation of eating, while in positive feedback the consequences enhance the behaviour, as in the early stages of sexual behaviour. Feed forward permits anticipatory action to minimize an impending discrepancy from an optimal or required state (e.g., McFarland, 1971; Toates and Archer, 1978).

Whilst the classical control systems approach has been especially valuable in analysing the relations between particular independent and dependent variables, in practice motivational factors for different types of behaviour compete for control, and any type of behaviour may have multiple consequences for the animal. McFarland (e.g., 1978) has therefore applied a 'state-space' approach which is better suited to the study of multivariable systems. The essence of this approach is not easy to convey in non-technical language: although the following paragraphs bypass the mathematical details, some readers may wish to proceed directly to p. 63.

The activities of an animal can be classed into a number of mutually exclusive categories – for instance eating, drinking and preening – each or which involves a number of identifiable units of 'actions'. Each action is influenced by a set of causal factors: for example eating is influenced by food deprivation and by the presence of food. Although each action may appear with more than one state of the causal factors (e.g., an animal will eat when more or less hungry), it is assumed that a particular state of the causal factors will always give rise to the same action. The animal's motivational state can be thus located in a 'causal factor space', each dimension of which represents a type of causal factor that affects the animal's behaviour. Causal factors may be relevant to more than one type of behaviour, but each point in the causal factor space can, by definition, cause only one action. For example, a simple model of the internal factors controlling drinking might involve two variables, the hydration of the blood and the gut water content. The state of the system at any instant could be represented by a point on a graph in which blood dilution and gut water content were plotted against each other. With drinking, that point would approach the origin. If not 2 but n variables were involved, a space of n dimensions would be necessary to pinpoint the state of the system at any one time, or to characterize its changes over time. Thus even where the behaviour varies along only one dimension (i.e., the possible measures are highly correlated with each other), it is possible to represent the multidimensional nature of the motivational system controlling it.

Using this approach McFarland and Sibly (1972, 1975) have developed a model of the motivational processes governing behaviour. In brief, they argue that within the total motivational system there is a command system relevant to the ongoing behaviour. The command state is represented by a point in a space of n dimensions: for example if hunger were determined only by the requirement for nutrients, the hunger command state might be represented by a point in a space of three dimensions corresponding to the amounts of carbohydrate, protein and fat required. The behaviour would be terminated when the point reached the origin, or came as near to it as possible.

Now in general the more strongly motivated (used here in an everyday sense) an animal is, the weaker the stimulus necessary to elicit a given response. A very hungry animal may eat almost anything placed in front of it, but a satiated one must be tempted with tasty morsels. Evidently the internal motivational state combines with the external stimuli present to determine the strength of behaviour shown. Now any one stimulus object may involve many 'characters' (see p. 43), but there is evidence that these usually are summated by the animal in a quantitative way (see pp. 38–40). This sum interacts with the internal factors to determine the 'motivational state'. An example concerned with the courtship of a common aquarium fish, the guppy *Lebistes reticulatus*, is shown in fig. 7. Here the male's internal state is indicated by changes in his colour pattern: the various colour patterns can be scaled in terms of the frequencies of various courtship activities given by males when showing each pattern. The effectiveness of a female in eliciting courtship increases with her size. Thus it is possible to plot the various combinations of internal and external factors necessary for each activity (Baerends *et al.*, 1955). The precise shape of the curves depends, of course, on the scaling of the axes, but the issues involved cannot be pursued here (Houston and McFarland, 1976).

Returning to the model, we now have a command space and the stimulus or cue strength, the latter being often, though not necessarily, unidimensional. These can be summed to give a causal factor space of n dimensions. If the animal were to pursue one activity, without interference from others, the point representing its motivational state would tend to move to the origin.

This may or may not be possible. Suppose an animal's hunger state were determined only by its need for protein and for fat. If two foods, one pure protein and the other pure fat, were available, it would be able to select foods in such a

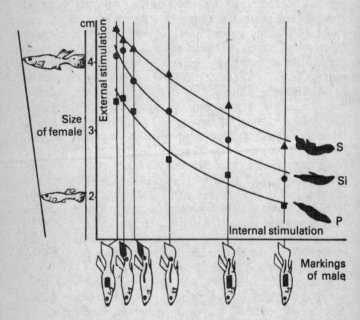

fig. 7. The relation between external stimulus and internal state as exemplified by a study of the courtship of the guppy. The effectiveness of a female in eliciting courtship increases with her size. This is shown on the ordinate. The male's internal motivation is revealed by his colour pattern, as indicated on the abscissa. Each curve represents the combination of external stimulus and internal state producing posturing (P), sigmoid intention movements (Si), or the fully developed sigmoid (S). (From Baerends *et al.*, 1955.)

way that its motivational state reached the origin, whatever its initial condition. However, if one (green) food was 50 per cent protein and 50 per cent fat, and the other (red) food was 90 per cent protein and 10 per cent fat, the animal could not reach the origin if its needs for either were too great. If it ate only red food, the motivational state could reach the origin if it started from anywhere along the line R in fig. 8, and if it ate only green the origin could be reached from any point along G. By combining the two foods, the origin could be reached from anywhere between the two lines, but not from the non-shaded area.

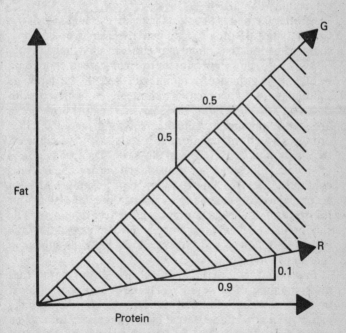

fig. 8.   Vectors in a consequence plane resulting from consumption of Green and Red food, when the environment is ambivalent. Only the points within the shaded area represent consequences that can be realized. (From McFarland and Sibly, 1972.)

Usually causal factors for more than one type of behaviour are present, and the animal switches to and fro between them. McFarland and his colleagues have used this to trace the routes by which motivational states approach the origin. Suppose we study two causal factors, y and z, relevant to two activities, α and β. These might for instance be hunger and thirst, relevant to eating and drinking. If both y and z have positive values, the animal is likely to show α and β (e.g., eat and drink) alternatively, its state tending to approach the origin. In practice 'behavioural inertia' causes it to overshoot a little on each change, but the changes in behaviour will mark out a 'switching-line'.

A better method is to assess the relative dominance of the two activities. If the ongoing activity is interrupted for a standard period, the animal may either resume that activity, or switch to the other. In the former case the ongoing behaviour is regarded as dominant, and in the latter as subdominant. Experimentally this can be achieved with doves by providing illuminated keys. When the dove pecks one key it obtains a small item of food, and the other produces water. Interruptions are produced by switching off the lights and disconnecting the keys. The behaviour is interrupted following each transition: if the new behaviour is continued after the interruption, the transition had been accompanied by a change in dominance, but if the behaviour reverts, the initial behaviour is held still to be dominant. The subdominant behaviour is thus largely suppressed, and the behaviour follows a trajectory towards the origin similar to that shown in fig. 9.

The special value of this approach arises from the fact that understanding the dynamics of behavioural control must involve knowledge of the nature of the relations between the values of internal and external factors necessary for a given behaviour to appear (e.g., fig. 7, leaving aside the difficulties arising in the scaling), and the values of the motivational state at which an animal will switch from one type of behaviour to another. However much we know about the

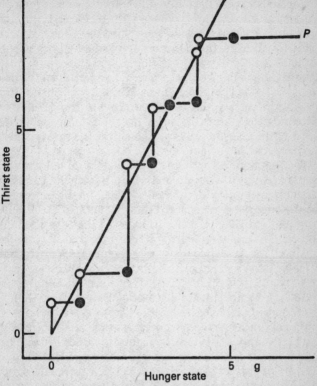

fig. 9. Trajectory in the hunger-thirst state plane resulting from the use of a double interruption test on a hungry and thirsty dove. From the initial state (P) the bird feeds, thus reducing its hunger state. On changing from feeding to drinking it is interrupted for one minute, and resumes feeding after the interruption, showing that hunger is dominant (filled circle). On being interrupted the second time it changed from feeding to drinking, showing that thirst is now dominant (unfilled circle). The procedure is continued until the satiation point is reached. The black circles tend to fall on one side of the boundary line (B), while the open circles fall on the other side. (From McFarland and Sibly, 1975.)

physiological machinery controlling each type of behaviour, we must also know the nature of these 'decision criteria', if we are to predict the course of its activities. But the techniques discussed above show that the animal can be made to tell us its decision rules – by studying behaviour, without analysing the physiological machinery, we can discern the relations between internal and external factors, and specify the conditions for switching. For instance it is possible to assess the effect on the switching rules of increasing the water content of the food, of changing the value of the cue stimuli, or of increasing the rate at which food rewards can be obtained.

The technique of opposing one behavioural tendency by another, coupled with the mathematical techniques necessary for integrating data on the effects of diverse causal factors on diverse responses, shows great potential. Because the total motivational space includes all the causal factors affecting the animal's behaviour, it is able to deal with, for instance, the fact that the causal factors relevant to one activity may change with other factors present (e.g., Fentress, 1976; see pp. 171–2). It has proved useful for a variety of maintenance and reproductive activities, though so far only in simplified laboratory situations. However even in the laboratory some phenomena would seem to require further assumptions before they can be incorporated into the model. For instance animals given both freely available food and the opportunity to work for it often prefer the latter (e.g., Duncan and Hughes, 1972) and animals may go on hunting even when they are satiated (Hinde, 1953c; Morgan, 1974). There is also considerable evidence that the earlier activities in a chain of behaviour, such as gathering material preparatory to building a nest, may have some autonomous control (e.g., Hinde and Stevenson, 1969; Roper, 1976). Further complexities arise from the fact that the causal factors for a variety of different patterns fluctuate partially independently, resulting in interference between competing acts: Slater (1978) has shown by computer simulation that potentially cyclical activities may cease to show cyclicity under such circumstances (see also Staddon and Ayres, 1975). But, given the diversity and complexity of behaviour, pointing to phenomena at the limits of a current theoretical scheme is seldom difficult, and profitable only in so far as it helps to pinpoint those limits.

(vi) Motivation: physiological approaches

The approaches considered so far involve solely behavioural analysis, and do not require consideration of what goes on beneath the skin. In the case of the second approach, it is even irrelevant whether the inability of two activities to appear together depends on competition for sense organs, effectors, or more central mechanisms. But for many purposes analyses of the internal processes involved may be essential – for instance studies of sensory mechanisms, of the role of hormones, of how hormones affect the brain, and so on. It is convenient to postpone discussion of examples until later chapters (e.g., chapters 8 and 9). However it is important to emphasize that the three approaches are not independent. Behavioural analysis and modelling can be pursued in their own right, but can also lead naturally to physiological analysis; and physiological analysis cannot be profitably pursued without adequate behavioural analysis. For many types of behaviour, however, the nature of the internal causal factors are quite unknown, and physiological analysis has not yet begun.

(vii) Conflict behaviour

At any one time motivational factors for more than one type of behaviour may be present. Indeed this is usually the case – a feeding bird must look out for predators, an incubating female must feed herself. Such 'conflict situations' may have a variety of outcomes. In attempting to understand the behaviour shown it is convenient to speak in terms of unitary intervening variables (see pp. 48–9) or tendencies even though, as we have seen, such variables may cease to be useful in more precise motivational analyses. In this context, the 'tendencies' may refer to causal factors either for a group of related activities (e.g., aggression, sexual behaviour) or for a rather specific act (e.g., approaching the other individual; see Blurton Jones, 1968; Andrew, 1972).

The first possibility is that one activity is dominant and suppresses or inhibits the other. We must note here that the postulation of a suppressing or inhibitory effect depends in part on the level of analysis with which we are concerned. Thus territorial defence, singing and sexual behaviour all occur at the same time of the year in the chaffinch and, at least early in the reproductive season, tend to occur in bouts interspersed with periods of non-reproductive behaviour – so that reproductive and non-reproductive behaviour appear to be mutually inhibitory. But during bouts of the former, sexual and aggressive behaviour are (partially) mutually inhibitory, and during bouts of sexual behaviour the several patterns are again mutually inhibitory (see also p. 23).

In general, the mechanisms involved in the change-over from one activity to the other may involve:

(a) Competition. Here the strength of the causal factors of the previously suppressed activity rises and it suppresses the ongoing behaviour. In competition the time at which the initially second-in-priority activity appears depends on the causal factors for that activity (fig. 10).

(b) Disinhibition. Here a lowering of the causal factors for the initially prepotent activity is responsible for the change-over. Thus changes in the causal factors for the second activity may influence its intensity, but not its duration. This means in effect that the second activity is under the control of the motivational factors relevant to the first. However, this may or may not persist: an initially dominant system which permits the occurrence of activity relevant to another system may either retain control and re-establish itself after a while, or it may lose control and cease to be dominant.

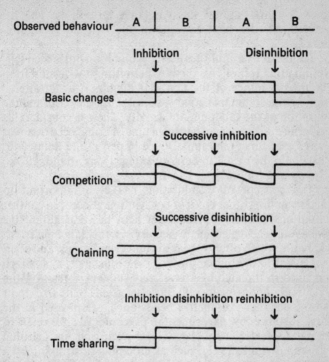

fig. 10. Three possible explanations of a simple alternating behaviour sequence, in terms of two types of behavioural transition. Lines represent schemetized levels of causal factors as a function of time. (From McFarland, 1974.)

The distinction has been illustrated by Halliday and Sweatman (1976) thus. A man with a small bladder must interrupt a car journey at intervals to urinate. Ordinarily he continues driving (the high priority activity) until the need to urinate is so strong that he is forced to stop to relieve himself (competition). But if he has to stop for fuel at a petrol station, he may take the opportunity to urinate even though his need is not compelling (disinhibition). And on a motorway he may pass a filling station knowing that he will be able to urinate at the next in half-an-hour's time (disinhibition).

If an activity establishes itself by inhibition but is then self-terminating (cf. p. 54), thereby permitting by disinhibition the reappearance of the first, but inhibits it again after a period, the dominant activity controls both the onset and the duration of the subdominant activity. There is considerable experimental evidence that such 'time-sharing' occurs, and it may be of functional importance in permitting animals to distribute their time to best advantage (McFarland, 1974a; Brown and McFarland, 1979).

The concept of disinhibition has been important in understanding other types of behaviour that occur in conflict situations, namely displacement activities and adjunctive behaviour. 'Displacement activity' is the label given to activities which often appear in conflict situations, and seem irrelevant to the human observer. For instance, a chaffinch engaged in threatening a rival may suddenly break off the encounter and wipe its bill: the latter seems quite irrelevant to the dispute. 'Adjunctive behaviour', a term used in the first instance by experimental psychologists to refer to apparently irrelevant behaviour occurring in learning situations (Falk, 1971), such as grooming or drinking by a hungry rat pressing a bar for food, probably refers to similar phenomena. The occurrence of the apparently irrelevant displacement behaviour appears to depend on disinhibition: for example, the preening shown by chaffinches at the points of balance in an approach/avoidance conflict is limited by the length of the pause – it appears when the other tendencies (approaching and flying away) are inhibiting each other. The occurrence of displacement activities may also be influenced by the causal factors normally appropriate to them: for instance the chaffinch's preening is increased by spraying the plumage with water (Rowell, 1961; see also Sevenster, 1961). A possible model of the processes involved is presented by Pring-Mill (1979). Displacement activities appear not only in conflict situations, but also in other situations where the ongoing behaviour is temporarily inhibited (e.g., frustration). Adjunctive behaviour also may be due to disinhibition (McFarland, 1966) though the drinking that occurs when rats have to work for food may be so excessive that other explanations are also required (Roper, 1978).

In many conflict situations inhibition of one activity by the other is incomplete. There may then appear 'intention movements' – that is, the incomplete preparatory phases of a movement, as when a bird crouches before take off; alternation between the two activities; ambivalent behaviour, in which elements of both are shown; or compromise behaviour, in which a behavioural element common to the two activities appears. Conflict situations are often accompanied by autonomic activity (e.g., feather movements, sweating), which may in turn lead to somatic activity, (e.g., scratching). In some cases one of the inhibited activities is redirected on to a new object, as when a bird which dare not attack a superior turns on an inferior. Occasionally sexual inversion, regression to juvenile behaviour, or immobility occurs in a conflict situation.

Much of the work on conflict behaviour has arisen from studies of threat and courtship behaviour. We may consider first the former. In the spring a male chaffinch attacks rivals which he encounters within his territory, and flees from those he encounters elsewhere. Prolonged skirmishes occur only along territorial boundaries. In these actual contact is rare, but each bird attacks and flees in turn, and shows an array of bizarre postures and movements (figs. 1 and 11). The facts suggest that the boundary is a line along which the tendencies to attack and flee from the rival are about equal, and that the postures are given when there is an even finer balance: the threat postures may be followed by movement either towards or away from the rival. Once the skirmish is seen to be associated with incompatible tendencies it becomes comprehensible. In a similar way, as we have seen (pp. 22–3), much courtship behaviour becomes comprehensible on the view that three conflicting tendencies are involved.

In general, evidence that a given display is associated with particular tendencies comes from the situation (e.g., the territorial boundary, see above); from behaviour accompanying the display (does the threatening bird edge towards or away from the rival?); from the nature of the display itself (it may for instance include an intention movement of striking); and from counts of the behaviour which precedes and follows the display. The latter involves the assumption that the motivational state common to several activities changes more slowly than the activities themselves: activities that are associated together in time more often than would be expected by chance are likely to depend on similar internal states. Thus a threat posture that is followed by attack on 40 per cent of occasions, by staying put on 50 per cent, and by fleeing on 10 per cent would be held to depend on a conflict between tendencies to attack, flee and stay. In some cases such data have been subjected to factor or principal component analyses. These are techniques which specify dimensions accounting for the variance in the initial correlations between activities: these dimensions correspond to the tendencies postulated on the types of evidence discussed above (Huntingford, 1976a).

Two experimental methods have been used to support such an interpretation of displays in terms of conflicting tendencies. One is to manipulate the tendencies experimentally, and assess the effects on the displays (Blurton Jones, 1968). The other is to assess the tendencies by an interruption technique similar to that discussed on pp. 60–1 (Cohen and McFarland, 1979).

It will be apparent that the behavioural tendencies invoked have the nature of intervening variables (see pp. 48–9),

fig. 11. Threat postures of black-headed gull, macaque, domestic dog, Siamese fighting fish, great tit and domestic cat. The gull is facing its opponent, the Siamese fighting fish is lateral to its opponent, and the great tit is displaying its yellow belly and broad ventral stripe to the opponent. Note the ambivalence evident especially in the postures of the mammals.

though they are postulated on the basis of correlations between types of behaviour, often without knowledge of the relevant causal factors ('treatments', p. 48). Whilst some displays are best understood as involving conflict between 'high level' tendencies, such as attacking and fleeing, others involve conflict between incompatible actions, such as approaching and fleeing, and yet others may appear when one tendency is thwarted (Blurton Jones, 1968; Andrew, 1972). This 'conflict hypothesis' for the causation of displays has found application in a wide range of species and types of behaviour (Baerends, 1975). We shall have cause to consider the nature of the postures again later.

(viii) Integration

We have seen that much behaviour occurs in functional sequences with appetitive phases leading to more or less consummatory ones. But complex activities like building a nest, and even more rearing young, demand the integration of diverse activities, and a variety of principles must be postulated.

First, different activities may share causal factors. For example administration of male sex hormone to a male chaffinch influences whether it will show courtship to a female, the frequency with which it sings, the probability that it will show aggressive behaviour to another male, and so on – all activities which increase during the breeding season. Similarly depriving a rat of water affects how hard it will work for water, how much water it will drink, and so on (fig. 5). A common causal factor may be positive or negative (i.e., consummatory): stimuli from the completed nest cause a decrease in all the nest-building activities of a female canary. Of course a multiplicity of consequences could arise from a single treatment or causal factor in a number of ways. Thus the factor could directly cause several activities, or cause a process (e.g., hormone secretion) or action which led to a number of other activities, or result in their disinhibition (pp. 64–5) without causing them directly.

Often activities sharing causal factors differ in their threshold of responsiveness to it. Thus a canary building a nest must gather nest material, carry that material to a nest site, and build that material into the structure. Early in the season a female shows gathering without carrying the material to the nest; later she often gathers and then carries the material aimlessly to and fro before dropping it; and later still she often completes the sequence. Two lines of evidence suggest that these activities involve successively higher values of an internal motivational state. First, nest-building can be affected by injections of female sex hormones (oestradiol), and successively higher levels of the hormone are more likely to produce complete nest-building sequences. Second, the greater the proportion of time involved in nest-building, and thus presumably the greater the internal state, the higher the proportion of sequences completed.

Another issue is that one activity may lead to stimuli which elicit the next ('chaining'). Gathering nest material presents a female canary with stimuli for carrying, and carrying with stimuli for placing though, as we have seen, the integration of this sequence depends also on common causal factors.

Usually chaining is not rigid, each response having a number of possible sequelae depending both on the external situation, and on the strength of the internal factors. A well-analysed case concerns the courtship of the smooth newt (*Triturus vulgaris*). This involves a sequence of activities leading to a tail-touch by the female which elicits spermatophore deposition by the male (fig. 12a). The male continues with further actions until the female picks up the spermatophore. A schematic summary of an interaction, pictured as a stimulus-response chain, is shown in fig. 12b (Halliday, 1976). However some of the groups of male activities shown in fig. 12b involve several alternatives: fig. 12c shows the frequency with which each of these appears in the presence of the three female states. Thus whilst what the male does is governed in part by what the female does, for

fig. 12a. Courtship of crested newts.

each female activity there are several possible male activities. By controlling the female's behaviour Halliday was able to show that variations in the early part of the sequence were correlated with variations in the later stages, so that all could be accounted for in terms of one causal factor, which he termed 'libido'. Sequences in which the males display high libido are characterized by rapid transitions from retreat display to creep to quiver, a small number of tail-touches to elicit spermatophore deposition, and a high probability of further sequences.

Animals do not usually do more than one thing at a time, implying inhibitory relationships between activities. Activities succeed each other as the causal factors for one become prepotent over those for another: we have seen that this may occur in at least three ways (pp. 64–5). But the influence of one activity on another may not be merely inhibitory – one type of behaviour may increase the strength of another. For example the three-spined stickleback sometimes breaks off from courting a female and shows nest-building behaviour: Wilz (1970) has suggested that this increases subsequent sexual behaviour.

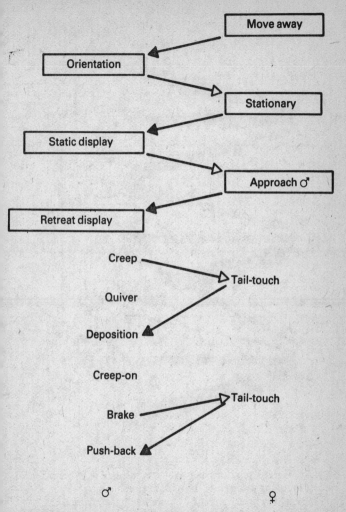

fig. 12b. The newt sexual sequence as a stimulus-response chain. Solid arrows indicate causal relationships established by experiment, open arrows those that are assumed. The earlier stages of the chain, which involve less stimulus-response specificity than the later ones, are enclosed in boxes. (From Halliday, 1976.)

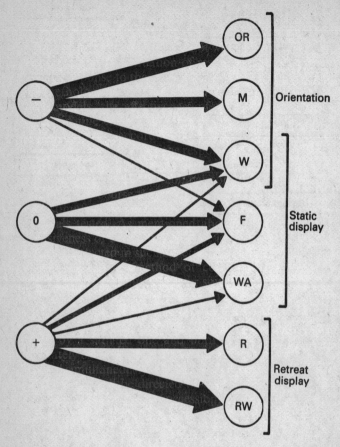

fig. 12c. Causal relations between the three female behavioural states of moving away from the male (−), remaining stationary (0) and moving towards the male (+), and male behaviour.
OR – orientation; M – move to the front; W – whip; F – fan; WA – wave; R – retreat; RW – retreat and whip.

The width of the arrows is proportional to the frequency of transition expressed as a proportion of all the transitions beginning with each female state. (Halliday, 1976.)

The principles mentioned so far may operate independently of previous specific experience in the situation: a canary will gather and carry material within seconds of being first exposed to it. But in other cases the integration of behavioural sequences depends crucially on learning. A consummatory stimulus may (though need not) act also as a reinforcer – that is, the presentation of the stimulus may increase the probability that the preceding phase will be repeated. And if successful performance of that phase always occurs in the presence of a particular stimulus (the discriminative stimulus), that stimulus may be used as a reinforcer for an even earlier phase, and so on. In this way a complex sequence of behaviour may be built up.

These principles can operate in relatively simple animals to build up quite complex chains of behaviour. They operate also in higher species, but additional principles, such as that of goal-direction, are also important. This requires a digression.

The behaviour even of a guided missile can be described as goal-directed, in the sense that its course at any moment is corrected according to the discrepancy between its present position and that of the target. It achieves this because some internal model or correlate of the target is compared with its present heading or position as indicated by sensors. Much animal behaviour can also usefully be described as goal-directed, though precise criteria for when the term can usefully be applied are difficult to specify (Hinde and Stevenson, 1969). Certainly, evidence that a situation brings a sequence of behaviour to an end is not in itself sufficient, since that would include all consummatory stimuli. Nor is persistence with varied action until the goal situation is achieved adequate, unless the actions are selected from a large repertoire in such a manner that they bring the animal nearer the goal: the most sophisticated goal-directiveness implies selection of the most economical course from starting point to goal, and thus lack of variability. However, we may be the more inclined to call behaviour goal-directed, the more starting points from which the goal can be reached.

But ultimately 'goal-directed' must imply that the animal has some model or correlate of the goal situation before that situation is achieved, and that behaviour is governed by the discrepancy between current and goal situations. Much complex behaviour in fact involves a succession of goals, which may be hierarchically organized with respect to each other.

An internal correlate of the goal can, but need not, imply complex cognitive abilities on the part of the animal. However, many of the phenomena on which ethology was nurtured – for instance the neglect by parent birds of young who have fallen just outside the nest rim – imply a marked lack of cognitive capacities. Partly for that reason, and partly in accordance with the principle of parsimony, most ethologists have been unwilling to impute cognitive capacities to animals. Recent work on the complex social behaviour of higher mammals, especially primates, and even more laboratory work designed to assess the cognitive capacities of the great apes (Sebeok and Umiker-Sebeok,

fig. 13. Model for the explanation of the inter-relations between activities shown during incubation by herring gulls. Fixed action patterns are shown to the right, first and second order control systems to the left. (N = System for nesting, incubation, etc.; E = System for escape; and P = System for preening.) The large vertical arrows represent orientation components with regard to the nest. Incubating is the consummatory act. Feedback stimulation from the clutch, after being processed in IP, flows to a unit (CU) where it is compared with expectancy, an efference copy or corollary on the input for incubation. This input is fed through a unit (I), necessary to explain the inhibition of settling and building when feedback matches expectancy. The effect of feedback discrepancy on N (and I), E and P can be read from the arrows. The main systems mutually suppress one another; P is thought to occur as interruptive behaviour through disinhibition of N and E. P can be activated directly by external stimuli like dust, rain or parasites, E can also be stimulated by other disturbances than deficient feedback from the clutch. (After Baerends, 1976.)

1980), has demonstrated clearly that parsimony has been overdone. Fear of the dangers of anthropomorphism has caused ethologists to neglect many interesting phenomena,

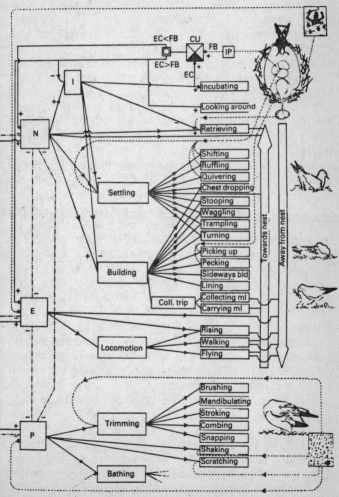

and it has become apparent that they could afford a little disciplined indulgence.

In human behaviour, goal-directed sequences may involve a succession of sub-goals. For example the goal of hanging a picture involves putting a nail into the wall, and that involves first finding a nail and second hammering it in. Hammering it in requires repetitive raising of the hammer, sighting and striking (e.g., Miller, Galanter and Pribram, 1960). Goal-directed sequences may incorporate elements that are not usually described as goal-directed but are more 'ballistic' in nature. Suitable means for describing the goal-directedness of behaviour have not yet been found even for human behaviour (Hinde, 1979) and we are still astonishingly ignorant of how widely the concept should be applied to animals.

It will be apparent that the integration of functional sequences involves a number of different principles. A concept that has proved useful here is that of the behavioural system. This is used with reference to the control of a group of behaviour patterns which are more or less closely causally (and often also functionally) related to each other. The concept approaches some usages of the old concept of 'instinct'. Such a concept has been applied, for example, to the nest provisioning behaviour of the wasp *Ammophila campestris* (Baerends, 1941); the reproductive behaviour of cichlid fish (Baerends and Baerends van Roon, 1950), the three-spined stickleback *Gasterosteus aculeatus* (Tinbergen, 1942), great tit *Parus major* (Hinde, 1953b) and herring gull *Larus argentatus* (Baerends, 1976). A behavioural system amounts to a blueprint of the relations between the several activities involved. As an example, fig. 13 shows Baerends's scheme for the systems which must be postulated to explain the patterning of incubation behaviour in the herring gull. The lower level systems controlling specific activities are shown on the right, and the systems postulated to explain the interrelations between the several types of behaviour are arranged hierarchically to the left. The highest order systems are labelled N (nesting, incubation and allied activities), E (escape activities) and P (preening). Whilst the scheme is derived from observations of behaviour, it is used in an explanatory sense to refer to systems postulated as controlling the behaviour. However, there is no implication that there are mechanisms in the brain isomorphous with the systems postulated: the explanation is a 'software' one, comparable to a computer program written with certain conventions to perform a certain job, but without specification of whether the computer into which it is to be fed employs valves, transistors or integrated circuits (Baerends, 1976; Dawkins, 1976a).

The details of fig. 13 do not matter for present purposes: the important points are that behavioural systems interact with each other and that each involves diverse patterns of behaviour related to each other causally and functionally. Some patterns may be appetitive to others, some consummatory. Some share positive causal factors, some negative. Some are alternatives. Some may be mutually facilitatory, others inhibitory. The behavioural system encapsulates the ethologist's knowledge about stimuli, responses and the general nature of the mechanisms relating to them. In a later chapter we shall see how the concept has been useful in studies of child development.

3   The Study of Development

(i) General

Not surprisingly, studies of causation and development often merge. A chaffinch's singing may be precipitated by the song of another male, but depends also on the fact that he is occupying a territory, which in turn depends on his having come into reproductive condition some weeks earlier, which in turn depends on even earlier experiences, such as finding enough food the preceding winter as well as on complex developmental changes even earlier in his history. Just which of these issues are to be regarded as involving immediate causation and which as ontogenetic is an arbitrary matter. It is usual, however, to treat the eliciting (e.g., song of the other male) and predisposing (e.g., reproductive condition, holding a territory) factors as matters of immediate causation, and earlier factors as involving ontogeny (fig. 14).

Study of the mechanisms of development must once again start with description – 'How does the behaviour change during development?' Observations made at this stage may provide important clues about environmental influences on development – for instance individual differences in experience may be correlated with differences in behaviour. But sooner or later an experimental approach is essential.

(ii) The development of chaffinch song

Experiments by Thorpe (1961) on the development of chaffinch song will illustrate some of the issues that arise. Adult male chaffinches have a repertoire of a few different

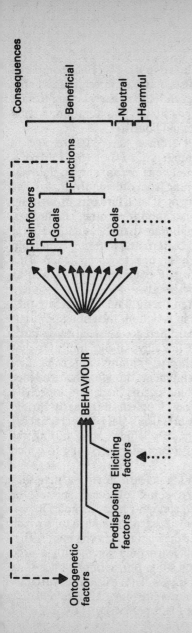

fig. 14. Relations between ontogenetic and causal factors and consequences. The distinctions between ontogenetic and predisposing and between predisposing and eliciting factors are often somewhat arbitrary. Among the consequences, the categories of reinforcers, goals and functions only partially overlap. Although a goal is normally achieved as a consequence of behaviour, an internal representation (anticipation) may contribute to causation (dotted line). Consequences may be beneficial, yet not provide material for the action of natural selection (functions, strong sense). Exceptionally, harmful consequences can be goals. The discontinuous line indicates evolutionary consequences on the next generation.

songs of the general type shown in fig. 15a. Each song lasts about 2.5 seconds and consists of two or three phrases and a terminal flourish. The songs develop in early spring from a rambling sub-song which has no definite duration, a wide range of notes, and no terminal flourish.

Chaffinches hand-reared from a few days of age in isolation develop only a simple type of song (fig. 15b), of a definite duration but with only one phrase and no flourish. Apparently, therefore, learning from other individuals plays some part in song development. If such birds are brought up in groups, still in auditory isolation from other chaffinches, they produce songs more elaborate than the isolate pattern, but conforming to a group pattern and differing both from normal song and between groups (e.g., fig. 15c). This indicates a stimulating effect of countersinging as well as learning from the other individuals.

If chaffinches are caught in the autumn, long before they start to sing, and then left in isolation, their song develops more or less normally. The difference between these birds and those isolated from a few days of age indicates that hearing adult song during the early months of life can suffice for near-normal song development, though other evidence indicates that further learning occurs later, and especially during the period of song development in the early spring. These views receive support from data on chaffinches exposed to tape recordings of chaffinch song during the autumn or winter: such birds reproduce the song to which they have been exposed.

However chaffinches will not learn anything that they hear. They will not learn songs of other species, or representations of chaffinch song in which the notes have a pure tonal quality, but they will learn a chaffinch tape which has been 'doctored' so that the ending is in the middle (fig. 15d). Apparently they will learn only songs with a note quality like that of chaffinch song. Furthermore, once song development has occurred, they will not learn fresh variants. Song-learning occurs much more readily during a 'sensitive period' than earlier or later (Thorpe, 1961).

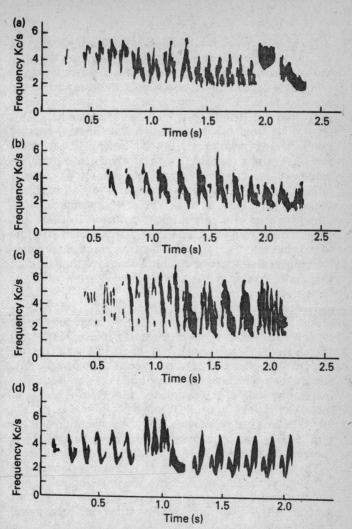

fig. 15. The song of the chaffinch. (a) A characteristic normal song. (b) Song of an individual reared in isolation. (c) Song of an individual reared in an isolated group. (d) Song produced by a bird reared in isolation, after tutoring with a re-articulated chaffinch song with the ending in the middle. (After Thorpe, 1961.)

These data suggest that chaffinches first learn what to sing and then, in the transition from sub-song during the early spring, learn how to sing it. In the latter case perfection of the song might depend on the bird being reinforced, during the period of plastic song in spring, by hearing itself produce a song like the template it had acquired earlier. Two predictions from this have been tested. First, if hearing chaffinch song is reinforcing, the chaffinch might learn other responses which enabled it to hear chaffinch song: chaffinches will in fact learn to perch preferentially on one perch rather than another if that permits them to hear chaffinch song (Stevenson-Hinde, 1972). Second, a chaffinch which cannot hear its own output might be unable to tailor that output to the template. Chaffinches deafened after exposure to song but before song development do indeed not progress towards the characteristic chaffinch song even though, once they have developed song, deafening does not affect its pattern (Nottebohm, 1967).

These conclusions about the development of song in chaffinches have been confirmed by data on other song-birds, though many details of the processes differ (e.g., Marler and Mundinger, 1971). For example whilst in chaffinches the constraint on what can be learned seems to involve the note structure, in other species young birds are predisposed to imitate the song of the male who rears them. The age of sensitivity varies. But nearly (though not quite, Marler l.c.), all of the data can be integrated on the assumption that the bird initially has a template, which may be modified by experience, and towards which it adjusts its vocal output.

The study of song development has thus revealed some of the complexities that may be involved in the ontogeny of a motor pattern. With that in mind, we may study some general issues that arise in the study of behavioural development.

(iii) Principles of development

A pivotal issue for early ethologists was the relative constancy of form of some movement patterns, especially those used in locomotion and signalling (see e.g., figs. 1, 3, 6, 11, and 15). As a result, they attempted to divide behaviour into that which is 'innate' and that which is 'learned'. There are a number of objections to such a dichotomy. First, it implies that the factors influencing behaviour are of two types only – genetic, and those associated with learning. This cannot be maintained: nutrition, 'stress' and many other factors are known to affect behavioural development in ways that would not come within any generally accepted definition of learning.

Second, such a dichotomy of behaviour was often supported by an 'isolation experiment': if the behaviour developed normally in an individual reared in isolation from the factors considered likely to be relevant, it was considered to be 'innate'. But whilst, for example, much behaviour (for instance many display movements) does develop normally in isolated individuals, isolation cannot eliminate *all* environmental influences. Again, sometimes practice seems to be unnecessary for the perfection of a movement pattern: the wing muscles of cricket nymphs show signs of rhythmic nervous impulses when the insect is suspended in a wind tunnel, even though the wings are as yet quite undeveloped. The discharges become more complex with each moult, and appear to be complete in the last instar before that in which the adult wings are developed (Bentley and Hoy, 1970). Once again, however, the finding that a particular form of environmental influence (here, the consequences of practice) is unimportant does not mean that all are.

Thus whilst relative constancy of form amongst individuals may indicate that the vagaries of their experience do not affect the pattern in question, whilst isolation rearing eliminates certain specific influences of the environment, and whilst practice may be unnecessary, none of these sources of evidence rules out all environmental influences. It is a truism that environmental influences are always there. For every pattern of behaviour, there are limits to the conditions of rearing which lead to its eventual appearance. For some patterns of behaviour, such as respiration, these conditions are co-extensive with those in which life itself is possible, and for others they are more restricted, but development always involves interaction between organism and environment.

The effects of internal (genetic) and external factors are closely interwoven. For example the 'seet' alarm call of an adult great tit causes nestlings to cease begging. The effect is found in all individuals, and does not require previous exposure to the call. Nevertheless the effectiveness of the call can be affected by experience. Exposure to the call in situations that are positive (just before parental feeding) decreases its effectiveness, whilst exposure in neutral or aversive circumstances (in association with simulated attacks on the nest) increases it. Furthermore prolonged exposure to artificial sounds resembling the 'seet' call reduces its effectiveness, so that it is at least possible that the normal response to the call depends in part on its acoustic contrast with the predominant sounds in the nestlings' auditory environment – namely their own begging calls (Ryden, 1978).

However it is not any practical difficulty in separating the effects of genetic and environmental influences that is the issue here. The view that it is not useful to attempt to understand the dynamics of development by dividing *items of behaviour* into those that are 'innate' and those that are learned or environmentally determined is one of principle. Every item of behaviour depends on preceding *interaction* between organism and environment, and which aspects of the environment influence the organism at each stage depends in part on its nature. It may sometimes be helpful to recognize a continuum from aspects of behaviour that are environmentally stable (i.e., unmodifiable by any environmental conditions within the viable limits) to those that are environmentally labile (i.e., varying greatly with environmental influences) (Hinde, 1959a). But then it must be remembered that behavioural development may be stable up to the time of first appearance of the behaviour in question and labile thereafter, as with the pecking of chicks, or labile up to the time of first performance and later become stable, as with chaffinch song (Bateson, pers. comm.).

Two asides are necessary here. First, while it is impossible to divide behaviour into items that are 'innate' and items that are solely experientially determined, it is possible to assess how far the variance in a character or item of behaviour is due to genetic variability and how far it is due to environmental variability. However even this is fraught with difficulty: because the environment an individual selects is influenced by its (in part genetically determined) nature, heredity and environment are not fully independent (Lewontin, 1975; Jaspars and Leeuw, 1980).

Second, students of behavioural development are not interested only in its dynamics. Some are concerned merely with the description of regularities in development (e.g., Overton and Reese, 1973), and others in the source of the 'distinctiveness' or 'specific adaptedness' of an item of behaviour. For instance it is possible to ask whether a character owes its specific adaptedness to a process of phylogenetic, cultural or individual adaptation: a propensity to learn only a particular song type would be a phylogenetic adaptation (Eibl Eibesfeldt, 1979) and on that basis some ethologists would label it 'innate'. It is important to note, however, that the question being considered here concerns the origin of distinctive characteristics of the behaviour in question, and not the interplay between the genetic and environmental factors in its development. Use of 'innate' to imply that distinctive characters are phylogenetically determined carries no implication that experience is not involved in their development.

Turning from behaviour to the processes involved in its development, it is sometimes convenient to distinguish consequences of 'maturation' from those of 'experience' (e.g., Schneirla, 1966), although here the dichotomy is only a convenient abstraction which depends on the universe of discourse. When applied to tissue growth and differentiation, 'maturation' is applied to processes that are unaffected by environmental factors because they occur within an environment whose characteristics are maintained within limits by regulatory mechanisms. When applied to behavioural development, it usually refers to environmentally stable (see above) characters which appear to be unaffected by differences in the environment during development. That stability may, however, be due to self-regulatory properties in the individual (see below).

A third type of dichotomy, and one with more heuristic value, concerns the sources of differences in behaviour. If we rear organisms, known to differ genetically, in similar environments, any differences in behaviour can be safely ascribed to genetic factors. For example, different species of finch, reared in closely similar environments, grow up to have different seed preferences. A role of genetic differences between the species in determining seed preferences thus seems highly likely. However this does not imply that learning is of no importance. In practice the seed preferences develop in part because species have differently sized beaks, and learn to select those seeds that they can open most efficiently with the beaks they possess (Kear, 1962).

Alternatively, if organisms of (actually or statistically) similar genetic constitution are reared in different environments, differences in behaviour can be ascribed to environmental factors. Thus the differences between the songs of chaffinches that have been reared in isolation and those that have been exposed to chaffinch song result from the environmental difference. Again this does not mean that genetic factors are unimportant: with a slight change in genetic constitution development might occur similarly in the two environments, for genes determine responsiveness to the environment.

Such a dichotomy between the causes of differences in behaviour poses further questions – how the genetic factors influence behaviour, what environmental factors operate, and how they produce their effects. An important issue here is that genetic differences may give rise to differences in predispositions to learn some things and constraints from learning others. The chaffinch is predisposed to imitate songs with a note structure resembling that of chaffinch song, and birds of other species are constrained in what they will learn in other ways (see p. 84).

In considering *how* inherited and environmental factors affect behaviour further classificatory categories may prove valuable. For instance, factors of either sort may have either specific effects on a rather narrow aspect of behaviour or more general consequences on much or all of the behavioural repertoire (e.g., Bateson, 1976a). Again they may act to initiate, to facilitate or to maintain processes involved in behavioural development (e.g., Gottlieb, 1976; Bateson, 1978a). This suggests that developmental determinants could be classified into twelve categories (inherited vs environmental, specific vs general, and initiating, facilitating or maintaining) but, as Bateson (1978) points out, many patterns of behaviour may well be determined by a combination from all twelve. Beyond that, the effects of any one determinant may vary with the others present. For instance a given factor may act in several ways, or be more or less general in its effects depending on the other factors present (e.g., Denenberg, 1979).

In considering the process of development, it must be remembered that development involves a continuing interaction between a changing organism and (usually) a changing environment. For example, female canaries are brought into reproductive condition by a change in daylength and other external stimuli. These result in a change in endocrine state, which in turn leads to nest-building behaviour. Stimuli from the resulting nest cause further changes in behaviour both directly and through endocrine intermediaries. Thus the bird changes its environment, and the environmental change induces further changes in the bird, and thus in behaviour (see pp. 162-7). More usually, perhaps, the change lies not in the actual environment, but in the perceived or effective environment. The environmental factors that matter to a one-month-old baby differ from those that matter at a year, and nest-induced hormonal changes make the canary increasingly sensitive to the nest that she has built, causing changes in her building behaviour (see p. 166).

Changes in the individual during development involve changes in its susceptibility to environmental influences. It is thus to be expected that some behavioural characteristics can be influenced by particular environmental events more readily at one stage than either earlier or later. Early on in the development of ethology some workers used the concept of 'critical periods' in this context. This came largely from experiments on 'imprinting' in birds: the young of many species will learn to respond to a moving object as they would normally respond to a parent, provided that the object is presented to them within a period starting a few hours after birth and finishing a few hours or days later (Lorenz, 1935). Lorenz regarded this period as immutable, and the process of imprinting as irreversible: the term 'critical period' became current in the literature (e.g., Scott and Marston, 1950; Hess, 1959).

However it soon became apparent that the limits of the period were not irrevocably fixed by inherent developmental processes (e.g., Moltz and Stettner, 1961), and that imprinting was not irreversible (e.g., Fabricius and Boyd, 1954). The term 'sensitive period' thus became more popular. Its implication is simply that a given event produces a stronger effect on development, or that a given effect can be produced more readily during a certain period than earlier or later. It does not imply that the period is necessarily closely tied to chronological age, nor that equivalent effects cannot be obtained (though perhaps with more difficulty) later (Clarke and Clarke, 1976). Seen in this way, 'sensitive period' refers to a characteristic feature of the development of many aspects of behaviour. It is of course crucial to remember that the processes involved in the changes in sensitivity are likely to differ from case to case (Bateson, 1979, 1981).

Given a continuing interaction between a changing organism and a changing physical and social environment, the question arises as to how far development is to be seen as proceeding smoothly and gradually, and how far as punctuated by periods of marked change in organization. Just because immature forms must be specialized for the tasks of growing and surviving to adulthood, we must expect some aspects of their structure or behaviour to be irrelevant to adult life: a caterpillar is adapted as a growing machine, and is also adapted to change dramatically to fulfill the functions of adulthood. In the same way, some of the behavioural characteristics of children can be seen as scaffolding, erected temporarily for the job of growing and subsequently demolished as the adult functions emerge in their own right (Bruner, 1978). But even where, as in insect metamorphosis, the tissues are almost completely broken down and the body is redeveloped in a new form, continuity is not totally absent: larval experience may affect the subsequent behaviour of the moth (Thorpe and Jones, 1937). Experience before metamorphosis is known to affect behaviour afterwards also in amphibians (Herschkowitz and Samuel, 1973).

In practice, evidence for less dramatic discontinuities is plentiful. It may involve marked alterations in the rate of development, such as the growth spurt just before puberty, or a sharp change in measures of behaviour accompanied by a change in the pattern of correlations between measures, as has been found in the play of kittens between seven and eight weeks after birth (Barrett and Bateson, 1978). Another type of evidence comes from sudden changes in the rank ordering of individuals assessed repeatedly for a particular behavioural characteristic: this can be important in studies of child development, for differences in performance at one age may not predict comparable differences later. Although apparent discontinuities may appear for quite trivial reasons (Bateson, 1978a), they may reflect important changes in organization. In this context a study showing profound changes between ten and twenty days of age in the way in which rats learn, changes which imply an increase in the importance of cognitive intermediaries, is of the greatest interest (Amsel and Stanton, 1980).

A related question which has engaged the attention of embryologists, ethologists and child developmentalists concerns the extent to which development is self-regulating. Does everything which happens to a young organism necessarily *matter* in the long run? Do all environmental factors which produce marked changes (or differences) in behaviour at one stage necessarily produce long-term effects? Over the last decade studies of rhesus monkeys have provided considerable evidence that apparently gross abnormalities produced by early social deprivation are susceptible to rehabilitation, at least in some degree (reviewed Suomi and Harlow, 1978a and b; see also Clarke and Clarke, 1976), and it has been emphasized that behavioural development often has a knack of returning towards its original track, even though it has suffered deviations along the way (Dunn, 1976; Bateson, 1976b).

Such recovery is usually ascribed to 'self-correcting features' or 'internal control' of development, the achievement of a particular end-state by diverse routes being labelled as 'equifinality' (e.g., Bertalanffy, 1968). For practical and conceptual reasons 'equifinality' is hard to prove (Bateson, 1976b; Dunn, 1976), but the occurrence of self-correcting tendencies cannot be doubted. But labels such as 'equifinality' have an almost mystical air, at least at first sight, and the systems theory with which they are often linked, though sometimes fertile in suggesting avenues of research (e.g., Bateson, 1978b), can appear more sophisticated than the crude behavioural data as yet available to us.

In practice, some examples of regulation in development may depend on very simple mechanisms. Given that only some aspects of the environment matter to the developing organism (see p. 35), there may be mechanisms for keeping the relevant environment more or less constant. If the mother leaves, a child may follow and thereby maintain proximity; if she disappears, attachment to another individual may be sought. In any case there is nothing mystical about regulation – it is to be seen only as a special form of organism/environmental interaction. Whilst progressive developmental change can depend on a response to environmental events producing change in the organism such that its responsiveness changes (pp. 82–4), so also can maintenance of the developmental track. The simplest case is perhaps that of habituation – stimuli which initially produce a response, and thus potentially divert development, produce a change in the organism whereby they cease to elicit a response.

In child development, many self-correcting mechanisms may lie in the child's relationships with others rather than in the child itself. That dyadic relationships and families have powers for self-regulation has been emphasized for many years by clinicians (e.g., Jackson, 1959; Watzlawick *et al.*, 1967; Wertheim, 1975): whilst stability within a defined range is ensured, limited change in particular directions may yet be possible. An example from rhesus monkeys is shown in fig. 16. After a short separation experience, rhesus monkey infants are often very demanding on their mothers, and spend much less time off them than before. In most cases, however, the relationship reverts to its original track. This occurs apparently because the mother at first accedes to the infant's demands: we can picture this as a deviance in one partner producing behaviour in the other which removes the deviance in the former. The marked oscillations in measures of the relationship in the days and weeks after reunion resemble those of a poorly damped homeostat and reveal the processes involved in the gradual re-establishment of the relationship. However dyadic regulation does not always occur, as shown by one dyad in fig. 16: the regulatory mechanism is effective only within limits (Hinde, 1974; Hinde and McGinnis, 1977; see Klopfer and Klopfer 1977 for another example). In man, Sameroff (1975; Sameroff and Chandler, 1975) has reviewed data showing that perinatal trauma produces significant long-term effects only in socially disadvantaged families, and Quinton and Rutter (1976) showed the same to be true of early separation

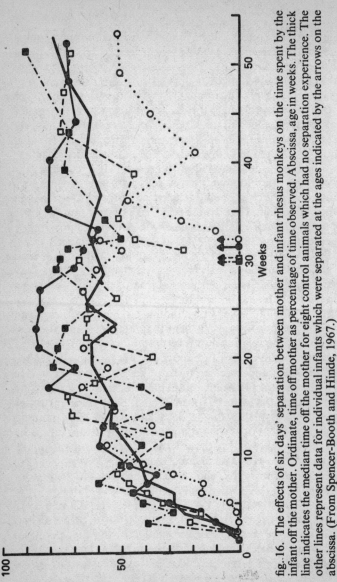

fig. 16. The effects of six days' separation between mother and infant rhesus monkeys on the time spent by the infant off the mother. Ordinate, time off mother as percentage of time observed. Abscissa, age in weeks. The thick line indicates the median time off the mother for eight control animals which had no separation experience. The other lines represent data for individual infants which were separated at the ages indicated by the arrows on the abscissa. (From Spencer-Booth and Hinde, 1967.)

experiences. Sameroff and Chandler proposed a continuum of caretaking effectiveness: at one end supportive, compensatory and normalizing environments appear to be able virtually to eliminate the effects of early problems, while at the other caretaking by deprived, stressed or poorly educated parents tends to exacerbate early difficulties. An unusual developmental course is thus likely to result either from an early above-threshold deviation, or from a continuing malfunction in the mechanisms of homeostasis. The latter could be due to the former, or to continuing environmental pressures.

(iv) Development of behavioural items vs development of behavioural systems

In studying the causation of behaviour, ethologists recognize the need not only to analyse the causal bases of particular aspects of behaviour, but also to re-synthesize the products of analysis in order to understand how functional systems of behaviour are integrated (pp. 76–8). The same issue arises in the study of development. We must understand not only how chaffinch song develops, but how singing becomes integrated into the complex of activities that lead to reproduction. The issue is highlighted by studies of young animals, which often show disconnected fragments of behaviour. A fledgling song-bird may peck at a small spot, give a snatch of sub-song, and show a fragment of copulatory behaviour in apparently inconsequential succession: how do the separate items become welded into the functional sequences seen in the adult? In adults the complex inter-relations between different types of behaviour necessitate the postulation of behaviour systems (fig. 13). But how do those inter-relations develop in the individual?

The gradual emergence of behavioural systems has been described in several cases (Kortlandt, 1955; Kruijt, 1964), but little experimental work has been done, and there is often an unstated assumption either that integration is a consequence of 'maturation', or that simple learning principles will suffice. However, a complex interplay between maturation and experience is more likely: the consequences of particular experiences depend on the nature of the experiencing organism, and may be more extensive and complex than simple learning principles would predict.

The evidence here is still anecdotal, but sufficient to indicate that important problems await investigation. For example, in a study of the gathering/carrying/building sequence shown by female canaries constructing a nest (see p. 71), birds, which had been deprived of nest material and whose only experience of carrying had involved attempts to carry their own feathers, were given grass. They picked up pieces of grass, carried them to a nest-site and built with them there within a few seconds. Their behaviour suggested the possibility that the earlier experience of incomplete nest-building sequences had facilitated the performance of complete ones as soon as that became possible. Again, in this case one might expect the later phases of the nest-building sequence to act as reinforcers (see p. 281) for the earlier ones. But while discrimination within a phase (gathering this material rather than that) is related to events within that phase (opportunity to pull or mandibulate material), no evidence that the performance of one phase (e.g., to gather) was affected by the opportunity to perform the next (e.g., to carry and build) could be found (Hinde and Steel, 1972).

Another example is provided by the maternal behaviour of mice. Adult mice respond more maternally to a live one-day-old baby than to a dead one, and much evidence suggests that the difference is due to the ultrasonic calls emitted by the former. However when naive mice were exposed to the ultrasonic sounds and smell of infants, even though they had no other contact with them, their subsequent responsiveness to a drowned infant was enhanced. While there may have been olfactory stimuli in common between the initial exposure and the test with the drowned infant, there was a strong suggestion that the initial exposure to the ultrasonic stimuli 'primed' the maternal behaviour in such a manner that it could be elicited by the drowned (and thus silent) infant (Noirot, 1964).

There is thus an urgent need for ethologists to undertake more work on the development of behavioural systems. An obvious candidate is the complex of responses involved in the relationship of infant or fledgling to its mother. While the imprinting (see p. 90) of the following response of young birds has been studied in detail (see pp. 193–6), we still know little about the precise way in which the relationship between chick and mother develops. The chick initially gives particular responses to specific stimuli emitted by the mother, but later responds to her as an individual. The latter could perhaps be understood in terms of the conditioning of the several chick responses to stimuli from the mother other than those that elicited them initially, so that each comes to be elicitable by rather general features of the mother. But is it possible that this process is facilitated by predispositions in the chick? Could responses which had never been elicited by the natural mother come to be elicitable by her as a consequence of experience with her as an elicitor of other responses in the chick's repertoire? Related problems are crucial in the study of child development (chapter 14), and there is an opportunity for ethologists to make a substantial contribution. In studies of the development of behavioural systems it must be remembered that not only does behavioural development involve a continuing interaction between a changing organism and a changing environment, but the organism itself has a changing behavioural repertoire, with response systems that interact in many ways: since the component responses may be appetitive, consummatory, alternative, facilitatory or inhibitory to each other, the development of one may affect that of others.

(v) Conclusion

This brief sketch has been intended only to indicate some of the issues currently controversial in the study of develop-

ment. But the nature of the controversies is worth noting.
The issues discussed – sensitive periods, continuity vs
discontinuity, and the like, involve vastly different types of
behaviour in diverse species, so that the mechanisms
underlying them are unlikely to be similar. Demonstration
of a sensitive period or discontinuity in development in one
species is of interest because it shows the *sort of thing* that
might be going on in another. It cannot be controverted by
data from another species, though such data might suggest
how the phenomenon was to be understood at a different
level of analysis.

4   The Study of Function

(i) Introduction

The third group of questions which ethologists seek to answer concerns the biological functions of behaviour. Trained as biologists, it was a basic presupposition of the early ethologists that behaviour, like structure, had been evolved by natural selection. As they observed new types of behaviour they were therefore prompted to ask 'What is this behaviour for?', or 'How do the consequences of that behaviour contribute to the survival and reproduction of the individual concerned?' Framed in the latter way, questions of function do not differ in kind from questions of causation: instead of asking what caused the behaviour, we enquire how the behaviour influences events that succeed it. However we shall see here that only some of the sequelae to a given item of behaviour are to be considered as functions (fig. 14). We shall also see that the form in which functional questions are usually asked has changed over the years, with important consequences for research.

We may consider first one group of examples from the early days of ethology. The work, carried out largely by de Ruiter (1956) and his colleagues, concerned the relations between colour and behaviour in caterpillars.

Many caterpillars are coloured in a way which makes them inconspicuous to predators. Usually they have a general colour resemblance to their environment. They are also coloured to conceal their solidity. Since the light in most environments comes from above, the underneath of a rounded object tends to be in shadow. This differential lighting of upper and under surfaces gives such objects an

appearance of solidity, and makes them more conspicuous –
an issue perhaps of special importance for caterpillars living
in an environment of flat leaves. The effect is largely
overcome if the animal is 'counter-shaded', that is, if it has
lighter coloration underneath than on top. Most animals are
in fact coloured in this way, but for the counter-shading to be
effective they must also orient themselves correctly with
respect to the light. Whilst most caterpillars are lighter in
colour on the anatomically ventral side, some are lighter on
their dorsal surfaces. This is associated with a difference in
behaviour: caterpillars of each species normally position
themselves in a manner that utilizes their counter-shading,
whether it be dorsal or ventral side uppermost (fig. 17).

The relations between the direction of the counter-shading
and the attitude (dorsal or ventral side uppermost) that
caterpillars normally adopt provides circumstantial evidence that the counter-shading facilitates concealment, but
is it effective? De Ruiter tested the matter experimentally by
allowing captive jays (*Garrulus glandarius*) to search for
caterpillars in an aviary. The jays found them less easily if
they were oriented correctly than if their counter-shading
was 'upside down'.

A number of other principles contribute to the camouflage
of animals in nature, but a behavioural component is usually
involved (Cott, 1940). For example some caterpillars
resemble natural objects, such as sticks, but for their
camouflage to be effective they must orient correctly with
respect to the twig on which they are situated, and remain
motionless. Experiments showed that if they move they are
much more likely to be eaten.

However well camouflaged caterpillars are, predators may
learn to locate them. If similarly camouflaged caterpillars are
present in abundance in a particular location, an individual
predator may become adept at finding them. Thus in
addition to correct orientation, camouflaged caterpillars
tend to be dispersed. Dispersal may result from the female's
behaviour when egg-laying, or from the caterpillar's own
movement (e.g., Ford, 1956; Tinbergen, 1958). Some other

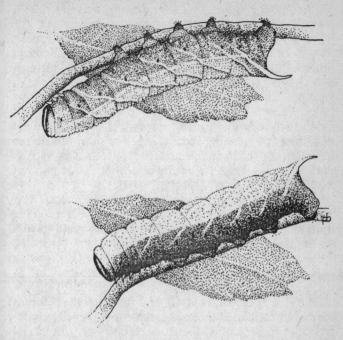

fig. 17. Counter-shading. The hawk caterpillar normally positions itself with its dorsal side downwards, and the counter-shading is reversed. Note how this increases its crypticity.

caterpillars rely on their own distastefulness to discourage predators. Such caterpillars tend to be conspicuously coloured. The success of this device depends on the predator, having tasted one, avoiding others. Here, therefore, safety lies in high density, and the caterpillars tend to aggregate.

(ii) The classical concept of function

Before considering the evidence used to establish function, we must consider the nature of the concept. When we say that a character is functional or adaptive, we mean that it enhances the survival or reproductive success of the individual (or, for reasons to be discussed later, his genetic kin): in brief, function implies enhancing (evolutionary) 'fitness'. But this ultimate function may be achieved through long chains of events consequent upon the behaviour in question. The male chaffinch's song has the immediate consequences of attracting females and repelling rival males, and these have further consequences which ultimately affect his chances of breeding successfully. The term function is thus often applied to more immediate consequences, such as repelling rivals, which follow the behaviour in question but precede the reproductive success.

Now every behavioural act has many consequences. These can in principle be classified according to their effects on the reproductive success of the individual and his relatives (fig. 14). Some are detrimental, some neutral and some beneficial. For example when a gull incubates its eggs it (a) probably loses time it could spend feeding, and exposes itself to predation (deleterious consequences or 'costs'); (b) slightly expands the egg-shell (neutral); and (c) keeps the embryos warm and facilitates their development (beneficial consequence) (Tinbergen, 1942). In a broad way, beneficial consequences are referred to as functions. A character of behaviour is said to be adaptive if its beneficial consequences outweigh the deleterious ones (i.e., the costs).

Natural selection can operate only through consequences that are achieved to a different extent in different individuals. (It is of course also necessary that the differences have a genetic basis.) For example, a bird's body feathers provide insulation, and also carry patterns and colours that are biologically advantageous. If the natural variation in the density of feathers is within the range which could affect insulation but does not affect coloration, natural selection can not act through the coloration to maintain the density of feathers at its present level. The coloration, though a beneficial consequence of having feathers, is not one through which natural selection can act to maintain feather density.

It is therefore useful to distinguish between beneficial consequences (or functions in a weak sense), and functions in a strong sense (s.s.) – namely those beneficial consequences through which natural selection acts to maintain the character in question (Hinde, 1956, 1975; Williams, 1966). Biologists often talk about the 'pressure' of natural selection on the various characters of an animal, but selection pressures can act only through consequences that are differentially achieved by the individuals in the population: these are functions in the strong sense.

To take another example, diverse functions have been ascribed to the territorial behaviour of song-birds. Some consequences of territorial behaviour seem to be deleterious – for instance the time used and exposure to predators in territorial defence. We must therefore ask what beneficial consequences outweigh them. Sometimes access to a nest-site is an important consequence of having a territory. But if nest-sites are superabundant, access to a site cannot be a consequence of territorial behaviour through which natural selection acts to maintain it at its current level (Hinde, 1956). This distinction, accepted by some biologists (e.g., Wilson, 1975; cf. also Curio, 1978), is regarded as generating confusion by others. For example Krebs (1976) writes, 'Natural selection today acts on all current consequences of territoriality, so any beneficial consequences must be in some sense a function.' However he provides no arguments in support of this view (see also Slater, 1976).

Of course an absolute dichotomy between beneficial consequences and functions (s.s.) would be an over-simplification. The extent to which the various beneficial consequences of a character of structure or behaviour provide material for natural selection varies along a continuum. And of course natural selection may operate through more than one consequence of a behaviour pattern: many patterns of behaviour have more than one function (s.s.). But the distinction does indicate that an answer to the question 'What is it good for?' *need* tell us nothing about selection pressures and the dynamics of the evolutionary process.

Thus to prove function in the weak sense it is necessary to show that a character has one or more beneficial consequences, though those beneficial consequences must also outweigh the concomitant costs. If in addition the beneficial consequence is realized to different extents by different individuals in nature (and of course if that variation has some genetic basis), the evidence for function in the strong sense begins to mount up. However there is still another difficulty. If the concept of function or adaptation is to have an empirical relevance, it must refer to a difference. If we say that the function of chaffinch song is to attract females, we imply that a non-singing male is less likely to get a mate than one which sings, or must obtain his mate by some other strategy. Unfortunately it is very difficult experimentally to alter one aspect of behaviour without also affecting others, and characters do not necessarily vary independently in nature. For example interpretation of field data on differences in breeding success between chaffinches who sing much and chaffinches who sing little may be complicated by other differences: those which sing little may have low sex hormone levels, and also be less aggressive. Again, parental feeding is elicited in many species by conspicuous markings in the gape of the nestlings. In a white variant of the zebra finch (*Taeniopygia guttata*) the gape markings are almost absent. Immelmann *et al.* (1977) have shown that such nestlings survive less well than wild-type nestlings, even when fed by wild-type adults, and thus conclude that the gape markings are indeed functional in eliciting parental feeding. But there remains the possibility that the genetic differences between the two strains also have other effects, which include lower viability of the white type. In addition, a deleterious effect of an almost total lack of gape markings indicates only a beneficial consequence of the markings: it does not show that such small differences as (presumably) exist between individuals in nature lead to differential survival.

This difficulty is minimized if we compare groups of individuals from the same population who differ only slightly in the character in question and can reasonably be assumed to be statistically similar in other respects. But the difficulty is greater, the greater the difference that is implied. When we are concerned with the function of a character possessed by all members of a species we imply comparison either with members of another hypothetical species identical in all respects except that it lacks the character in question, or with another real species that differs in many respects. Whereas the difficulty in comparisons within a species lies in causal links between characters, those between species involve also functional ones: the characters of a species form an adaptive complex such that evolutionary change in one will have ramifying consequences through the whole.

A slight digression is necessary to make this clear. Whereas most gulls nest on flat grassy or marshy areas, the kittiwake (*Rissa tridactyla*) nests on cliff ledges, a trait which no doubt protects it from predation (fig. 18). The kittiwake's behaviour also differs from other gulls in other ways – for instance in the nature of territorial defence, in nesting, copulatory and parental behaviour, and in various aspects of the behaviour of the young. Many of these can be regarded as evolutionary consequences of cliff-nesting. For instance the nest is more elaborate than that of ground-nesting species, and the young do not run away when attacked. Gull species which can nest either on cliff ledges or on level ground show characteristics intermediate between those of the kittiwake and those of ground-nesting gulls (Cullen, 1957; N. G. Smith, 1966). Thus the function of any particular character of kittiwakes must be considered together with a whole complex of other characteristics, including cliff-nesting. Comparisons with other species must be made within the context of the adaptive systems to which they contribute (e.g., Nelson, 1975; Tschanz and Hirsbrunner-Scharf, 1975; Birkhead, 1978).

We shall return to this important concept of the adaptive

fig. 18. Kittiwake sitting on its nest on a cliff ledge.

complex later. The point being made here is that when two species or groups differ in a number of respects, the significance of a difference in any one character must be considered in relation to the total complex.

One final point must be made. Evidence that a given trait has consequences that are beneficial bears not at all on how that trait is acquired in individual development. It could be an environmentally stable character (p. 86), whose features are little influenced by individual experience. But, at the

fig. 19. A blue tit opening a milk bottle by tearing the foil cap.

other extreme, it could be individually acquired. For
example blue tits (*Parus caeruleus*) in England have
developed a habit of opening milk bottles and drinking the
milk – a habit presumably beneficial (fig. 19). It depends on
the fact that milk bottles present stimuli for certain motor
patterns which are used in acquiring natural foods and can
be used for opening the bottle, and on propensities to feed
where other individuals have been seen feeding and to learn
from experience (Hinde and Fisher, 1951). Thus, while the
difference between tits who have and who have not acquired
the habit does not in general depend on genetic differences,
the differences between species who do not acquire the habit
(given the opportunity) does – namely on genetically-based
differences in motor patterns and learning propensities. We
may presume that those motor patterns and learning
propensities are maintained in the repertoire of the species
through a variety of consequences: it is an open issue
whether differences in milk drinking are amongst them (i.e.,

are functions s.s.), but it is reasonable to suppose that they could be.

However it is also clear that those same abilities play a part in another trait which is unlikely to be beneficial. Blue tits sometimes enter houses and tear paper, pull down wallpaper, tear up books, and so on. This behaviour varies much in frequency, but simultaneous outbreaks have occasionally been recorded all over the United Kingdom. The behaviour involves one of the movements used in opening milk bottles, and a similar learning propensity, but no food is obtained and no beneficial consequence is apparent (Hinde, 1953c). This example has been spelled out in some detail because it provides an animal example of how propensities which are in general beneficial to the species can produce behaviour which is not. Another more well-known case is the reed-warbler which feeds a cuckoo in its nest: in general it is advantageous to put food in a gape in your own nest, but the cuckoo exploits this. Similar considerations apply to some aspects of human cultures (pp. 250–65).

(iii) Evidence for the classical concept of function

With that as background, we may turn to some types of data used as evidence for function. Often the first evidence comes from observations of the consequences of behaviour. If we see a female moving towards, or a male retreating from, a singing male chaffinch, we may speculate that attracting females or repelling males are probably beneficial consequences of singing. This leaves open such issues as whether it is useful to repel other males, what the costs of singing are, whether there may be other beneficial consequences, and so on. But we are the more likely to presume a selection pressure, the more closely the character in question seems to 'fit' a problem presented by the environment (Tinbergen, 1963; Williams, 1966). In the case of the singing chaffinch we might examine whether he sings more or less often once he has a mate, whether he is more likely to sing near territorial boundaries where trespassing often occurs, and so on.

A related type of evidence comes from correlations between a character of structure or behaviour and environmental factors. If distinctive coloration and display are common in male birds living in areas where closely related species are present, but where only one species is present, both sexes tend to be cryptic, it seems likely that the distinctive features have a function related to the presence of related species: the prevention of inbreeding is an obvious candidate (Brown and Wilson, 1956; Lack, 1966, 1968).

Another approach involves looking for correlations between a range of characters across a range of species. For example examination of the relations between population density, group size, breeding system and sexual dimorphism in mammals suggests that variations in food supply determine differences in population density and distribution, that these determine differences in breeding systems, and that differences in breeding systems determine a wide variety of morphological and physiological traits (Clutton-Brock and Harvey, 1978): we shall discuss a specific example of some of these issues later (chapter 7).

There are of course many problems with the use of correlational evidence, including the dangers of falsely inferring causation. Furthermore there is a real danger that the focus is on the wrong consequence. For example when a group of animals is first put together there is often much fighting, but after a while individuals become organized into an hierarchical dominance order in which each submits to the one above it. Since a stable hierarchy is correlated with a reduction in aggression, it has sometimes been suggested that the reduction in fighting is the function of the hierarchy. The implication is that stability and lack of overt aggression is in the interests of the group. A proper approach, however, must be to consider the consequences of the formation of a dominance hierarchy for the individuals involved, including both those high and low in the order (see pp. 143–4). A relation between high dominance and reproductive success has been established at least in some cases (e.g., Hausfater, 1975;

Packer, 1979). However a stable hierarchy implies that it must also be beneficial to acknowledge inferiority or to submit to those stronger than you if you thereby avoid an attack (Lack, 1954, 1966; Hinde, 1972): this is less easy to substantiate.

Further progress can be made by means of simple field experiments. We may consider some examples from the pioneering work of Tinbergen and his colleagues on various aspects of gull behaviour. The gulls in question nest colonially on flat ground, but defend territories within the colony. The territory owners spend much time displaying on their territories, and we may ask whether these displays do in fact deter intruders. By comparing the behaviour of intruders into territories in which the owners were present but had been immobilized by a stupefying drug, with that of intruders into territories on which the owners were behaving normally, Patterson demonstrated that the displays do have a deterrent effect (see also e.g., Smith, 1979). Accepting for the moment that this is beneficial for the territory owner, the experiment demonstrates the effect, but does not show that natural selection acts through that consequence in maintaining display at its present level: it could be that such displays have other consequences, and that repulsion of males is incidental. In fact other observational evidence renders this unlikely.

Another experiment concerned predation on black-headed gull chicks. The gulls remove fragments of egg-shells from the nest after the young have hatched. In doing so, they may leave the nest temporarily unguarded, but Tinbergen and his colleagues (Tinbergen, 1967) nevertheless suspected that the removal of the egg-shell could function in reducing predation. The outsides of the eggs and the chicks are cryptically coloured, but the lightly coloured inner surfaces of egg-shells could make the nest conspicuous. Comparative evidence supported this view: in those avian species which nest on the ground and do not remove the broken egg-shells, the young usually leave the nest very soon after hatching; and amongst gulls and terns those species with camouflaged young tend to remove the shells, while those with conspicuous young do not. Accordingly the hypothesis was tested by laying out eggs in the colony with or without a broken shell nearby. The former were taken by predators more rapidly than the latter. This again demonstrates a beneficial consequence, but does not in itself show that natural selection operates through it. It could be that egg-shell removal has consequences as or more important than concealment of the chicks from visual predators. For instance the broken edges of the egg-shells might injure the chicks, or provide a focus of infection. Tinbergen argued that, since the cliff-nesting kittiwake, whose nest and young are not cryptic, does not remove the egg-shells, such issues are unlikely to be important. Once again, comparative evidence is used in addition to experimental data.

Yet another issue concerned the function of territorial behaviour in the black-headed gull. Given that the displays help to repel intruders, they also consume time and energy. What use is the territorial behaviour in this species? Several issues may be involved here. First, the spacing out of nests may make it more difficult for visual predators to find the cryptic eggs and young: a predator who finds one will not find another close by (cf. pp. 100–1). This effect was demonstrated experimentally. Second, black-headed gulls eat each other's newly hatched chicks: possession of a territory may thus reduce intra-specific predation. However egg and chick survival tends to be better in the centre of the colony than on the periphery, because the mobbing of colony members can deter ground predators of other species (Patterson, 1965; Tinbergen *et al.*, 1967). It thus seems that the degree of nest dispersion is the resultant of diverse conflicting consequences. The difficulty of pinning these down will be apparent. Even if it could be shown in nature that the more widely spaced nests are less subject to intra-specific predation, this could be because such nests are on the periphery of the colony, and neighbours are likely to be less aggressive there.

It will be apparent that proof of function in the narrow

sense is extremely difficult. Tinbergen (1967) was properly cautious about this, but his caution has not always been emulated.

(iv) Studies of optimality

Recently, questions about function have been asked rather differently. Instead of starting with the behaviour, and asking 'What is it for?' or 'Through what consequence is it maintained by natural selection?', it has become customary to look at the issues from the other end, assuming functions (e.g., inseminating females, foraging efficiently) and asking how, or how well, they are achieved. The approach is potentially able to take into account the fact that the character may be subject to several different selective pressures, though in practice attention is usually focused on one.

The basic supposition is that animals are adapted in such a manner that their biological inclusive fitness is maximised.* Maximizing inclusive fitness involves achieving many short-term consequences – acquiring adequate food, a mate, a nest-site, and so on. It is on these that attention is usually focused, since it is usually impracticable to measure inclusive fitness under field conditions. The questions studied are thus of the form 'Is the animal foraging as efficiently as it could?' or 'Is it selecting that mate who will provide the greatest potential number of offspring?'

One relatively simple but elegant example from a study of foraging behaviour may be mentioned first. Crows (*Corvus caurinus*) forage on whelks (*Thais lamellosa*) by dropping them from a height to break them open. Large whelks break more easily than small ones, but several drops may be

* That is, that not only their own reproductive success measured in terms of their descendants in subsequent generations is maximized, but also that those of relatives (who share a high proportion of their rare genes) is maximized to an extent devalued according to their degree of relatedness (see pp. 145–7).

necessary. Zach (1979) showed that the crows (a) selected large whelks; (b) minimized the energetically expensive ascending flight before dropping; (c) persisted with individual molluscs until they broke: this was economical, because the percentage breaking on successive drops was constant; and (d) dropped the whelks only on rock. Crows gained about 1.49 Kcalories per whelk, enough to open another 1.5 whelks. Thus the crow's behaviour seems to be organized to maximize efficiency.

In general, the study of optimality in foraging behaviour requires concomitant behavioural analysis (e.g., Krebs and Davies, 1978; Collier and Rovee-Collier, 1980). The relative availability of different prey items, and indeed what counts as available food, depends on the nature of the forager, and this may change with age or experience, differ between individuals, and so on. Food must be found, selected, prepared and digested before it can be assimilated, and behavioural aspects are crucial at each stage. Foragers may selectively take the more abundant prey items, perhaps because the formation of a 'search image' (L. Tinbergen, 1960; Dawkins, 1971) facilitates the search. They may adjust their foraging according to the patchiness of the distribution of foods (Royama, 1970): the behavioural rules that determine how long they continue to search in one place or for one type of prey (e.g., Krebs *et al.*, 1974; Krebs *et al.*, 1978) will be crucial to their success. The complexity of the behavioural problems is indicated by the consideration that, in order to maximize feeding efficiency, an animal must know what is available, and must thus spend some time in less than maximally productive search (Smith and Sweatman 1974). And parents may be influenced in choosing a less nutritious readily available food over a better but less accessible sort by the immediate hunger of their young (J. Tinbergen, 1980). Further issues arise in dealing with the food once found. Many food items must be prepared before they are eaten, and this may require skills that are individually acquired (e.g., Hinde, 1959c; Vince, 1964). Often the course of skill acquisition is determined by the morphological tools available (e.g., Davis, 1957). And the capacity to deal with prey items may change with time, not only through skill acquisition but simply through growth: many fish take larger prey items as they grow larger, presumably as a consequence of learning, the optimal food reward for energy expended in taking it increasing with size of fish (Hinde, 1959c). The availability of food may also be influenced by other animals (e.g., p. 107) (Hinde and Fisher, 1951; Krebs *et al.*, 1972) and foraging strategies may change in a manner which minimizes competition when competition is severe (e.g., Hartley, 1953).

The issues now being tackled include not only foraging behaviour, as discussed so far, but virtually everything animals do, including the complex issues of mate selection and other aspects of reproduction (e.g., Krebs and Davies, 1978). In general, to tackle such problems it is necessary to calculate how the animal should behave in order to optimize the consequence in question, and then see how closely the behaviour actually shown approximates to that expected (e.g. MacArthur and Pianka, 1966; Pyke *et al.*, 1977). This approach can in theory be applied not only to particular types of behaviour, but to the relative importance of external stimuli and internal factors in controlling behaviour, the relative prepotence of different types of behaviour (see pp. 63–6) and so on. One approach is to assess the costs and benefits incurred in the behaviour, and to combine them into a cost function. This is used to calculate an optimal control law which will generate a supposedly optimal behaviour sequence. In practice, hypotheses about the cost function, derived from observation of behaviour on the assumption that behaviour is optimal, are used to predict behaviour sequences under a wide variety of conditions. These are compared with the behaviour actually observed in those situations, and the discrepancy used to reformulate the initial hypotheses (McFarland, 1976).

One complication, implicit in what has been said already, is that the optimal behaviour may vary with circumstances. As a simple example, a tit should choose a nest hole that is inaccessible to predators, with an entrance only just large enough for it to enter. Given artificial nest-boxes, which meet these requirements, great tits choose them. But they can also accommodate to circumstances, and if insufficient nest-boxes are available inferior sites are accepted. The benefits of accepting any particular site depend on what is available (Hinde, 1959c). As another example, the stability of a dominance hierarchy depends on the facts that it is better to be at the top if you can, but if you cannot achieve dominance it may be better to bide your time than struggle against hopeless odds. In other words, the best course of action depends on what other individuals do. This is an issue which comes up repeatedly: the best way to behave in a fight depends on what the opponent does; the amount of energy to expend on territorial defence may depend on the pressure from neighbours.

In such cases a stable situation can arise if all individuals have appropriate conditional strategies, or if some individuals have one and some have another. To take the fight case, if all individuals in a population used conventional threat signals, retreating from a contest if there was any real danger, a new mutant who fought viciously would be at an advantage. But in a population of vicious fighters, someone is liable to get hurt in every encounter; if the gains of winning are less than the costs of losing, it may be better not to be a vicious fighter. Maynard Smith (e.g., Maynard Smith and Price, 1973; Maynard Smith and Parker, 1976; Maynard Smith, 1976) has shown that, given certain assumptions, a stable situation can arise when there are particular proportions of vicious and conventional fighters in the population, or when each individual adopts each strategy for a particular proportion of the time. Such mathematical models can be compared with the situations which actually occur, and modified in the light of the comparison and of further theoretical considerations (e.g., Grafan, 1979). They have provided a powerful stimulus to research (review Dawkins, 1980).

Thus the device of asking 'Is the animal behaving as well

as it could?' has proved remarkably fertile. There are however some conceptual issues which deserve consideration.

First, it is not immediately obvious which, or how many, short-term functions should be studied. Consider, for instance, studies of foraging. As Krebs (1978) points out, animals are probably selected to feed efficiently, but 'efficiently' could mean achieving a maximum net rate of food (or energy) intake, a maximum rate of intake of some specific nutrient, a maximum rate of intake per energy expended in searching, and so on. The difficulty here is related to the distinction, discussed above, between functions (s.s) and beneficial consequences. Natural selection can act only if variation within the normal population affects survival or reproduction. If some individuals only manage to obtain a diet providing so little energy that their chances of survival are affected, but even they obtain adequate supplies of a particular nutrient, natural selection cannot operate to maximize or augment intake of that nutrient.

The importance of this issue becomes apparent when a beneficial consequence, which is at one time achieved easily and adequately, becomes crucial. For example the foraging behaviour of spotted flycatchers is normally compatible with the view that they maximize energy gain, but they seek out calcium-rich prey when reproductive needs require it (Davies, 1977): presumably at other times their calcium needs are taken care of in the course of maximizing energy intake.

A second issue concerns the complexity of the relations between the short-term beneficial consequences of a behavioural sequence and inclusive fitness. The former must first be assessed against the costs, including the costs of not doing all the things the individual might have been doing instead of the behaviour in question, and it is not always easy to know what these are, let alone to measure them. An example where considerable progress has in fact been made may clarify this. As sticklebacks become less hungry, they prefer to feed in less dense swarms of water-fleas (*Daphnia*). This shift would not be expected if the fish were optimizing their capture rate (or energy intake) throughout the time they were feeding. However in addition to feeding, the fish must look out for predators. Heller and Milinski (1979) suggested that the 'confusion effect' of feeding in dense swarms of water-fleas lessened the ability of sticklebacks to detect approaching predators. Since additional prey become less valuable as satiation approaches, the stickleback should slow its capture rate by moving to an area of lower prey density and thereby reducing the costs of confusion. A mathematical model taking account of this cost of feeding in high density swarms predicted that the fish should always choose the lowest prey density in which it could achieve a feeding rate sufficient to satisfy its hunger. Some of the predictions of the model were experimentally verified (see also Sibly and McFarland, 1976).

A related matter is that the short-term benefits and costs that are measured in practice (e.g., in terms of caloric value of food per time spent foraging, or survival of own young) could be related in diverse ways to benefit as measured in terms of inclusive fitness. A male bird may incur heavy costs by engaging in territorial defence today, but will presumably reap dividends in the long run (Davies, 1977). Again, it does not necessarily follow that an increase in foraging efficiency will increase fitness – the efficiency may be more than adequate already. We shall see later that the optimal (in terms of biological fitness) number of eggs for a female bird to lay is not the maximum, and is determined in a complex way by the food available at various points in the season, the length of the day in which to find that food, and so on (p. 137).

Even the relative prepotence of different types of behaviour may depend on outcomes in diverse behavioural contexts. For instance in many birds the initial response of a male to a potential sexual partner is aggressive. Just why this should be so is itself a problem. It has been suggested that it is advantageous to the male because it deters females who are not highly motivated to engage in reproductive activities (Trivers, 1972; Zahavi, 1977) or who have recently mated. In the latter case aggression could delay ovulation beyond the period for which sperm from any other male would be viable (Erickson and Zenone, 1978): whilst the male courtship of doves stimulates ovulation, the period from pair formation to egg-laying is 5.25 days with relatively unaggressive courtship but 8 days with a highly aggressive male (Hutchison and Lovari, 1976). Presumably an even more aggressive male would in nature drive the female off altogether. Thus the degree of aggression shown by the male must be adjusted rather finely. However there are further complications, for animals that are highly aggressive in one context tend to be so in another (Huntingford, 1976a and b); and Tinbergen (1952) has suggested that aggressive propensities, important in the territorial defence of herring gulls, may interfere with pair formation. Assessments of the cost of aggression in the context of pair formation may therefore be inadequate: it is necessary to come to terms with the whole adaptive complex.

These are problems of complexity: it may well be that, in due course, with increasing refinement of measures for recording behaviour, analysing data and model building, it will be possible to cope with them. Mathematical models and computer simulation can play an important role here. Thus the field worker may propose evolutionary causes in terms of selection pressures to account for the type of behaviour that he observes, but since the behaviour lies within an adaptive complex (p. 105 and pp. 137–42), direct tests may be ruled out by the impossibility of finding individuals, groups or species who differ, and differ only, in the aspects of behaviour under consideration. While circumstantial evidence of various sorts may support the hypothesis, mathematical models and computer simulation can provide evidence as to whether the proposed selection pressures would be sufficient to account for the observed behaviour (Maynard Smith, 1977, 1978). An example arises from the possible beneficial consequences for females in breeding synchronously. Amongst a number of possibilities, it has been suggested that if females breed synchronously, philandering males will find no available females. It will thus pay each male to become more involved in helping the female he has fertilized to maximize the chances of survival of her young, rather than trying to inseminate other females. Computer simulation enabled Knowlton (1979) to specify the factors that would influence this effect. Such studies, carried out with a realistic appreciation of their relation to real-life data, may greatly augment understanding of species biology (see e.g., Parker and MacNair, 1979).

Meanwhile many workers are properly cautious (e.g., McCleery, 1978). There is always the possibility that the wrong consequences have been assessed, or that some have been omitted, or that the assessments have been made in the wrong circumstances. However although Krebs (1976) cautiously wrote 'No one expects simple optimality models to work, they provide predictions for experimental test', they have in fact fitted the behaviour observed in a surprising number of cases. The approach has the great advantage that the same mathematical model can apply to quite different problems. For instance the same model has been used to understand how long a bee feeds on a flower, how long a tit feeds on a pine cone, and how long a dungfly copulates: all involve the problem of how best to exploit a diminishing resource (N. Davies, pers. comm.). And just because the models make quantitative predictions, they are easier to test, and thus to reject, than the qualitative hypotheses of the earlier approach to functional questions. But we must bear in mind that, just because of the many difficulties in focusing on the pertinent consequence(s) and in finding the 'right' model, there is also a difficulty in showing that the basic supposition – namely that individuals are acting in a way likely to maximize inclusive fitness, is wrong.

A final problem arises from the relativity of questions about function: 'Does this animal achieve X as well as it could' always implies 'Given the animal is the sort of animal that it is': if it achieved X 'better' in some sense, it would be a different sort of animal. This can be illustrated from studies of foraging behaviour. The beaks of seed-eating birds like the chaffinch differ between species, in conformity with the size of seeds taken. The older view was that beak size was adapted to the diet (e.g., Lack, 1947) but, as we have seen, Kear (1962) showed that the size of seeds taken was influenced in part by the beak size, individuals learning to take the seeds they could open most efficiently. The questions of whether a bird has an optimal beak size, or whether it takes the optimal size of food, can not be considered independently. Studies showing that animals select food items that they can handle most efficiently assume the given nature of the bird.

This difficulty is in effect an extension of the old problem of phylogenetic inertia: a flying fish does not fly as well as it might because of its fishy ancestry; insects are limited in size by the nature of their respiratory system. Whilst the issue does not affect the validity of most current studies of function, it is one of principle, and must not be lost sight of. It relates, of course, to the necessity of discussing questions of function in terms of differences. The question 'Does this animal behave in a manner that maximizes fitness?' must be reformulated as 'Will this animal achieve greater inclusive fitness than that hypothetical other animal which behaves differently?' But, because of the inter-relations between functions, no other animal could differ in just one way, so we must be wary of confronting ourselves with a question as meaningless as 'Is this species better adapted than that?': in so far as questions about function imply questions about differences, one cannot prove an animal is doing as well as *it* can by comparing it with a (by definition) different alternative.

Finally, it must be stressed that not all differences have a functional explanation, and not all behaviour is perfectly adapted. Differences may result from genetic drift, or may be by-products of selection acting through other consequences. Environmental effects may produce non-adaptive phenotypic effects. Behaviour may be used inappropriately, or be a relic of behaviour formerly adaptive in another context (e.g., Hinde, 1975; Gould and Lewontin, 1979). In addition, differences between individuals within a species may represent alternative 'adaptive peaks' – that is, alternative solutions to the same problem. The task is thus not to show that fitness has been optimized, but to assess how, and how effectively, natural selection has acted.

5.   Behaviour and Evolution

The fourth group of questions addressed by ethologists is concerned with the evolution of behaviour. 'How have characters of behaviour changed in evolution?' 'Can they be used in the same way as morphological characters to help us understand the course of evolution?'

Confronted by such issues, the student of behaviour is in a position quite different from that of the morphologist, for no palaeontological evidence is available to him. Yet from the earliest days of ethology, it was apparent that even quite closely related species differed in ways that demanded evolutionary explanation. The only approach available is the comparative one. This involves first comparison between taxonomic units (species, genera or higher categories) on the basis of a large number of characters. This can lead to hypotheses about the phylogenetic relationships between the units. As a first approximation, the more resemblances are found, the more closely related the taxonomic units are likely to be. Of course similarities between species could be due to convergent evolution resulting from similar ecological requirements, but the hypothesis is more likely to be reliable if the characters are numerous and diverse. A classic example, Lorenz's (1941) study of the ducks and geese, is summarized in fig. 20. The species are represented by vertical and/or oblique lines, while the horizontal lines refer to characters. Some of these, such as the 'lost piping' call of chicks (EPV in fig. 20), are common to all the species. Some, such as the 'displacement shaking' used in display, are found in nearly all ducks but not in geese. And some are present only in particular groups of ducks. Although the ducks and geese had been well studied anatomically, in some cases behavioural evidence has led to a reassessment of systematic relationships.

As another example, discussions about the phylogenetic relations of the chaffinch, whose behaviour has been discussed in several contexts already, include evidence of this sort. The genus *Fringilla*, to which it belongs, contains only one other species, and differs in a number of respects from the main groups of seed-eating finches, the *Carduelinae* (which includes the Goldfinch and Canary) and the *Emberizinae* (the buntings and New World sparrows). Whilst certain anatomical characters clearly distinguish *Fringilla* from the Carduelines, the behavioural evidence indicates that it is more closely related to them than to the Emberizines. Such evidence involves the form of the tail flicks made during locomotion, the movements made in mobbing predators, and the nature of male threat displays and of male and female courtship displays: on all these issues *Fringilla* resembles the Carduelines more closely than the Emberizines. Although the Carduelines show courtship feeding and feed their young by regurgitation, whilst *Fringilla* and the Emberizines do not, these characters are patchily distributed amongst the groups of song-birds and unlikely to be of phylogenetic significance. The behavioural evidence is supported by the fact that *Fringilla* × Cardueline hybrids are commonly bred in captivity, but *Fringilla* × Emberizine hybrids are unknown (Mayr *et al.*, 1956).

Of course in such studies, as everywhere else, there is difficulty in specifying just what constitutes a 'character', and some characters are more useful to the systematist than others. The characters chosen must show appropriate diversity, bearing clear resemblance between some taxonomic units and clear differences between others; and the differences must not be solely environmentally determined. It is also necessary to assess the extent to which similarities between characters could be the result of independent evolution for a similar function, and how far dissimilarities could be due to selection for divergence as such. Similarities between species must be evaluated according to whether the

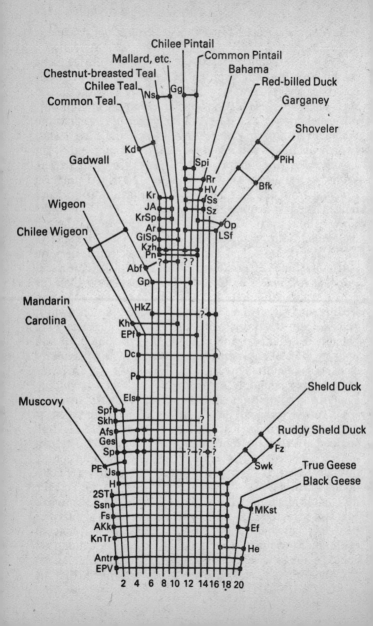

Chilee Pintail
Mallard, etc. — Common Pintail
Chestnut-breasted Teal — Bahama
Chilee Teal — Red-billed Duck
Common Teal — Garganey
Shoveler

Ns Gg

Kd

Spi
Rr
HV
Ss
Sz
Op
LSf

Gadwall
Kr
JA
KrSp
Ar
GlSp
Kzh
Pn

Wigeon
Chilee Wigeon

PiH
Bfk

Abf   ?   ? ?
Gp

HkZ
?

Mandarin
Carolina

Kh
EPf

Dc

P

Els

Muscovy

Spf
Skh
Afs
Ges
Sp

?

?

?–?–?–?

Sheld Duck

Fz

Ruddy Sheld Duck

Swk

PE   Js
H
2ST
Ssn
Fs
AKk
KnTr

Antr
EPV

MKst

Ef

He

True Geese
Black Geese

2 4 6 8 10 12 14 16 18 20

characters concerned are functionally linked, and thus liable to change in concert (see pp. 105 and 137–42), or can be treated as functionally independent. It will be apparent that the appropriate 'weighting' of characters is a matter involving considerable systematic expertise, and cannot be discussed in detail here. In spite of these difficulties behavioural characters, used in conjunction with others, have been of considerable value in assessing relationships between species. The most useful characters have been fixed action patterns, but other characters have also been used (see e.g., Cullen, 1959).

If the relationships between taxonomic units are reasonably firmly established, comparisons between behavioural characters can provide evidence about the course of evolution. Here again the study of fixed action patterns has been especially valuable. It is first necessary to recognize formal similarities between fixed action patterns in closely related taxonomic units. These similarities suggest a common evolutionary origin. If the movements are basically similar, it is then necessary to describe the slight differences that occur. If there are reasonable grounds for supposing that the differences have a genetic basis, it may then be possible to erect hypotheses as to which variants are phylogenetically older. Such a hypothesis may use additional information, such as knowledge about the causation and function of the movements, and their distribution amongst the taxonomic units. For example if a movement is used in biting in a number of species, but has a variant used in threat in others, it is likely that the former is more primitive. Given hypotheses about which forms are the more primitive, it is

fig. 20. The use of behavioural characters in taxonomy, as exemplified by Lorenz's study of the Anatinae. The vertical and oblique lines represent species and genera. Each horizontal line represents the behavioural character present in the species whose line it crosses. A cross indicates that the character is absent in the species in question, and the circle that it is exceptionally differentiated. (After Lorenz, 1941.)

possible to speculate about the nature of the evolutionary changes which have occurred.

Ethologists are not blind to the possibilities of circular argument, and to the tentative nature of the conclusions that can be drawn. The dangers can be minimized by the simultaneous study of as many species as possible, and by the use of many independent sources of evidence about the phylogenetic relationships between them. The endeavour is worthwhile because this is virtually the only way to assess the detailed course of behavioural evolution.

Some of the most interesting material has come from studies of the stereotyped movements used in threat and courtship. As we have seen, these serve as signals (p. 23), and are often associated with ambivalence (pp. 67–9). Comparative studies indicate that such movements in birds and fishes (figs. 1 and 11) come from three main evolutionary sources. Some have come from intention movements – the incomplete movements that are made when the motivational factors for a particular activity are too low for the complete movement to appear, or when its expression is partially inhibited (pp. 67–9). Many avian displays, for instance, incorporate elements of the intention movements of taking flight. Others appear to have evolved from 'displacement activities' – the apparently irrelevant movements which often appear when motivational tendencies are in conflict and more or less evenly balanced (p. 66). The third source lies in the consequences of activity in the autonomic nervous system. For instance many displays involve movements of the hair or feathers, urination or defecation, changes in skin colour, and so on. Furthermore autonomic activity may give rise to somatic movements, such as scratching or preening, and these have evolved into signal movements.

Comparative study indicates how display movements have changed in evolution. The changes are usually such as to make the movement more conspicuous or distinctive ('ritualization'). They may involve changes in the movement, including exaggeration, changes in tempo, changes in the relations between its components, increased stereotypy, and so on. The comparative data indicate that such evolutionary changes have often been accompanied by the development of conspicuous structures which enhance the signal, such as the stickleback's red belly (see p. 35). Comparisons across a number of species often show a correlation between the extent to which a signal has been developed and the development of the accompanying structures: evidently evolution of the signal and of the structures which enhance it have proceeded in parallel.

A comparable methodology has been used with reference not only to the evolution of signal movements, but also to that of more mundane activities such as the grooming movements used by insects (Jander, 1966), and the movements used by mammals in settling into and rising up from the resting position (Zannier-Tanner, 1965). Although the conclusions must always be tentative, they are often extremely compelling.

We see, then, that on the one hand behavioural evidence, taken with evidence of other sorts, can contribute to our understanding of the phylogenetic relations between species and higher systematic categories. And on the other, knowledge of relations between species can indicate the probable course of evolution of some behavioural characters.

6. Core Ethology – Relations between the Four Whys

Selection of issues discussed in the preceding chapters as representative of 'core ethology' has of course been influenced by my own interests, and I acknowledge that others, with equal justification, would have chosen differently. Furthermore it is a central thesis of this book that the boundaries of ethology can and should be only loosely defined: some ethologists will find issues that they consider central discussed in later chapters.

In the meantime it is necessary to emphasize that the organization of material under the four questions of Causation, Development, Function and Evolution does not mean that they are necessarily independent: they can be both interdependent and interfertile. Clear distinctions between them are necessary because, for instance, items of behaviour that share causal factors need not have the same function, and vice versa (e.g., Beer, 1963). Nevertheless they often do, and a functional classification of behaviour is often a good first guide to a causal one.

Indeed it has recently been argued that the causal analysis of systems controlling behaviour can profit greatly from functional considerations. At a simple level, this is obvious enough. The problem of how stimulus strength interacts with motivational state to influence the intensity of behaviour is a causal problem, but likely to be facilitated by functional considerations relevant to the particular case: selection affects not only the types of behaviour in an animal's repertoire, but also the criteria by which it decides when to use them. Thus as we saw on pp. 114–15, the relations between nest-building motivation and the stimuli determining nest-site selection by great tits must have been modulated by natural selection acting through the consequences of building in holes of different properties. In the same way, if food availability is erratic, animals which feed whenever they get the chance (i.e., were guided by external factors) would be favoured; while the extent to which internal factors (hunger) were important would be influenced by the individuals' tolerance for starvation (McFarland, 1976). The same principle applies to decisions between alternative types of behaviour. The relative importance of feeding, territorial defence, etc. will vary with the species and its circumstances. Whilst attempts to specify the decision rules in terms of the physiological mechanisms involved – i.e., in causal terms – is likely to be defeated by the sheer complexity of the task, an alternative approach in terms of consequences may be possible. Sibly and McFarland (1976) argue that, if the animal is adapted to its environment, the decision criteria will be such as to optimize survival and reproductive success (or, more generally, inclusive fitness, see p. 112). In other words, the costs and benefits of engaging in different kinds of behaviour can be measured along a single yardstick – that of evolutionary success. As we have seen, if the costs and benefits of alternative courses of actions are estimated, they can be combined into a single cost function which, assuming that the animal behaves in an optimal fashion, permits predictions of its behaviour in specified circumstances. Comparison with how it actually behaves may enable the cost function to be reformulated. This is an ambitious procedure, and it has so far been tested out only in one or two cases (see McFarland, 1976).

Of course inter-relations between causal and functional questions are not the only ones possible. That causal and ontogenetic questions may be inextricably interwoven is indicated by the frequent difficulty we have in differentiating between ontogenetic, predisposing and precipitating factors (see fig. 14). And Tinbergen (1963) emphasized that questions of ontogeny must be viewed in functional and evolutionary terms. There are at least three issues here. First, the young organism must be adapted to the specific needs of its situation – to assimilate food, to disperse, to find a suitable environment and/or whatever requirements are specific to its nature. Second, those adaptations will also be constrained in part by phylogenetic considerations – by the sort of organism it is. Indeed the special requirements of development may limit the probabilities of evolutionary change leading to forms with a different life style – as demonstrated most clearly by the limitations placed on amphibian radiation by the susceptibility of their eggs to desiccation. And third, many aspects of development must be determined by selective forces acting through the adult characteristics that they determine. In general this is obvious enough, but a recent example is of great interest. Adult male quail (*Coturnix c. japonica*) copulate preferentially with females which resemble, but yet differ from, the individuals with which they have been reared. This is presumably adaptive, fostering within-species mating but preventing too close in-breeding. It requires the learning of the siblings' characteristics during a particular sensitive period – namely after they have acquired adult-type plumage but before the brood disperses (Bateson, 1978c). Thus ontogenetic, causal, functional and evolutionary issues are inter-related (see also Richard, 1979).

As another example, the study of animal communication involves interactions between all four approaches. As we have seen, causal analysis shows that many signal movements are given when the animal is subject to conflicting tendencies to behave in incompatible ways (pp. 67–9). Evolutionary considerations permit hypotheses about the probable origins of the signal movements, and about the way in which they have been ritualized for a signal function (pp. 126–7). Functional analysis raises questions about the extent to which they can properly be described as conveying information to, deceiving or manipulating the other individual (chapter 13 [i]). And developmental questions concerning how the signal movements develop, and how the motivational conflicts arise in the life of individuals (e.g., Kruijt, 1964) also arise.

It will be apparent that, whilst for much of the time it is essential to recognize the distinctions between the four whys, full understanding requires consideration of all four, and the questions themselves are often inter-fertile.

PART II

Ethology and the Biological Sciences

7. Behavioural Ecology

(i) Ecology and animal behaviour

Since ethologists have an interest in functional and evolutionary questions as well as in causal and ontogenetic ones, it is not surprising that the boundary between ethology and behavioural ecology is now impossible to define. Many of the conceptual issues that arise have already been discussed in chapter 4. But the history of the relations between behavioural ecology, sociobiology and ethology are of some interest – though I realize that my perspective of that history is a personal one.

Ethology and ecology have not always been close. Ecology was in fact well established as a branch of zoology when behaviour studies were still regarded by many as disreputable natural history. In Europe the *Journal of Animal Ecology* branched off from the *Journal of Ecology* in 1932, years before the leading ethological journals *Behaviour* (1948), the *Bulletin of Animal Behaviour* (1938) and *Zeitschrift für Tierpsychologie* (1937) were founded. During the thirties ecological studies thus had little reference to behavioural analysis. An ecological text influential at that time (Elton, 1927) was concerned largely with the interrelations between species in communities, the control of populations, and the relations between ecology and evolutionary studies. In a diagram at the end 'social science', 'sex biology' and psychology were mentioned as relevant to the study of animal communities, but behavioural matters played a small part in the text.

A similar situation persisted in the late forties. An anecdote may be illustrative. The Edward Grey Institute of

Field Ornithology in Oxford, where I was a graduate student, was next door to Charles Elton's Bureau of Animal Populations, and the two held joint seminars. Elton had earlier done important research on animal communities, and the Bureau was currently concerned with studies of predator-prey interaction and of vole population cycles. At one meeting Dennis Chitty described how the populations of voles that he was studying showed an approximately four-year cycle of peaks and troughs. He remarked incidentally that, at the time of each population crash, many voles were found to have torn ears. This was ascribed to intra-specific fighting, but Elton remarked, 'Sheer cussedness, I suppose', and the matter was dropped. Only some time later was the possible importance of this observation recognized by the appointment of Clarke (1953) specifically to study the problem.

At that time, the impact of ethology was only just beginning to be felt in the English-speaking world. However, as we have seen, much of Tinbergen's early work showed a constant concern with how behaviour contributed to survival or reproduction: his pioneering use of field experiments to study function has already been discussed (pp. 110–11). Tinbergen's interest in functional issues was partly a product of his early biological training, but it may have been augmented by his field study of Snow Buntings in Greenland, where the brevity of the summer placed special constraints on the breeding cycle (Tinbergen, 1939). It may have been further facilitated by his move to Oxford in 1949. Also at Oxford was David Lack, who had earlier carried out one of the classic field studies of bird behaviour (Lack, 1939) and had provided some of the best examples of the mutual interfertility of ecological, evolutionary and behavioural work. He made, for instance, a detailed study of a group of finches (*Geospizinae*) on the Galapagos Islands which had much interested Charles Darwin (Lack, 1947). There are about fourteen species on the Islands, differing in structure, notably that of the beak, in feeding habits, and in other aspects of behaviour. Many of the species occur as morphologically distinct subspecies on different islands. Lack showed that many of the interspecies' differences in structure and distribution could be accounted for by competition between closely related species. Beak size was related to the size and nature of the food items that the species took (see p. 88). The variability of beak size within a population was related to the presence of potential competitors. Competition led to the population specializing in a type of food item not taken by other populations in the same area, and thus to a reduction in the variability of beak dimensions. Some examples are shown in fig. 21.

(ii) The adaptive complex

Much of Lack's work was concerned with such questions as 'Why (in functional terms) do different species of birds lay different numbers of eggs in their clutches?' 'Why does the average clutch size of a species vary from place to place, with time of year, and from year to year?' He showed that many of the differences could be explained on the supposition that natural selection had operated to produce a clutch of such a size and at such a time that the maximum number of healthy young would be produced. Thus species whose young find their own food lay large clutches, but in other species clutch size is limited by the ability of the parents to find enough food for the nestlings. For temperate zone species, clutch size tends to be greater in the northern parts of the range, for there the days are longer and more time is available for finding food. Clutch size tends to vary with the season, and from year to year, according to the food likely to be available at the time when it is most required by the parent(s) to support the developing eggs or young.

Throughout his work Lack was constantly forced to consider the aspect of behaviour in which he was interested against a background of the whole biology of the species. Consider for example the three species he studied most intensively. The robin (*Erithacus rubecula*) is a relatively

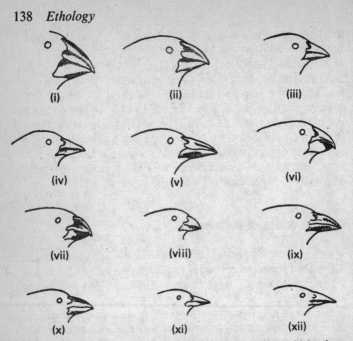

fig. 21a. Beak differences in Darwin's finches on Central islands.

(i) *Geospiza magnirostris* (ii) *Geospiza fortis* (iii) *Geospiza fuliginosa* (iv) *Geospiza difficilis debilirostris* (v) *Geospiza scandens* (vi) *Camarhynchus crassirostris* (vii) *Camarhynchus psittacula* (viii) *Camarhynchus parvulus* (ix) *Camarhynchus pallidus* (x) *Camarhynchus heliobates* (xi) *Certhidea olivacea* (xii) *Pinaroloxias inornata.* (After Lack, 1947.)

inconspicuous bird laying five or six eggs in a more-or-less open nest in thick cover. The great tit lays in a hole in a tree, where the incubating female is much less vulnerable. Perhaps for this reason, the female need be less cryptically coloured. Robins and great tits feed their young on similar food items, mostly caterpillars and other arthropods, but the great tit young develop more slowly, spending about nineteen days in the nest instead of fourteen: this is correlated with their lower vulnerability in the nest hole. And in turn, presumably

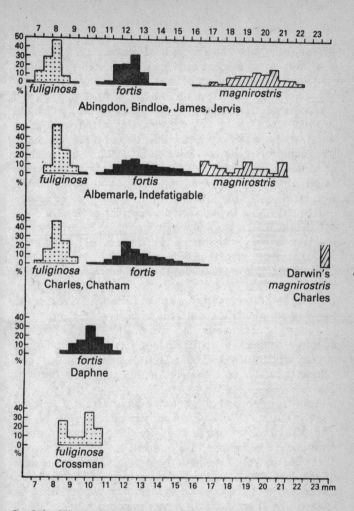

fig. 21b. Histograms of beak depth in the species of *Geospiza* on different islands. Note that the beak size varies with the presence vs absence of other congeneric species. (Too few specimens were available for a histogram of the extinct *magnirostris* on Charles.) (After Lack, 1947.)

because each young bird needs less food per day, the great tit can afford to lay five to eleven eggs, considerably more than the robin. The abundance of food for the young of these two species is consistent from day-to-day: their developmental physiology seems to be such that they cannot withstand protracted starvation. By contrast the swift (*Apus apus*), another hole-nester but laying only two or three eggs, feeds its young on airborne insects. Depending on weather conditions, these may be abundant one day and almost totally absent the next. The time that the young spend in the nest is not only long in comparison with the other species (35–56 days), but highly variable depending upon the food supply: the nestlings are much better able to live on reserves over a period of starvation than are those of robins and great tits. There is also a marked difference in the breeding seasons of these species: great tits and robins hatch in April-June when caterpillars are available, but swifts not until late June, when airborne insects are more plentiful. Such data illustrate the way in which the different aspects of the structure, physiology and behaviour of each of these species form an adaptive complex – an issue that has been emphasized already (pp. 105–6). The adaptive significance of one character cannot be considered in isolation from those of others.

Another important milestone was John Crook's work on weaver finches. Working under the direction of W. H. Thorpe, Crook set out to compare the nesting and other reproductive behaviour of a number of species of weaver finch. But his work led him to the view that these issues were inseparable from those of the ecology and population dispersion of the species concerned. The weavers that he studied (1964) appeared to have developed four relatively discrete grades of adaptation resulting from the interaction of numerous selection pressures. Each grade was characterized by the feeding behaviour (insectivorous/granivorous), population structure (solitary/gregarious and monogamous/polygamous) and types of display used in territorial defence, advertisement and pair formation.

In general the insectivorous species were forest-dwelling, monogamous and defended large territories, whilst the seed-eating species tended to inhabit savannah or grass-land, and to be colonial and polygynous. Crook argued that the primary adaptations concerned the utilization of the food supply. The food of the forest insectivores was scattered, not superabundant, and located in defensible areas. In addition their nests were susceptible to predation. All these issues favour territorial behaviour, for this results both in defence of a food supply and dispersion of nests. Since food is not superabundant, neither male nor female can entrust parental care to the other, and monogamy persists. The savannah species depend on temporarily locally super-abundant food, so that territorial defence would bring no selective advantage with respect to food. There may in fact be advantages in feeding in flocks, such as reduced susceptibility to predation and spread of information about food, and clumped nesting may be in part dictated by the scarcity of well-protected nest-sites. Temporary food abundance permits polygyny, for the female alone can raise the brood. Convergence between unrelated species, and the behaviour of species with intermediate diets, support these generalizations.

Similar approaches were being developed by such workers as J. L. Brown (e.g., 1964, 1975), Emlen and Oring (1977) and Orians (e.g., 1969). They have led to considerable progress in our understanding of the adaptive bases of inter-species differences in a number of groups, including birds (e.g., Nelson, 1975), primates (Clutton-Brock and Harvey, 1977), ungulates (Jarman, 1974) and carnivores (Kruuk, 1975). Of course comparative studies can lead only to correlations between characteristics of social organization, it cannot sort out which is cause and which effect. For instance Clutton-Brock and Harvey showed that primates which go about in large groups have large home ranges, but their data could not show which was cause and which effect.

Thus by the 1960s a rapprochement between studies of animal behaviour and studies of the relations of animals with their animate and inanimate environments was already well under way. Lack saw himself first as an ornithologist, and although concerned more with ecological than behavioural problems, in writing about adaptation he made no distinction between the two approaches – 'Crook's comparative method is that used throughout this book . . . and I find myself in virtually complete agreement with what he established earlier, while Tinbergen's experimental method points the way ahead' (Lack, 1968). Similar views were voiced in the USA (Park, 1961).

(iii) Population control: group vs individual selection

However there were also other forces contributing to a close liaison between ethology and ecology. This requires a digression.

One of the central controversies in the 1950s and 1960s concerned the way in which animal populations are controlled. Animal populations have the potential for extremely rapid increase. Occasionally this occurs: six pheasants placed on an island in 1937 increased to 1898 individuals in only six years (Einarsen, 1945). More usually, however, populations remain fairly stable or fluctuate between limits (Malthus, 1803; Darwin, 1859; Nicholson, 1933; Lack 1954). The question thus arises, on what mechanisms does this relative stability depend? In the 1950s there were three main views. Andrewartha and Birch (1954) believed that the numbers of animals were limited by shortage or inaccessibility of material resources, and by fluctuations in the rate of increase caused by weather, predators, etc., such that periods when increase occurred roughly balanced periods of decrease. They laid considerable emphasis on the occurrence of local population decrease or extinction during unfavourable periods, followed by increase or recolonization by a population expanding from another locale. Competition between individuals for essential resources was, however, thought to be as most a minor issue.

The second view, due to Wynne-Edwards (1962), was that though populations are ultimately limited by shortage of food, situations in which food was actually short, so that competition for food occurred, were rare. He supposed that individuals dispersed in such a way that local populations remained near the optimum. Thus he held that each species controlled its own density by emigration or non-breeding of individuals. His thesis thus depended on the view that such non-breeding individuals acted against their own biological interests. Such behaviour would be explicable only in terms of selective forces which acted on groups of individuals as a unit – 'group selection'.

The third view, espoused especially by Nicholson (1933), Lack (e.g., 1954, 1966) and Williams (1966), is that natural selection acts primarily on the individual, favouring those individuals which reproduce most successfully. However, populations remain steady because mortality factors are density dependent. When populations are high, a larger proportion die than when populations are low. Lack held the view that for birds starvation outside the breeding season is the most important density dependent factor, but emphasized that this did not necessarily apply to other species.

It is not possible to pursue this controversy here, but the evidence is heavily in favour of the last view. The crucial issue is the strong evidence for competition between individuals both within and between species for necessary resources (Lack, 1947). Lack (e.g., 1966, Appendix) argued convincingly that there is a logical necessity for postulating density dependent mortality, and that Andrewartha and Birch's attack on the evidence for such an effect was groundless. He further pointed out that the concept of an optimum population is irrelevant to natural populations, that there is no reason to suppose that reproductive rates have evolved to balance mortality rates, that dispersion benefited the individuals concerned rather than the group, and that group selection could operate only for close kin (see below).

In general, group selection is unlikely to be important in

most circumstances because its consequences would be susceptible to invasion by an individual who 'cheats' (Williams, 1966). For example, a number of studies show that newcomers to an area may not attempt to settle if the population density has already reached a certain level. Wynne-Edwards explained this by selection for the good of the population as a whole: intruding latecomers might so reduce the availability of resources that no one had enough. But such a mechanism is unlikely to work if one latecomer 'cheated' by remaining to breed, his genes might be perpetuated more effectively than those of his colleagues who searched elsewhere. However an explanation in terms of individual selection is possible: it may be better for the latecomers to go elsewhere than to attempt to defy the established residents. Whilst there are some situations in which group selection may operate, evolutionary change must be seen primarily as a consequence of individual selection (Lack, 1954; Williams, 1966; Maynard Smith, 1976b). Thus it is now generally recognized that selection acts primarily on individuals, and that group selection can be important only in certain very restricted circumstances. Indeed Dawkins (1976b) goes further and lays emphasis not on individuals seeking to perpetuate their genes, but on the genes themselves. He sees the genes as the essential replicators, seeking to perpetuate themselves and using the bodies of their host to that end. Whilst this approach has advantages in some contexts, we need not pursue the argument here.

The issue of individual vs group selection was not especially important to most ethologists in the fifties and sixties, but the view that all ethologists always thought in terms of group selection, sometimes espoused in the recent literature, is not true. Some perhaps did, and many were not always so precise over these matters as it is now apparent that they should have been. But by and large those influenced primarily by Tinbergen tended to think in terms of individual selection, while those influenced by Lorenz sometimes wrote as though selection acted on the group.

Returning to the question of population control, this has been mentioned for two reasons. First, it provides our first example of the way in which the heat generated by academic controversy can clarify the issues. The Wynne-Edwards hypothesis, though based on misinterpretations of the evidence in many respects, focused attention on the issue of individual vs group selection, and facilitated attempts to define the circumstances in which group selection might operate. Wynne-Edwards, whose attractive personality brought many friends even amongst those who disagreed passionately with him, stuck to his guns over some issues, such as the importance of dispersion, but eventually agreed that, over most issues, selection must act on the individual. Second, the emphases on the possible importance of competition and of dispersion focused attention on behaviour, and brought realization that ecology and ethology were inseparable.

(iv) Inclusive fitness and sociobiology

During the late sixties and early seventies yet another issue arose which brought ecologists and ethologists together. Whilst most biologists recognized that natural selection acted at least primarily on individuals, some facts had long failed to fit. Some insects produce specialized castes of workers or soldiers which are completely sterile. It seemed impossible to explain the evolution of such highly specialized yet non-reproducing individuals in terms of Darwinian selection. And the evolution of forms of behaviour which were costly to the performer (in terms of reducing his chances of surviving and reproducing) even though beneficial to others seemed inexplicable. Why, for instance, should a bird utter an alarm call if doing so increased his own susceptibility to the predator? Except in the special case of parents protecting their offspring, how could such behaviour be shaped by natural selection?

The germ of an answer had been around for a long time.

Darwin (1859) had pointed out that sterile castes and altruistic behaviour benefitted the group or family in which the individuals concerned lived, and so perhaps group selection could operate. Attempts were made to specify the circumstances in which group selection could operate (Haldane, 1932; Wright, 1969), but by and large such circumstances seemed very unlikely to have occurred often (Maynard Smith 1976b). Haldane (1932) came near to the point when he argued that altruism would be selected for if it prompted the survival of descendants and near relations, and a related point was made by R. A. Fisher (1958, p. 178). But the issue was not worked out in detail until Hamilton (1964), in a seminal paper, pointed out that selection must operate not only through the advantages or disadvantages conferred by a genetic difference on a particular individual, but through those conferred on other genetically similar individuals in the population (see also Maynard Smith, 1964). A genetic change disadvantageous to one individual might yet be selected for if it benefited sufficiently others who were genetically closely related to it.

This is obvious enough in the case of parental care, for the following reason. The individuals in any population are on the whole genetically very similar to each other, but differ in certain relatively rare genes or gene combinations. These rare genes are more likely to be similar between parent and offspring than between any two individuals taken at random, for each offspring will have obtained half its genes from each parent. Thus it will be to the evolutionary advantage of a parent to care for his offspring so long as the costs for him (in terms of the effect on his chances of survival and further reproduction) are less than half the benefit (similarly measured) to his offspring (Trivers, 1974).

However this is not the only issue. On average full siblings will also share half their rare genes, grandparents and grandchildren (assuming no inbreeding) will share one quarter, and cousins (in a monogamous species) one eighth. Thus a given act will be to an individual's evolutionary advantage if its cost to the actor is less than half its benefit to a sibling, or one eighth its benefit to a cousin. Individuals are thus selected to act not to maximize their own fitness (measured in terms of their own survival and reproduction) but their inclusive fitness (measured in terms of their own survival and reproduction *and* that of their relatives, though devalued in the latter case by the degree of relatedness). Imagine a gene which, in some way, programmed an individual to give up its life for others. One copy of the gene would disappear from the population when the altruist died, but if the act saved the life of more than two offspring, more than two siblings or more than eight cousins (etc.), then the altruistic gene would still increase in frequency.

This way of thinking provides a possible explanation of the evolution of castes of individuals who cannot themselves reproduce, such as worker bees and ants. In these species the males develop from unfertilized eggs, and are therefore haploid, while the females develop from fertilized eggs. The latter become either reproductive queens or sterile workers according to the food they receive from the workers: normally there is only one queen in each colony. Now each of the queen's genes stands a 50 per cent chance of being transmitted to each offspring, male or female. If the queen has mated with only one (haploid) male, all workers will carry the same paternal genes. And the chance that they will share a rare maternal gene will be one half. Thus sisters will be related more closely to each other (on average 0.75) than they would be to their own children (assuming they mated with a male other than the one who mated with their mother). Thus it is more to the evolutionary advantage of the workers to help the queen rear their own sisters than it would be for them to mate and breed themselves. Given the reproductive arrangements of these species, the workers increase their reproductive fitness by looking after their potentially reproductive sisters more than they would by looking after their own offspring.

But although the workers are related by 0.75 to each other, they are related only by 0.25 to their brothers. Thus if brothers and sisters were equally common, sisters would be on average related to their siblings by 0.5. They would in fact do just as well to rear their own offspring. If they are to do better by helping the queen, the sex ratio must be biassed towards three reproductive females to one male. If that is the case, brothers will be three times as likely to reproduce as reproductive sisters, and hence the benefit to workers from rearing reproductive brothers and sisters will be equal. But since the queen shares equal numbers of rare genes with her sons and daughters, it would be adaptive for her to produce equal numbers of reproductive sons and reproductive daughters. In practice, the ratio is usually close to three to one, as would be predicted if the workers were in control (Trivers and Hare, 1976). Although all the initial assumptions are not always met, and other explanations of the sex ratio are possible (Alexander and Sherman, 1977), the crucial importance of Hamilton's concept of inclusive fitness in understanding the evolution of sterile castes will be apparent (but see Noonan, 1978).

The view that individuals are selected to maximize not their individual fitness but their inclusive fitness can also explain some examples of apparent altruism. An altruistic act will confer a profit (in evolutionary terms) to the actor if the cost incurred is less than the benefit to the recipient by a factor equal to the degree of relatedness between them. We may consider one specific example. In Belding's ground squirrel the males are polygynous and move between breeding seasons, but the females are sedentary and live in related groups (Sherman, 1977; in press) (fig. 22). Co-operation occurs between mothers and daughters, and between sisters, in that such individuals fight little, co-operatively protect neonatal young, and allow each other access to normally defended areas round nest-sites. Thus very close relatives are favoured. The incidence of alarm calling can be understood in similar terms. Reproductive females with close female relatives living close by give more alarm calls than do reproductive females who have no relatives other than their own young, and the latter give more than non-reproductive females without relatives. The differences appear to be due primarily to differences in speed of response to a predator, and to the fact that females refrain from calling if another female has already called. Thus alarm calling, which entails increased risk from the predator, is related to the number of offspring and close relatives likely to profit from the warning.

However traditional kin selection theory does not explain all the facts, for males who had copulated frequently were not more likely to call than males who had copulated less often, even though they might be expected to have more

fig. 22. Belding's ground squirrel.

(potential) offspring. Furthermore females did not show preferential treatment of more distant kin: aunt–cousin, first cousin–cousin and grandmother–granddaughter pairs behaved as if unrelated. Sherman suggests that such dyads occur so infrequently that natural selection has presumably not operated to promote recognition within them.

A second point concerns the proximate factors determining the probability of alarm calling. There is no necessary implication that the presence of relatives has a *direct* influence on the likelihood of an individual calling. It will be apparent that calling is also related to the individual's familiarity with the area, and this could be the immediately determining factor. Thus the kin selection hypothesis provides a genetical framework for interpreting the data, but does not provide complete understanding of the mechanisms involved (see also Cheney and Seyfarth, 1980).

Of course not all examples of apparent altruism are to be understood in terms of inclusive fitness. In some cases a good turn is worthwhile because it is likely to be reciprocated (Trivers, 1971). For example male baboons who do not have a consort female sometimes form a temporary alliance with another similarly situated male. Whilst the latter attacks a male who is consorting with a female, and thus distracts the male's attention, the first male mates with the female. Those males who often give aid appear to be more likely to receive aid in return, so that reciprocation occurs (Packer, 1977), though this is not always the case (Rasmussen, 1980). Similarly young baboons direct their grooming behaviour towards individuals who will later benefit them: young females tend to groom dominant adult females, who may later be powerful allies in the troop; but the young males, who will later leave the troop, tend to groom the more subordinate females, with whom they are likely to have a chance to practise mating (Cheney, 1978; see also Crook, 1980). Yet other cases of apparent altruism are to be understood on the view that individuals get better benefits by co-operating with others. It pays two pied wagtails (*Motacilla alba*) to defend a winter feeding territory to gether, even though they are not related, because each thereby can achieve a higher feeding rate (Davies and Houston, 1981).

Hamilton's ideas about inclusive fitness provide insights into many types of social behaviour, including strategies of mate selection, reproduction and dispersal (see e.g., Krebs and Davies, 1978). Whilst so powerful an explanatory tool has been misapplied and misunderstood, as Dawkins (1979) has pointed out, its value is now generally recognized. But recognition took time, and it was not until the early or mid-seventies that there was a real flowering of studies which utilized the idea to throw light on social behaviour. An important landmark was the publication of E. O. Wilson's *Sociobiology* (1975). This is a masterly integration of material from population biology, ecology, ethology and related disciplines, and has done much to bring evolutionary theory and behavioural biology into alignment with one another. The many achievements of this book have been widely discussed, and at least some of the criticisms have been symptoms of reviewers' disease – the tendency to criticize an author for not doing something which he did not set out to do. But it is necessary to comment on the relation of Wilson's *Sociobiology* to the theme of the current volume, because issues relevant to the nature of scientific growth arise which we shall meet repeatedly in other contexts.

The main aim of Wilson's book was to interpret features of social organization from a knowledge of population parameters (i.e., demography and genetic structure) and from knowledge of the behavioural constraints imposed by the genetic constitution of the species (Wilson, 1975, p. 5). However in seeking to establish the young discipline of 'sociobiology'*, Wilson made the bellicose claim that sociobiology would in due course engulf current disciplines such as ethology and comparative psychology. He found it necessary to launch an attack on ethology and psychology. For instance he argued that many of the concepts used in ethology (e.g. aggression, drive) were 'panchrestons' that 'becloud the behavioral literature', neglecting that the limits of their usefulness have been the subject of careful and constructive debate, and that in many cases they have been operationally refined (Miller, 1959). At the same time he continued to use concepts like 'instinct' which ethologists had effectively thrown out, continued himself to use some of the ethological terms he despised (e.g. drive), and rested much of his discussion on concepts like 'the multiplier effect' and 'preadaptation' which are of basically similar status but the limits of whose usefulness have been less carefully defined. He similarly caricatured psychology as involving an 'ad hoc terminology, crude models, and curve fitting'. For a while it seemed as though the strong words could set back the increasingly intimate relationship between ethology and ecology.

The need for this attack is not immediately apparent, since the 'behavioural constraints' to which Wilson referred both influence and are influenced by the genetic structure of the population, and embrace the problems of ontogeny and causation, whose prior solution is thus necessary if Wilson's principal goal is to be achieved. Indeed some of his book consists of masterly surveys of particular problems in the causation and ontogeny of behaviour. In reply to reviewers he argued (1976) that questions of ontogeny and causation could be regarded as modules which could be 'temporarily decoupled' in order to provide the degree of simplification necessary for models in population biology. Here he neglected the lessons of his predecessors and failed to see the shape that work in behavioural ecology would take only a few years later (see pp. 135–6). To cite but one example already available to Wilson, in many sea birds the understanding of social structure includes the *demographic* issue

* This was incidentally an unnecessary new term, since 'Behavioural ecology' was already in the field and is more appropriate given the relations between feeding behaviour and social structure (pp. 140–1). If 'sociobiology' is to be used it is more appropriately limited to consideration of selection for inclusive, as opposed to individual, fitness. Whilst Hamilton's contribution certainly opened up new possibilities for understanding social phenomena, nothing is gained by attempts to stake out territories in science.

of why many individuals, though apparently fully adult, do not breed. One suggestion is that this depends on the *ontogenetic* question of how long it takes to acquire feeding skills adequate to make a breeding attempt *functionally* worthwhile. Decoupling, in the way Wilson implies, is simply not possible.

It is clearly best not to judge either Wilson's unnecessary broadsides at the behavioural sciences, nor his subsequent justifications for them, by the same sort of criteria as lead us to admire the grandeur of his achievement as a whole. But science is not separable from scientists, and this aspect of Wilson's work becomes more understandable if it is seen as a polemical move to establish the importance and facilitate the exploitation of an important new route for biology. We shall meet other examples of interdisciplinary jousting in later pages.

One other aspect of Wilson's work is relevant to the theme of this book. Part of his attack on behaviour involved the reductionist implication that behaviour is nothing but neurophysiology and sensory physiology (1975). But behaviour has emergent properties not found in neurones, and the successive levels of interactions, interindividual relationships and social structure have each further properties, properties which simply do not apply to the behaviour of individuals in isolation (see pp. 204–7). Competitiveness and altruism, issues of crucial concern for understanding social structure, can only apply to a dyad or group, not to an individual. Yet such properties have functional consequences for individuals. The recognition that science must concern itself with phenomena at many levels is as true of the study of social behaviour as anywhere (see also Rosenblatt, 1976). We shall return to this issue later.

8. Behavioural Endocrinology

(i) Introduction

Recent advances in behavioural endocrinology probably owe more to F. A. Beach than to any other single investigator. Weight must therefore be attached to his recent view that, in this field, 'The rapidly increasing precision and sophistication in endocrinological and neuroendocrinological techniques has not been accompanied by comparable advances in the definition and measurement of behavioral variables' (Beach, 1976, p. 105). Though he has never called himself an ethologist, Beach was engaged in ethological type research before European ethology was known in the USA. His launching in 1969 of a new journal *Hormones and Behavior* has done much to advance the field, and large numbers of investigators are now analysing either the effects of hormones on behaviour or the effects of behaviour on the secretion or effectiveness of hormones. In this chapter I shall try to demonstrate by example how some of the issues that arise in the study of hormone/behaviour interactions can be resolved only if endocrinological studies are combined with ethological analysis.

(ii) The necessity for behavioural analysis

The first example here comes from Beach's own work. For many years, most studies of the hormonal induction of oestrus involved a simple differentiation between oestrous and non-oestrous females. However behavioural studies (e.g., Michael, 1971; Beach, 1976) have indicated the need to distinguish at least three aspects of female sexuality:

(a) Female attractivity. This refers to the female's stimulus value, as inferred from the male's behaviour to her. It includes the full range of stimulation provided by the female, from that which attracts males from a distance to that which promotes ejaculation, i.e., behavioural as well as non-behavioural cues.

(b) Female proceptivity. Oestrous females are not only attractive to the male, they are attracted to him. Whereas many earlier studies, especially those based on laboratory mating tests, had assumed an essentially passive female receiving a sexually aggressive male, the concept of proceptivity emphasizes the importance of female initiative in a mounting sequence. In some species the female's behaviour may be quite complex (Burley, 1980).

(c) Female receptivity. This refers to the consummatory phase of the mating sequence. At a minimum, it includes those responses necessary and sufficient for fertile copulation, including active co-operation in intromission.

Beach (l.c.) surveyed evidence for differences between the neural and hormonal bases of these aspects of female sexuality. For example, total removal of the rat neocortex does not reduce receptive behaviour but seriously disorganizes proceptive behaviour. So far as hormonal control is concerned, the attractiveness of female rhesus monkeys is enhanced by an oestrogen-dependent pheromone acting in the vagina, the action of which can be antagonized by local administration of progesterone. Proceptive behaviour is stimulated by a central nervous action of androgens, while any central effects of either oestrogen or progesterone on the female's receptive or proceptive behaviour remain to be determined. The hormonal basis of receptivity has not yet been established (Herbert, 1978).

The effects of experience and of situational variables on the three aspects of female sexuality may also differ. Thus distracting stimuli may interfere with the proceptive behaviour but not with the receptive behaviour of female rodents; and the receptivity of bitches is less affected by

experience than their proceptive behaviour (Beach, 1976).
Thus proper understanding of the control of female sexual
behaviour depends absolutely on previous behavioural
analysis.

A second example also concerns female rodent sexual
behaviour. Most earlier studies made an absolute distinction
between the female's behaviour at the time of oestrus and
that shown during the rest of the cycle. At oestrus they adopt
a passive 'lordosis' posture in the presence of the male, but
otherwise they appear to be either uninterested in, or
aggressive to, the male. Recently, however, Steel (1979,
1980) has shown that the behavioural changes shown by
oestrous female hamsters are the culmination of more
gradual changes occurring throughout the four-day cycle.
Her analysis depended on finding a behavioural measure
which was correlated with lordosis on the day of oestrus, but
was available also on other days of the cycle. This was a
measure of the role of the female, relative to that of the male,
in establishing or maintaining proximity. Male and female
were confined in concentric runways, separated from each
other by wire mesh: this permitted the female to show
proceptive behaviour more fully. An index of the female's
role in the maintenance of proximity was obtained by
counting how often the female approached (as judged by
objective criteria) the male or left the male, and how often he
approached or left her. The data, shown in fig. 23, show a
gradual change through the cycle.

Some recent work by McClintock (in press) raises the
possibility that some of the traditional experimental techniques used in the study of rodent sexual behaviour may
have been inappropriate. In most experimental work, male
and female are placed together in an arena and their sexual
behaviour observed. The most conspicuous female behaviour is the static lordosis posture she shows when
approached by the male. The male mounts the female,
dismounts and mounts again until, after a number of
intromissions, ejaculation occurs. McClintock studied the
behaviour of rats mating in multi-male multi-female groups

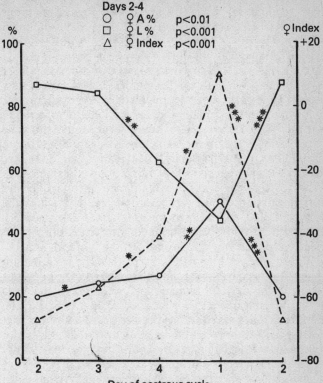

fig. 23. Changes in the sexual behaviour of the female golden hamster with the oestrous cycle. The points represent the proportion of occasions on which distance between male and female decreased from more than 10 cm to less than 10 cm that were due to an approach by the female (–o–, A%); the proportion of occasions in which the distance between male and female increased from less than 10 cm to more than 10 cm that were due to the female leaving (–□–, L%); and the difference between the percentage of approaches and the percentage of leavings due to the female, an index which indicates the female's responsibility for proximity (–△–). The data for oestrous day two are shown twice. (From Steel, 1979.)

in a seminatural environment. Under these conditions monogamous pairings did not occur. The males mounted different females in turn, so that the female with whom a male ejaculated was not the female whom he had mounted earlier in the series. Each female received intromissions from several males. Who mounted whom was determined at least in part by females, since a female might 'intercept' a male following another female and induce him to mount her instead. If two males were present, the dominant male achieved more intromissions before ejaculation and more ejaculations than the subordinate male. And dominant females were more successful at intercepting other females in order to receive the male's penultimate intromission and thus ejaculation. However, the orderliness with which the dominant and subordinate males alternated ejaculatory series was striking, each beginning to mate during the quiescent period which followed the other's ejaculation.

We do not yet know for certain that the rat's mating system was selected for the context of such social groups, but detailed analysis of the temporal pattern of sex behaviour is in fact helping to resolve some previous paradoxes in the literature. For instance it has been reported that intromissions spaced at three-minute intervals are the most likely to bring a male to ejaculatory threshold. However, the optimal value of this same behavioural parameter is different from the females' perspective: intervals greater than ten minutes are most effective for inducing the progestational state which the female requires to become pregnant. Now when rats mate in small cages, they generally display one-minute intervals between intromissions. Thus the optimal value of this parameter is not only different for the two sexes, but also not even close to what pairs of rats actually do in a small standard testing cage. However, during group mating in a larger environment, there is no longer a compromise enforced by mating in a pair: the larger and more complex environment allows each individual the opportunity to pace its own mating. Under these conditions each sex mates at intervals which match the temporal parameters of its neuroendocrine system. This match is achieved only in the apparently more natural context of group mating.

Even in studies of the influence of hormones on the brain, behavioural analysis may play an essential role. For example male doves show a fairly complex series of courtship displays when placed with a female. Furthermore the nature of the courtship changes through the breeding cycle. Early in the cycle the courtship contains many aggressive components (cf. p. 118), but later nest-orientated components come to predominate. Having established that courtship was controlled by male sex hormones, Hutchison (e.g., 1978) proceeded to investigate whether the hormone affected the brain directly, and if so where. This was achieved by implanting pellets of hormone into the brains of male castrates: such pellets release hormone in minute quantities at rates which vary with their surface area. Doves receiving low diffusion implants showed only the nest-orientated components, while those receiving high diffusion implants showed aggressive and nest-orientated components. Such data suggested that the several components of courtship depend on brain mechanisms with differing thresholds to androgen, and that the predominance of nest-orientated components later in the sexual cycle was due to a fall in male androgen levels. Such a fall was in fact later found (Feder *et al.,* 1977).

Even this may not be the whole story, however. It is known that the male sex hormone can be converted to oestrogen in the brain, so either could be the active agent. Implantation of oestrogen leads to the nest-orientated components, but not to the aggressive elements. Thus there may be not only a lowering of androgen levels as the cycle advances, but also a change in conversion levels (Hutchison, 1978).

Furthermore, by analogy with other species, the changes in the nature of the courtship through the cycle may involve changes in the relative strengths of different tendencies in the male – for instance to attack, flee from, and behave sexually to the female (see p. 23). A further step, therefore, would seem to be an assessment of the effects of the different steroids in different loci on these aspects of male behaviour.

(iii) The diverse modes of action of hormones on behaviour

A related issue, mentioned already in the context of rhesus sexual behaviour, concerns the finding that hormones may affect behaviour by a number of quite different routes. The technique used by Hutchison was in fact derived from Harris, Michael and Scott (1958), who showed that oestrous behaviour could be induced in female cats by minute amounts of oestrogen implanted in the hypothalamus. The oestrogen affected nerve tissue locally, and thereby affected behaviour, but was present in such small amounts that it produced negligible peripheral effects.

However, hormones can affect behaviour by producing peripheral changes, feedback from the periphery then affecting behaviour. Thus the effects of male sex hormone on the male sexual behaviour of mammals depends in part on a direct effect of the hormone on the brain, and in part on a hormone-induced change in the glans penis which mediates tactile stimulation during intromission (Beach and Levinson, 1950).

A similar finding was made by Lehrman (1955) in a study of parental feeding in ring doves. Doves feed their squabs on 'pigeon's milk', produced by sloughing off the cells on the internal surface of the crop. The crop enlargement which occurs at this stage in the breeding cycle is produced by the pituitary hormone prolactin. Lehrman showed that doves treated with prolactin would feed squabs. However if the crop was anaesthetized with a local anaesthetic they would not. Apparently it is stimuli from the engorged crop that cause the doves to be responsive to the begging of the young.

Even these are not the only ways in which hormones affect behaviour. They may influence particular types of behaviour by affecting the development of effectors, such as the pad used by male frogs in mating, or of peripheral structures used as signals, such as the cock's comb. Or they may have more general effects, mediated for instance by the reticular activating system or by the processes of perception. Thus by careful behavioural analysis Andrew (1976) and his colleagues have shown that testosterone increases the persistence of certain types of behaviour in chicks and mice (such as searching for a particular type of food object), and that the effect is best described as representing greater persistence in the use of particular rules of selection. For example, testosterone-treated chicks show more sustained search for a particular type of stimulus in the presence of alternative targets than do non-treated controls. Exogenous testosterone reduces the effect of additional stimuli that are not selected and enhances the effect of those that are, and it also prolongs the period of attention to a novel object. Clearly such effects, which could have been discovered only through detailed ethological analysis, must be taken into consideration in future studies of the effects of hormones on behaviour.

(iv) Hormones and sex differentiation

Yet another important way in which sex hormones affect behaviour is by influencing the developing nervous system. Embryonic rats develop to show the cyclicity and sexual behaviour characteristic of females unless they are exposed to male sex hormone during a sensitive period around four days after birth – if they are, they develop as males. Androgen is normally secreted by the male testis for a brief period at this age. Thus if female rats are treated with androgen at four days they show no oestrous cycles or sexual behaviour in adulthood, whereas neonatally castrated males show ovarian cycles and female sexual behaviour if given an ovarian transplant (Goldman, 1978; Plapinger and McEwen, 1978).

The issues are in fact more complex than this, the embryonic or perinatal hormone affecting the nervous system and the somatic secondary sexual characters at different stages, and at different ages with respect to birth or hatching, in different species. Furthermore the story does not end there, for subsequent environmental influences may affect the nature of the sexual behaviour shown. For example male rhesus monkeys indiscriminately mount males and females during their first one to two years of life. Young females kept in heterosexual groups show much less mounting behaviour than do young males. Females kept in all-female peer groups show a higher level of mounting, though it is still less than that of males. Evidently the presence of males has an inhibitory influence on mounting by females. Similar evidence suggests that the presence of the mother has an inhibitory influence on mounting in both males and females. The mounting rate of females raised in isosexual groups subsequently reverts to normal – apparently another example of developmental regulation (see pp. 92–4) (Goy, 1979).

In man, of course, further issues arise, again depending on experimental and behavioural factors. The nature of the parental behaviour received and the gender assigned by the parents to the infant at birth (which may not be the same as its genetic sex) influence subsequent psycho-sexual development (e.g., Ehrhardt and Meyer-Bahlberg, 1979; Green, 1979).

(v) Endocrine-behaviour – environment interactions

Most early work in behavioural endocrinology was concerned with the problem of which hormones affect behaviour. But a moment's reflection indicates that this is a very one-sided view. Successful reproduction, for instance, depends on correct timing with respect to environmental factors and adequate co-ordination with the mate. The ground work for understanding the role of environmental stimuli was laid by such investigators as Rowan (1926) and F. H. A. Marshall (1942), while G. W. Harris (e.g., 1955) was largely responsible for uncovering the mechanism whereby neural events influence endocrine changes. Against this background, more recent ethological studies have been able to uncover some of the complexities of the interactions between the environment, behaviour, and the endocrine system.

We may consider two groups of studies of the integration of reproductive behaviour in birds. Each was aimed at disentangling the complex interactions between the external stimuli that control reproductive development, the hormonal changes that occur, and the behavioural changes involved. The first concerns the work of D. S. Lehrman and his colleagues on the ring dove, and is summarized in fig. 24a. Egg-laying and incubation in the female is stimulated both by male courtship and by participation in nest-building. The effect of courtship depends on both visual and auditory stimuli, and it is important that the male and female should be synchronized through each being able to respond to the other's courtship behaviour (Friedman, 1977). Males likewise become ready for incubation as a consequence of their participation in courtship and nest-building. In both sexes, incubation is maintained by stimuli from the nest and eggs.

The subtlety of some of the issues involved can be illustrated by some more detailed findings. Females apparently distinguish between unfertilized and fertilized eggs. The former are incubated until the normal time of hatching, but then the female starts immediately to recycle, whereas if the eggs had been fertile recycling is delayed for a fortnight. The difference is reflected also in elevated plasma luteinizing hormone (LH) and decreased prolactin during the incubation of infertile eggs (Cheng, 1977).

As noted above, the young are fed on pigeon's milk formed by sloughing off the crop epithelium. Crop gland development begins during incubation, but recedes unless stimuli from squabs are received. Here there is a subtle

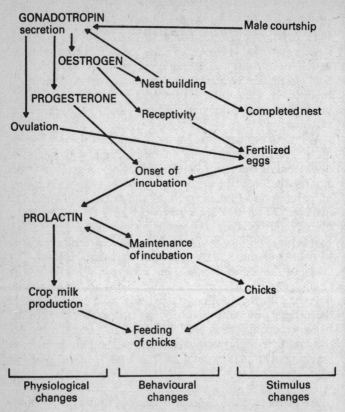

fig. 24a. Diagrammatic representation of the stimulus changes, behavioural changes, and physiological changes in the reproductive development of the female ring dove. Based on the work of the late D. S. Lehrman and his colleagues. (From Slater, 1978.)

difference between females and males. The former, who provide the early morning feed when the chicks are hungry and begging actively, release the prolactin necessary for crop function on receipt of visual stimulation from the chicks. The males, who are usually concerned with only mildly hungry squabs, respond only to tactile stimuli.

Thus achievement of successful reproduction depends on a complex series of changes in endocrine state and behaviour, related to changes in the external situation, themselves in part determined by the endocrine and behavioural changes.

Comparable data are available for the female canary (fig. 24b). For example, environmental factors (long daylength, male song), acting via the hypothalamo-pituitary-gonad system, result in gonadal development and the release of oestrogen. Oestrogen has a positive influence on nest-building behaviour. The external factors also influence the effectiveness of oestrogen in influencing behaviour. For example oestrogen-treated gonadectomized females build more if exposed to male song or longer days (see below). Nest-building results in a nest, and stimuli from the nest result in a change in the selection of nest material (from grass for the outside to feathers for the lining), a decrease in nest-building behaviour, and further reproductive development. These stimuli from the nest are received through the ventral areas of the skin . Their sensitivity to stimuli from the nest is increased by the development of a brood patch, itself under complex hormonal control. It will be noted that the stimuli from the nest are received as a consequence of and in the course of nest-building behaviour (Hinde, 1965; Hinde and Steel, 1966).

That similar principles apply also to mammals is shown by, for instance, the finding that stimuli from a female monkey influence the levels of sex hormone in a male (Bernstein *et al.,* 1977), and not only does testosterone promote the mating behaviour of male rats, but mating (or at least a concomitant of exposure to females) augments testosterone levels (Thomas and Thomas, 1973; see also Keverne *et al.,* 1978).

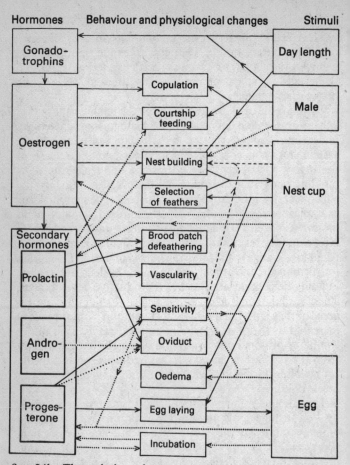

fig. 24b. The relations between external stimuli, hormonal changes, and behaviour in the reproductive development of the female canary. The continuous lines represent positive effects, the discontinuous lines negative effects, and the short dashed lines probable relationships not yet established with certainty. Where the extent to which an effect may be indirect has not yet been established, only the direct effect is shown. The diagram includes reference to three aspects of brood patch development (defeathering, vascularization and sensitivity to tactile stimulation, such as that provided by the nest).

(vi) Changes in the behavioural effectiveness of hormones

We have seen that, in higher vertebrates at least, the steroids to which the brain is exposed during embryonic life or the perinatal period may affect its subsequent responsiveness to steroids. However even later in life the long-term hormonal environment of the brain cells may affect the influence of current hormone levels on behaviour. If male doves (e.g., Hutchison, 1978) are castrated, the effect of implanting steroids into their brains decreases with time since castration.

However the individual differences in responsiveness to steroid hormones, found by earlier investigators (e.g., Young, 1969), are not due only to long-term differences in the hormonal environment. For one thing, experience may play a role. Thus doves can be induced to show incubation behaviour by injections of progesterone, but the treatment is effective only if they have had previous experience of courtship and nest-building (Michel, 1977).

Another issue here is that external stimuli may influence the effect of given (plasma) steroid levels on behaviour. In domesticated canaries and budgerigars the length of the day, and stimuli from the male (e.g., song), influence nest-building behaviour. There is strong evidence that this influence is mediated primarily by an effect of external stimulation on the pituitary gland, which in turn causes the gonad to secrete steroid hormones, which then enhance nest-building behaviour by an effect on the brain. However such stimuli also have a more direct effect, for if that route is eliminated by removal of the gonads, they still influence the effectiveness of exogenous oestrogen. For example, gonad-ectomized canaries, injected with the female sex hormone oestrogen, show more nest-building behaviour, and more nest-building per hour of daylight, if they are kept on long daylengths than if kept on shorter ones. At least some other external stimuli which affect reproductive development also have this more direct influence on the effectiveness of hormones. Thus gonadectomized canaries injected with oestrogen build more if exposed to canary song than if exposed to budgerigar song or to no song. The effectiveness of song is greatest at intermediate daylengths (Hinde and Steel, 1978). Evidently there is a good deal more lability in the hormone/brain cells behaviour system than had previously been suspected. Recent evidence suggests that changes in the ways in which steroids are metabolized in the brain may be implicated (Steimer and Hutchison, 1980).

(vii) Conclusion

In conclusion, therefore, current work is now showing that the older simple measures of sex behaviour, obtained in artificially simplified situations, can be misleading. Comparable data are available for aggression and maternal behaviour. Detailed analysis of behaviour is necessary if we are to understand both the influence of the endocrine system on behaviour and the effects of behaviour on the endocrine system.

9. Neurophysiology

(i) Introduction: historical perspective

In the early days of ethology it was for contact with neurophysiology that hopes were highest. The gradual demise of purely reflex theories of behaviour, coupled with the growing emphasis on the continual activity of the nervous system, provided a climate which seemed congenial to the ethologists. Lorenz (e.g., 1950a) had used von Holst's neurophysiological data to support his own views on the spontaneity of behaviour. Tinbergen (e.g., 1951) translated Lorenz's 'energy' model of motivation (see p. 266) into terms which seemed compatible with neurophysiology, and suggested that the reproductive behaviour of sticklebacks might depend on a hierarchically arranged series of mechanisms which he identified as 'centres'. He related these to the hypothalamic loci which, on localized electrical stimulation, had been found to produce specific types of behaviour in mammals (e.g., Hess, 1943). Emphasizing 'the fundamental identity of the neurophysiological and the ethological approach' (p. 122), he called for the training of ethophysiologists.

Von Holst started to study the behavioural effects of stimulating the brains of freely moving domestic fowl (von Holst and von St Paul, 1963), but this enterprise came to an end with his death in 1962. However the von Holst/Lorenz emphasis on spontaneity in motor mechanisms also resonated with the work of Kenneth Roeder, a neurophysiologist in the USA. He had earlier shown that the locomotor and sexual behaviour of the praying mantis, which in the intact insect occur only with specific stimulation, become continuous after the removal of the two main parts of the brain, respectively the supraoesophageal and suboesophageal ganglia (Roeder, 1935). Such findings suggested spontaneously active nervous centres in the ventral nerve cord normally inhibited by the 'higher' circumoesophageal ganglia.

Roeder (e.g., 1963) argued that many of the proposed bridges between neurophysiology and behaviour had an impractically wide span. Most involved attempts to find the neurophysiological bases of learning, and Roeder (1963, p. 434) thought that 'To reach this point from what we now know about the behaviour of nerve cells is comparable to trying to derive the theory of evolution from a knowledge only of Amoeba and of man'. He felt that ethology provided a more realistic approach because it opened up problems of intermediate complexity. Roeder became an active collaborator in ethological endeavours, and his studies of the neural mechanisms whereby moths detect and avoid bats involved a fascinating marriage of neurophysiology and field ethology (Roeder, 1966). Much other work on the neurophysiology of invertebrates owed its character directly to the ethology of the early fifties, the work of Huber (e.g., 1978) and his colleagues on the courtship and other behaviour of the cricket being a notable example. A similar approach was adopted by neurobiologists who would not have called themselves ethologists, and progress towards the understanding of some relatively complex behaviour patterns has been made (e.g., Kandel, 1978).

But in spite of the successes, both ethological and physiological analyses revealed unexpected complexities, and progress towards a rapprochement was slower than had earlier been hoped. The view that it would be possible to isolate specific neural centres which controlled functionally related groups of activities proved naive, and Tinbergen's hierarchical model, though well supported at the *behavioural level*, was coupled with an energy-model of motivation, and became unfashionable by association with it (see p. 266). That this was unfortunate for the development of ethology has recently been emphasized by Dawkins (1976a).

To say that the optimism of the fifties has not been fulfilled is not to deny the enormous progress in the neurophysiology of behaviour of the last three decades. But whilst the neural bases of some of the simpler behaviour patterns of invertebrates are becoming quite well understood, we are far from comprehending the mechanisms of even such well-studied patterns as eating or sexual behaviour (e.g., Hutchison, 1978) in higher vertebrates. This may be because the 'ethophysiologists' called for by Tinbergen have been slow in coming forward. It may also be because physiologists have forgotten Sherrington's injunction to examine function as well as mechanism. But a major issue has certainly been the naiveté of premature searches for parallels between the products of ethological analysis and phenomena at the neuronal level.

Partly for that reason, some ethologists and zoologists took a rather different route, attempting to specify behavioural processes in systems theory terms (e.g., Hassenstein, 1961; Mittelstaedt, 1962; Horridge and Sandeman, 1964; McFarland, 1974b). But whilst this proved a powerful tool for increasing understanding at the behavioural level, it was less successful in paving the way for neurophysiological analyses. Some ethologists (e.g., Baerends, 1975) now emphasize the dangers of premature links between behavioural and physiological data, arguing that the laws of complicated behaviour must be deduced from behavioural data alone. The force of this view is becoming even more apparent as it is realized that the products even of behavioural analysis are often more elusive than appears at first sight (Fentress, 1976). The boundaries between behavioural systems (see pp. 76–9) are hard to define, the systems overlap, influence each other, and so on. The extent to which a behavioural system depends on factors external to it, and the extent to which it is self-activating and self-integrating, vary with time and with its current state. And since systems influence each other, again to an extent which varies with time, the conventional distinction between factors that are specific to particular aspects of behaviour and factors that are general breaks down. These are important new perspectives, and require us to look for relations between behavioural and physiological data in a new way.

But whilst research over the last thirty years has demonstrated the difficulties of building bridges between neurophysiology and behaviour, it remains the case that, in relatively simple systems, behavioural and physiological analyses can mutually facilitate each other; and that understanding of the mechanisms of more complex behaviour must be preceded by adequate behavioural analysis. In that spirit, we may consider two examples of recent progress in the neurophysiology of behaviour which came, and could only have come, from ethological beginnings.

(ii) The neural bases of bird song

Thorpe's work on song-learning in the chaffinch was discussed in chapter 3 (pp. 80–4). We may consider here an important series of studies on the neural mechanisms underlying singing carried out by Nottebohm (e.g., 1980) and his colleagues. These started from the behavioural data, and have continued to use behavioural end-points at almost every step.

We saw earlier that experienced birds can continue singing after deafening. Since the control of human speech is influenced by the speaker's perception of himself speaking, the finding that deaf birds could sing normally was surprising. One possibility was that the deafened bird was using feedback from the muscles. Nottebohm therefore investigated the effects of severing the nerves to the bird's vocal organ, the syrinx (fig. 25).

Bilateral denervation of the syrinx by section of the hypoglossal nerves rendered chaffinches effectively aphonic. But unilateral operations produced a rather surprising result. Whilst section of the left hypoglossal nerve in adult

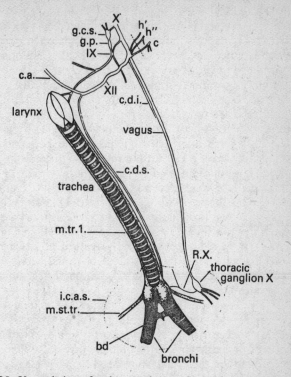

fig. 25. Ventral view of syrinx, trachea, and attendant musculature and innervation of the chaffinch. Three hypoglossal roots are indicated (h', h" and c), the last corresponding to the first cervical nerve. In the experiments described here the routes of the hypoglossal nerve were cut on one or both sides proximal to the hypoglossal/vagus (x) anastomosis. (From Nottebohm, 1971.)

birds led to loss of most of the components of the song, section of the right hypoglossal had only minor effects. If nerve regrowth was prevented, these effects were permanent.

Still more surprising was the finding that unilateral operations on birds which were still developing their songs produced effects that were similar but partly reversible.

Some of the lost song elements were redeveloped by the intact side, though abnormalities remained. At an even earlier stage, before song development had started, section of either hypoglossal nerve was followed by the development of normal song by the intact side. Thus control by the left and right hypoglossal nerves is initially equivalent, left dominance being established during normal song development. If the left hypoglossal nerve is sectioned early on, the right becomes dominant without any loss of effectiveness.

The data have interesting implications concerning the bases of laterality. If unilateral hypoglossectomy in adulthood is followed by functional reinnervation of the syrinx, the lost song elements are reinstated to varying degrees. But if nerve section is performed while the song is still plastic, song production comes to be controlled solely through the intact nerve, whether or not the sectioned nerve regrows. 'It would seem that early section of one hypoglossus leads the CNS to discard the operated nerve as an instrument of vocal control even if that nerve regrows and reinnervates the syrinx' (Nottebohm, 1971, p. 258).

Actually, song learning is the culmination of a long series of processes involving the acquisition of other vocalizations. There is evidence that the two hypoglossi are associated with sounds of different physical characteristics, and differentiation of function may occur in the early food-begging calls.

Nottebohm *et al.* (1976) have shown that similar principles apply to a number of other species, including the domestic canary. By a combination of unilateral lesions, assessment of the vocal output and histological assessment, they have been able to identify many of the neural structures involved in the control of song. Left hemisphere lesions have more pronounced effects than those in the right.

What must be especially emphasized is that this important work stems from a thorough-going behavioural analysis of song ontogeny, and continues to use behavioural dependent variables. Progress would have been impossible were this not the case.

(iii) Neural correlates of learning

Attempts to relate the phenomena of learning, as manifested by changes in behaviour, to changes in the central nervous system, constitute one of the most exciting frontiers of modern biology. However the difficulties, as Roeder foresaw (see p. 170), are profound. One issue is that whilst studies of relatively simple examples of plasticity in relatively simple organisms permit considerable progress (e.g., Horn and Hinde, 1970; Kandel, 1978), their relation to learning as we know it in higher organisms is obscure. But the latter involve phenomena so complex that progress depends not only on the growing sophistication of neurophysiological techniques but also, and crucially, on adequate behavioural analysis. We may consider some issues relevant to the latter.

(a) The definition of learning. Whilst it is generally agreed that learning refers to relatively permanent changes other than those due to maturation or senescence, fatigue, or sensory adaptation (themselves all hard to define), many problems remain (Hinde, 1970). Psychologists tend to use the term with reference to behaviour, physiologists to a change in neural substrate. Biologists may limit its use to 'adaptive' change, but the psychopathologist does not. Learning usually is implicitly related to changes within the nervous system, but most behavioural adjustment involves both intra- and extra-neural changes which interact with each other. Learning usually implies considerable specificity in the behavioural outcome, but no absolute distinction can be made from more general changes consequent upon experience (Schneirla, 1966). Furthermore, the bases of any behavioural change probably depend on a number of intervening processes, which may be analysed in terms of short-term memory vs long-term storage, information acquisition and storage vs retrieval, and so on.

In the face of such issues, some psychologists have erected definitions which clearly delimit a range of phenomena but have the disadvantage that the limits are arbitrary and/or depend on a particular theory of how learning occurs. For instance Kimble (1967) limits learning to changes which occur 'as a result of reinforced practice'. A preferable point of view, taken for instance by Kling (1971), is to acknowledge complexity and diversity by regarding learning as merely 'a heading for a set of chapters in a textbook' (p. 553), a classificatory term for a range of psychological/physiological issues (see also Kandel, 1976). But if this latter view is accepted, attempts to identify the neuronal bases of changes in behaviour must specify those issues rather precisely.

(b) Side effects of training. Experiments aimed at establishing the neuronal bases of learning almost inevitably involve controlled training conditions leading to a specified change in behaviour. The investigator must then attempt to identify some change in the neural substrate which is associated specifically with the change in behaviour being studied. But the training procedures are likely to have effects on the animal in addition to those specific to the learning process (Bateson, 1974, 1978a) (fig. 26). They will certainly involve activity in sensory pathways, and may include exposure to stressful stimuli or require motor activity. These will have widespread neural and endocrine consequences, some of which may be quite irrelevant to the learning process, while others will be necessary for the learning but similar to or identical with the consequences of many other training procedures. And even the necessary neuronal events may have side effects which are irrelevant to the specific behavioural changes in question.

(c) Side effects of learning. In addition to the side effects of training, the learning processes themselves may have consequences – for instance on the general activity of the animal. These also will have neuronal correlates which must be dissociated from those specific to the learning process itself.

Bateson pointed out that most attempts to establish relations between learning and neuronal changes have failed to control for one or more of these issues, and could therefore make only limited progress. In attempts to overcome these difficulties, a neurophysiologist (Horn), an ethologist (Bateson) and a biochemist (Rose) have collaborated in a study of the neuronal bases of imprinting based on a sophisticated behavioural analysis, with full awareness of the difficulties in interpretation that are involved.

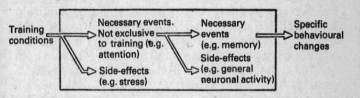

fig. 26. Events intervening between training and the consequent behavioural changes in a learning experiment. (After Bateson, 1974.)

As is well known from experiments on imprinting (see p. 90), chicks are attracted towards a wide range of conspicuous objects if they have been exposed to one during a sensitive period after hatching. The process can be studied by confining the chick in a running wheel and exposing it to a rotating, flashing light (training). Its preference for that light over others differing in colour, flashing pattern, etc. can be tested subsequently. The principal experiments conducted by Bateson, Horn and Rose (e.g., Horn, 1979) can be summarized as follows.

(a) Chicks were hatched in the dark, and 14–19 hours later, maintained either in the dark (dark controls), or in constant light (light controls), or exposed to a flashing light (experimentals) for 105 minutes, after which each chick was killed. Each chick was injected with (^{3}H) lysine 90 minutes before death. Lysine is an amino acid likely to be involved in any synthesis of protein, which would be expected if structural changes in the brain were produced by the experience of the flashing light. The amount of radioactive lysine incorporated into protein was measured in three brain regions. The only significant effect was that incorporation into the forebrain roof was higher in the experimentals than in the controls. This effect was of course not necessarily a correlate of the learning process, but could have been due to any of the side effects mentioned earlier: however it pointed the way ahead.

(b) In a similar experiment, the period of exposure to light was, for separate groups of experimentals and light controls, 38, 76 and 160 minutes. (^{3}H) uracil (a precursor of RNA which is required for protein synthesis) was injected 150 minutes before death. Incorporation in the forebrain roof was higher in the experimentals than in the controls after 76 minutes. After 160 minutes it was higher in all three brain regions in both experimentals and light controls compared with the dark controls. This suggested that specific effects of the imprinting procedure may emerge quite rapidly in the forebrain roof, but are eventually overlain by non-specific effects of exposure to light. However, the early change could also be a consequence of differences in motor activity or levels of stress between the various groups, and to control for these side effects another experiment was devised.

(c) This experiment was conducted with chicks after one cerebral hemisphere had been surgically isolated from visual input to the other. By covering one eye with a patch, it was possible to train such 'split-brain' chicks on one side only. Behavioural experiments showed that chicks would approach the training stimulus preferentially when tested with the trained eye uncovered. The incorporation of (^{3}H) uracil was higher in the forebrain roof of the trained than of the untrained side; there were no other regional differences between the two sides. It is reasonable to ascribe the biochemical changes to the differences in visual experience between the two sides of the brain since, in these experiments, general effects of motor activity or hormonal changes can be discounted. Whilst this is a further step, biochemical changes could result from short-lasting effects of sensory stimulation influencing, for example, levels of synaptic transmitter enzymes, rather than, or in addition to, any specific effects of learning. In the next experiment an attempt was made to tease these factors apart.

(d) Chicks were trained on the first day after hatching for either 20, 60, 120 or 240 minutes, and then for 60 minutes on the second day. The supposition was that birds which had been exposed for longer on the first day, and thus learned more about the stimulus, would learn less on the second day. If incorporation was a function of the amount learned on day 2, such birds should show a lower rate of incorporation then. However if incorporation was a function of short-lasting effects of sensory stimulation, incorporation should be the same for all groups on the second day, since each group was exposed to the stimulus for the same length of time on that day. It was in fact found that incorporation of (^{3}H) uracil in the anterior part of the forebrain roof on the second day decreased with the time of exposure on the first day. No such relationship was found for other brain regions. This experiment excludes short-lasting effects of sensory stimulation and further supports the view that the bio-chemical changes are related to the learning process itself. It was pointed out that these changes could be correlated with differences in vigilance in the young birds as they learn, but this seems unlikely as an explanation because the birds trained for longer on the first day approached the stimulus no less vigorously on the second day. In this experiment a general effect on the rate of neural development could not be discounted. However, if the biochemical changes are related to learning, then the stronger the preference, the higher should be the level of incorporation. Is this so?

(e) 106 chicks were all exposed for the same time (72 minutes) to a flashing light. They were subsequently tested for their preference for the light on which they had been trained over another light. The only significant correlation between radioactive uracil incorporation and behavioural measures in training or testing was with preference for the familiar stimulus on testing. This indicates that the biochemical changes observed are unlikely to be a con-sequence of either sensory stimulation or motor activity.

(f) In further studies the region of incorporation was localized to the medial part of the hyperstriatum ventrale, and it was shown that lesions of this region have a specific effect on the stimulus preference resulting from the imprinting procedure. Structural changes in this area have been identified (e.g., McCabe *et al.,* 1980; Bradley *et al.,* 1980).

These experiments thus involve the successive elimination of possibilities. The 'split-brain' experiment eliminates the consequences of motor activity and stress, the two-day experiment short-lasting effects of sensory stimulation and differential vigilance, and the correlation experiment the consequences of differential stimulation. Real progress towards specifying the neuronal correlates of one case of learning has thus been made, progress that would not have been possible without careful behavioural analysis and continuous consideration of the possible side effects of training or of learning.

(iv) Conclusion

Progress in understanding the neurophysiological bases of complex behaviour has been slower than was earlier anticipated, in part because the necessary integration between physiological and behavioural studies was not achieved. However advances are now being made. On the one hand, ethologists have disowned their earlier naive implications of isomorphism between behaviour and neural machinery. On the other, physiologists have begun to recognize that, in this field, physiological sophistication is not enough. Analysis must be accompanied by resynthesis, and physiological study accompanied by comparable behavioural investigation.

But there are still formidable obstacles to be overcome. Even with apparently stereotyped fixed action patterns, invariance in the movement does not necessarily involve invariance in the neural input. And the relative importance of internal and external factors in their control may vary with speed of performance, practice, and many other factors. The finding that the items of behaviour in an animal's repertoire can be hierarchically organized does not necessarily mean that the controlling mechanisms are, and the ethologists' behavioural systems may be a poor guide to the neurophysiological machinery. The extent to which behavioural systems are independent, the extent to which they can be seen as self-integrating, even their own internal properties, may change with the degree of activation of other systems. For such reasons, Fentress (1976, 1980) calls for caution and emphasizes the need for new conceptual sophistication in attempts to integrate behavioural and neurophysiological data.

10.   Comparative Psychology

As with behavioural ecology, comparative psychology and ethology have passed through a period of sharp divergence and debate to become almost indistinguishable. Once again a historical approach is of interest, even though the events are seen from a personal perspective.

American comparative psychology had already had a distinguished history when Lorenz and Tinbergen started their work. In the 1930s it was perhaps best represented by Maier's and Schneirla's (1935) textbook, published in the same year as Lorenz's *Kumpan* paper. Some comparative psychologists entered into discussion or collaboration with ethologists, a notable example being F. A. Beach. Beach's Ph.D. thesis had been entitled 'The neural basis for innate behaviour', and in 1935 he had independently developed methods for using models to analyse the stimuli controlling species-characteristic behaviour. It was thus not surprising that, when he first met Tinbergen in 1938, the two men had a common language. Shortly afterwards Tinbergen and W. H. Thorpe approached Beach and invited him to join the editorial staff of *Behaviour*. Tinbergen's most recent description of his impressions at that time says much about both men:

> Although at that time I was not at all attracted to Frank's 'laborientedness', nor to his inclination to measure simple components of the 'causal web', he on his side was open-minded enough (I am sure not merely polite enough) to express interest in what we were then doing. And he did influence us, much to the good, by his insistence on the need for measurement. I think that it was a combination

of our respect for his research, for his open-mindedness and for his friendly and truly co-operative attitude that made us (W. H. Thorpe and N. Tinbergen) approach him for representing *Behaviour* in the US (Tinbergen, pers. comm.).

Beach has never called himself an ethologist, perhaps because he viewed the early ethologists' 'field-orientedness' as 'fine, but not for me', but he continued to be both a fellow-traveller and a friendly critic.

However other comparative psychologists were strongly opposed to the new discipline. Foremost among these was T. C. Schneirla, Beach's successor in the department of animal behavior at the American Museum of Natural History. In the post-war years deep differences of opinion existed between Lorenz and Tinbergen on the one hand, and Schneirla on the other. There were a number of issues, but three were paramount. First, Schneirla was bitterly opposed to Lorenz's distinction between innate and acquired behaviour, arguing that the distinction is not empirically useful because there are no hard-and-fast rules for making it, and that it is not heuristically valuable in that it leads to a neglect of the complex processes intervening in development (see pp. 85–7). Ethologists, in his view, were dodging the important developmental problems. Bringing up animals in social isolation was not, as some ethologists claimed, an adequate demonstration that the behaviour which appeared was 'innate', but merely showed it was independent of some of the sources of external influence that ethologists thought might be important in its development.

Second, ethologists at that time used models of motivation that stemmed from the view that behaviour depended upon the discharge of hypothetical 'reaction specific energy' generated and stored in reservoirs in the nervous system, and discharged in action. Similar models were used by McDougall and earlier comparative/experimental psychologists, and of course by Freud. Tinbergen, in an effort to forge links with neurophysiology, had translated the energy into 'motivational impulses' and the 'reservoirs' into hierarchies of 'nervous centres', but the structure of the model was essentially similar. Schneirla rightly regarded such models as remote from probable neurophysiological reality.

Third, Schneirla stressed the importance of recognizing the differences between levels in the cognitive capacities of animals. He was thus wary of terms which embraced aspects of behaviour phenomenologically similar across species (see p. 20) because the underlying mechanisms might be very different. Aggressive behaviour, to mention one with which he was much concerned in later years, involves very different mechanisms in ant, goose and man. Many of the terms used by ethologists, such as 'fixed action pattern', involved in his view the mere reification of description, and were not of any explanatory value.

On their side, the ethologists had their own reservations about psychology, though they did not always distinguish too clearly between its branches. They argued strongly against the use by American psychologists of a very small number of mammalian species, most usually just the laboratory rat, as a basis for far-reaching generalizations (e.g., Tinbergen, 1951). They felt that the adjective in 'comparative psychology' was a sham, for contrasting distantly related species as representatives of different phyletic levels did not constitute comparison in a biological sense. Some of the ethologists' criticisms were, it must be admitted, based on ignorance. Lorenz, better acquainted with European than with current American psychology, as late as 1958 described 'psychology proper' as 'the science dealing with subjective phenomena'.

Whilst it is possible to pick out a few issues that seemed primary in the disputes between ethology and comparative psychology, the basic issue was perhaps a difference in attitude to the enormous complexity and diversity of animal behaviour which both sides recognized. Both saw the need for refining the questions asked – for instance Schneirla (1940) was just as scornful of answers to questions of causation given in functional terms as were the ethologists But whilst the ethologists tried to abstract simple principles embodied in such concepts as the 'fixed action pattern' or 'sign stimulus', and assess the extent of their generality, Schneirla felt the need constantly to emphasize complexity and diversity. Neither approach is right; both are necessary.

Schneirla's criticisms tended to be published in journals which were not widely read by ethologists, who were in any case still mostly European. Furthermore his prose style was difficult. However in 1953 his pupil, Lehrman, published a 'Critique of Konrad Lorenz's theory of instinctive behavior' in the *Quarterly Review of Biology*. Although Lehrman had toned down his article on the advice of Ernst Mayr, Frank Beach and others, it was a hard-hitting attack on ethology. That it led to a permanent rapprochement between most ethologists and most comparative psychologists was almost entirely due to personal factors. Lorenz has described how, after reading the Critique, he pictured Lehrman as a pinched, shrivelled little man. Nothing could have been further from the truth. Lehrman weighed more than he should have, had an infectious geniality, and an ebullience and enthusiasm for natural history that matched Lorenz's own. Tinbergen, Lorenz and Lehrman were all bird watchers with a common interest in natural history and compatible personalities. Each side learned from the other, softening its more extreme views, and the protagonists became close friends.

On the ontogeny issue, both sides changed their emphasis: comparative psychologists withdrew from their extreme emphasis on the role of experience; the dichotomy between maturation and experience, suggested by Schneirla as a substitute for that between innate and learned, proved no more valuable; and most ethologists modified their views about the usefulness of classifying behaviour into elements that were innate or learned (see pp. 85–7). Thorpe's work on song-learning in chaffinches (chapter 3), not yet published at this time, greatly facilitated this.

Ethologists had in fact already started to have doubts about their motivational models. For example von Holst and Mittelstaedt (1950) had introduced the idea of negative feedback to ethologists. Whilst this was applied at first mostly to invertebrates or 'lower level' mechanisms in vertebrates, its general importance became clear when Moynihan demonstrated the role of feedback stimuli in controlling incubation behaviour. Although this was first published in a paper which still leant heavily on an energy model of motivation, the change had begun. Behaviour sequences could be brought to an end not by the discharge of energy in action, but by stimuli received as a result of the behaviour. At the same time I was studying the waning of the mobbing response of chaffinches to owls in what had initially been an attempt to specify the dimensions of the Lorenzian reservoir, but the data made me realize the inadequacies of the Lorenzian model (see p. 28). Furthermore whilst the field data on great tits I had collected could be described in hierarchical terms, postulation of a hierarchy of nervous centres would have gone far beyond the evidence. Lehrman's strictures about the ethological approach to motivation thus fell on receptive ears.

On the 'comparative' issue, the differences in approach were recognized. Both the problem of accounting for the diverse levels of complexity within the animal kingdom, with which the comparative psychologists had been concerned, and the problems of microevolution on which ethologists had focused, were recognized as important.

Thus at one time at least some ethologists and some comparative psychologists saw themselves as bitterly opposed to each other. Lehrman's 'Critique' established a dialogue which, largely because of the personalities of the participants, was constructive and led in the main to a permanent rapprochement between members of both groups. On the whole the relations of comparative psychologists to Tinbergen and others influenced by him was closer than that to Lorenz and his colleagues. Lorenz, at first apparently susceptible to new ideas, later (1966) defended a position on the innate vs learned issue only marginally different from that he had occupied earlier. Some debate between Lehrman (e.g., 1970) and Lorenz continued (see Beer, 1975), but Lehrman effectively joined the ethologists. Whilst at the present time some comparative psychologists influenced by Schneirla still reject ethology and there are a few ethologists who perpetuate the notion of innate behaviour (see p. 87), on the whole the distinction between the two groups barely exists. This came about not through one group proving the other wrong, though this happened over some issues, but by a combination of tenacity by members of each side where they continued to believe themselves to be right with humility and a willingness to learn.

11. Experimental Psychology

(i) Introduction

The germination of ethology more or less coincided with the flowering of learning theories within experimental psychology. Tinbergen (1951) was critical of such theories because they were based on studies of one or two species in unnatural laboratory environments: he urged the need for a broader basis for generalizations. In this chapter I have selected two issues to exemplify the growing contacts between ethology and experimental psychology. The first concerns the impact of studies of a broader range of species and responses on learning theories, the second the value of detailed study of the phenomenon of imprinting, provided that the analysis is linked to the natural context and is not too blinkered by theory.

(ii) Constraints on learning

During the thirties and forties, when ethology was just beginning to grow, learning theorists were optimistic about the possibilities of constructing a comprehensive theory of behaviour. It was assumed that learning was of one or two basic types and, by many but not by all, that the occurrence of learning depended on events that could be labelled as reinforcers. The early ethologists, by contrast, being by training biologists, were conscious of the diversity of organisms and of the diversity of mechanisms within organisms. In the fifties and sixties they found numerous examples of limitations within and differences between species in learning abilities in particular contexts. For example Tinbergen (1953) noted the clumsiness of the way in which herring gulls (*Larus argentatus*) retrieve eggs which have rolled out of the nest by niggling them back with their beaks, and remarked on their apparent inability to use their wings and feet (cf. fig. 3). He also observed that the herring gull does not learn to respond differentially to its own eggs, but does recognize its own chicks: this appears to be adaptive because, with the spacing of nests in a herring gull colony, mixing of eggs is very improbable but chicks can and do stray. In two species which live in dense colonies where mixing of eggs is possible, the cliff-nesting guillemot *(Uria aalge)* and the densely nesting royal tern *(Sterna maxima)*, egg recognition does occur (Tschanz, 1959; Buckley and Buckley, 1972). Another case has been mentioned already (pp. 80–4): while some birds develop a near-normal vocal repertoire if reared in acoustic isolation others, like the chaffinch, have to learn the species-characteristic song but can learn little else, whilst yet others learn a wide range of sounds.

Studies of the capacities of honey-bees provide some further examples. If food is presented in association with different stimulus objects, honey-bees will learn to respond reliably to an odour after only one approach, but need three to learn to return to colour, and over twenty to respond to characters of form. Furthermore some types of odour, namely those associated with flowering plants, are learned more readily than others. And when bees of different races are compared, each race learns most readily the odours that are characteristic of its native flora. The evidence that the differences in learning preference are genetically determined is considerable (Lindauer, 1975).

Similar conclusions were reached in laboratory experiments. In studies of operant conditioning, a particular stimulus (e.g., a yellow light) sets the occasion for an operant response (e.g., pecking a key). If that response produces an event, such as the arrival of food in a dispenser, the event is called a reinforcer. But the effect of the reinforcer on the operant response is not always so great as in Skinner's classic experiments of food-deprived pigeons pecking for food; and the earlier view that if an event, such as the arrival of food or access to a female, acts as a reinforcer for one response it will do so for any, proved untenable. For example chaffinches will learn to sit preferentially on a particular perch to turn on a playback of adult song (though not to turn on white noise). Thus by that criterion song is a reinforcer. But playback of song is much less effective in getting them to peck a key, although food does reinforce key-pecking by food-deprived chaffinches (Stevenson-Hinde, 1972; Stevenson-Hinde and Roper, 1975).

These and many other studies showing that animals often have remarkable learning abilities limited to specific contexts (e.g., Baerends, 1941) led ethologists (e.g., Lorenz, 1965; Tinbergen 1951; Hinde 1970; Hinde and Stevenson-Hinde, 1973) to emphasize that, quite apart from differences in learning ability, what a species learns is determined by its nature – it has predispositions to learn in some contexts, and is constrained from learning in others. Some learning theorists had themselves expressed doubts about the generality of learning theories (e.g., Koch, 1954; Logan, 1959; Miller, 1959; Tolman, 1959), and evidence for constraints and predispositions came from within (e.g., Breland and Breland, 1961; Glickman and Schiff, 1967; Shettleworth, 1972; Seligman and Hager, 1972; Razran, 1971) as well as from outside their ranks.

In 1972 ethologists and learning theorists came together to discuss the issues (Hinde and Stevenson-Hinde, 1973). It was apparent that differences in what is learned could depend on diverse factors – differences in cognitive ability, differences in predispositions to form particular associations, differences in the availability of motor patterns, or differences in relations between stimulus, response and reinforcer. In attempting a partial synthesis, Stevenson-Hinde (1973) classified constraints on reinforcement in terms of the place in the learning sequence at which they acted:

(a) The 'causal factors'. This was used in a very general

sense to refer to antecedent manipulations or to any conditions that hold throughout the period of testing. For example, age and early experience affect whether or not a chick will sit on a pedal when that response is followed by the opportunity to approach a flashing light.

(b) The relation between the stimulus and the operant response. The stimulus may or may not elicit aspects of the operant response initially. If it does, learning will be facilitated. Thus the success of many studies of learning in neonates has depended on the use of nipples which elicited sucking from the start: reinforcement was made contingent upon responses that exceeded a criterion amplitude.

(c) 'Relevance' of the operant response to the reinforcer. In chaffinches, song is a better reinforcer for perching than for pecking. This may be related to the fact that, in the natural situation, perching can bring the bird closer to song, but pecking can not. The influence of 'relevance' may be related to a sharing of motivational factors between operant and consummatory responses (e.g., Breland and Breland, 1961).

(d) The relation between stimuli associated with the consummatory stimuli and their physiological consequences. This refers specifically to the manner in which animals can learn to avoid substances whose poisonous consequences appear with considerable delay after their ingestion (e.g., Revusky and Garcia, 1970). If ingestion of a sweet-tasting solution is followed by toxicosis, the solution is subsequently avoided. But if, instead of a flavour, external stimuli (flash of light and a click) accompany drinking, there is no such avoidance. Such a finding suggests that the 'relevance' of the stimulus to the physiological consequence is an important issue (Revusky and Garcia, l.c.). On such a view, a flavour has a high associative strength with respect to physiological consequences, but exteroceptive stimuli do not. Such relevance may be acquired (Mackintosh, 1973).

(e) Compatability between recent performance of the consummatory response and repetition of the operant response. Sevenster (1973), studying three-spined sticklebacks *(Gasterosteus aculeatus)*, compared the reinforcing effects of an opportunity to court on two operants, swimming through a ring and biting a rod. The interval between courtship and the next performance of the operant was much longer for biting, and this was shown to be due in part to a form of behavioural inhibition between courting and biting.

Of course such a classification is not absolute. More or fewer constraints might be recognized, depending on the level of analysis. Indeed there is now evidence that the same responses and reinforcers may interact differently under different circumstances (Rice, 1978), and it is apparent that the problems are only just broached. But it is clear that we can no longer expect a variety of reinforcers to control a variety of operant responses in similar ways, and that understanding of such operant sequences requires some knowledge of the behaviour in natural contexts.

It is important to be precise about the role of the ethological approach here. As stressed above, many learning theorists had themselves expressed doubts about the generality of their theories. The importance of constraints and predispositions would no doubt have been fully recognized without ethological intervention. And indeed the ethologists had themselves been naive about learning phenomena. But the fact is that a mammoth enterprise, involving innumerable scientists in diverse laboratories over several decades, almost came to grief because the importance of observation before experimentation, and of comparison before generalization, were not recognized.

Recently Rozin (1976), by training an experimental psychologist, has suggested a framework for synthesizing these data on situational differences in learning ability. He contrasts the view, held by most experimental psychologists, that the evolution of intelligence involves the gradual accretion of new general learning capacities, with the view that animals evolve first adaptive specializations for particular contexts. Initially each adaptive specialization, being as it were a solution to a particular problem, tends to manifest itself only in the narrow set of circumstances in which that problem arises. These specializations may involve mechanisms ready to perform particular tasks, or the capacity to profit from experience in particular situations, or any intermediate between the two. Thus the bee's capacity to learn associations with particular flower scents, and the rat's ability to associate past tastes with digestive discomfort, are seen as elements in systems evolved specifically in the context of feeding behaviour. Rozin cites such phenomena as the navigational abilities of birds, the ability of bees to use the sun as a compass, and the memory of hunting wasps for the location of several different nest-holes, as abilities evolved for specific tasks in specific situations. The constituent mechanisms are, to varying degrees, inaccessible for use in other contexts. Rozin suggests that the evolution of intelligence has involved the harnessing of abilities initially specific to one context for other purposes – an extension of function which may utilize the same genetic blueprint to duplicate the neural machinery, or involve easier access to that machinery by other inputs. Thus higher mammals may differ from most other species not so much in the plasticity of their behaviour in any particular situation, as in the range of situations in which they can display their capacities for plasticity. Rozin further suggests that a similar extension of access is involved in development, drawing a parallel with the Piagetian scheme of movement from concrete to abstract abilities. Conversely many of the symptoms of senility can be regarded as a reduction of access. Rozin's scheme requires a new perspective on the nature of intelligence, and could have important educational implications.

(iii) Imprinting

Chicks, ducklings and goslings exposed to a moving object during a certain sensitive period soon after hatching will learn to follow it, responding to it as they would to their own parents. After relatively little experience with one object, their responsiveness becomes more or less limited to it. Lorenz (1935) called the learning process involved 'imprinting', and although he was probably wrong in regarding it as a special form of learning, the context in which it occurs gives it a number of special properties. The detailed studies stimulated by his earlier work are of considerable importance for the study of learning in general. We have already seen how the imprinting paradigm has been applied in studies of the neural bases of learning (chapter 9, pp. 175–80): the following further issues may be emphasized:

(a) Imprinting occurs during a sensitive period. Within that period learning occurs much more readily than outside it. The concept of a sensitive period, and its limitations, were discussed in chapter 3 (p. 90). Whilst the factors limiting sensitive periods clearly differ from case to case, the concept has proved to be a useful one. It arose from studies of imprinting.

(b) The importance of perceptual learning. Lorenz emphasized that imprinting was independent of any of the conventional reinforcers. Later Bateson (e.g., 1966; see also Sluckin and Salzen, 1961; Hinde, 1962) demonstrated that it is operationally similar to 'perceptual learning', as studied by experimental psychologists such as Gibson and Walk (1956). The latter had shown that exposure of rats to metal shapes in their home cages facilitated their subsequent learning to discriminate one of them from another shape, whether or not the second was one they had seen before and whether the familiar shape was the rewarded or the non-rewarded one in the discrimination task. Bateson showed that exposure of chicks to a colour pattern in their home pens both subsequently facilitated imprinting to that pattern and facilitated discrimination learning involving that pattern. Procedurally, therefore, the two could be described in similar terms: they appear to involve stimulus-stimulus association independent of any response-contingent reinforcement. 'Learning about the stimulus' was demonstrated in a number of ethological studies, including song-learning (see chapter 3, pp. 80–5), and the importance of perceptual learning was emphasized by Thorpe (1963). Similar phenomena were studied by psychologists under the rubrics of 'sensory preconditioning', 'two-stage discrimination learning'; and 'place learning', but a sole reliance on experiments that isolated parts of the learning process did not facilitate general acceptance of their importance until relatively recently (e.g., Sutherland l.c.; Mackintosh, 1973).

(c) The interdigitation of learning paradigms. Attempts to classify studies of learning under a small number of learning paradigms may not have done justice to the variety of learning phenomena (Razran, 1971), but have been valuable in reconciling different studies (Kling, 1971), for diverse learning experiments on a variety of species can be classified in terms of three basic procedures – exposure (or perceptual) learning, classical conditioning and operant conditioning. However Thorpe (1963; see also Konorski, 1948) argued that 'associative' learning as studied in most experimental situations has features in common with both classical and operant conditioning, and that perceptual learning is ubiquitous. Studies of imprinting supported his view, for all three procedures could be used to portray aspects of imprinting (e.g., Bateson, 1964; James, 1959; Bateson and Reese, 1969). This interdigitation of learning paradigms has now become apparent also in other contexts, such as 'autoshaping' (Moore, 1973).

(d) Response to discrepancy: response to novelty. Whereas marked novelty elicits avoidance or a negative response, slight novelty may be attractive and elicit positive responses. For example, novelty is a potent elicitor for smiling in human infants (McCall and Kagan, 1969). A comparable phenomenon occurs in the imprinting situation, where a variety of lines of evidence indicate that, even while the chick's readiness to approach is being progressively narrowed to the most familiar class of objects, they prefer slightly novel stimulation. On the basis of empirical data, Bateson has suggested that the relations between the period of exposure to one of two stimulus objects, the preference shown for that object over the other, and the difference between the two objects, can be represented as in fig. 27 (Bateson, 1973b). The view is also in harmony with the predictions of a theoretical model (Bateson, 1973a). Although detailed testing of this model has been hindered by the difficulty of finding a stimulus continuum in which stimulus effectiveness shows no marked discontinuities, it has been valuable in reconciling a number of apparently discrepant experimental findings.

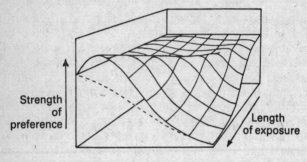

Strength of preference

Length of exposure

Familiar ⟶ Unfamiliar

fig. 27. Theoretical model showing how the preference of chicks for an unfamiliar model varies with its difference from a familiar model and the chick's length of exposure to the familiar model. (Bateson, 1973a.)

(e) The fertility of questions of adaptedness. Lorenz (1935) emphasized that the nature of the imprinting process, for instance its rapidity and irreversibility, varied between species in an adaptive way. More recently ethologists have asked why such a chancy way of learning the species characteristics should have been selected at all. Why are not young birds born with a capacity to respond appropriately to their parents? They must of course learn to recognize them as individuals, but surely the species characteristics need not depend on learning? One suggestion is this. Whilst adult animals can respond similarly to a given stimulus object no matter (within limits) what its distance or their angle of regard, this ability probably depends on experience. Since a particular parent bird would present diverse stimulus configurations to a young chick, and the hatchling presumably does not yet have these 'perceptual constancies', any recognition mechanisms that did not depend on experience would have to be very complex (Hinde, 1961).

Of more interest is a recent suggestion by Bateson (1978b and c). It depends on the finding that the learning determining that the chick will direct its filial responses to its parent occurs earlier than the learning that determines the direction of its sexual responses in later life (Schutz, 1965). Bateson suggests that the latter involves characteristics of the siblings as well as of the parent, and has the function of ensuring that the individual will both breed with a mate of the same species and also not breed with a very close relative. On this view, pair formation is more likely to take place with an individual slightly different from those on which the chick was imprinted. Experimental and comparative evidence support this hypothesis (see p. 130).

The issues mentioned here are varied. However they all stem from a detailed analysis of one issue, an analysis pursued with an eye not just to one problem, but to a variety of problems concerned with development, causation, function and evolution.

(iv) Conclusion

It is beginning to be apparent that more and more of the phenomena initially studied independently by ethologists and by experimental psychologists are related, at least at the behavioural level. Displacement activities may be related to adjunctive behaviour (see pp. 66–7); the phenomenon of supernormal stimuli (p. 38) to the peak shift phenomenon (Stevenson, 1966; Terrace, 1968; Hogan *et al.,* 1975); the ethologists' 'releasing mechanism' to the psychologists' 'analyser' (p. 39); and habituation to extinction (Kling and

Stevenson, 1970). The prospects for increased co-operation in the future seem bright. And the need for such co-operation is emphasized by a traditional difference in orientation between ethologists and psychologists. The former, although they have long discarded classical instinct theory, still like to classify types of behaviour into groups on causal or functional grounds – for instance into sexual, aggressive or feeding behaviour. In so far as the relations between these categories, or between their constituent members, are discussed, the emphasis is on their mutually inhibitory or facilitatory influences. Psychologists, by contrast, have been concerned with characteristics of processes such as perception, motivation or learning which permeate the ethologists' categories. The ethologists' bias may lead to shortcomings in their approach to development, where such categories can be misleading, and in studies of the behaviour of higher organisms, where cognitive functions may link causal or functional categories of behaviour. The psychologists' bias retarded their recognition of the importance of response or situation-specific constraints on learning. Integration between these approaches is clearly essential.

PART III

Ethology and the Human Social Sciences

12.   Introduction: Ethology and the Social Sciences

(i) General issues

Ethologists have been concerned primarily with non-human species. That their work could be in any way relevant to studies of human behaviour might well be doubted. However I shall argue in the following chapters that, provided the dangers of false parallels are recognized, ethologists have much to contribute. In fact just because many ethologists were trained as biologists, most are fully conscious of the diversity of nature and recognize that projections from one species to another can be misleading. This is especially true of comparisons between animal and man. Human capacities for cognitive functioning, and particularly for language, introduce new dimensions, including a possibility for cultural diversity of a different order from that encountered amongst animals. For that reason alone, ethologists know (or should know) that direct parallels between animal and human behaviour are rarely appropriate. For another, the very diversity of human cultures, coupled with the diversity of animal species, often make it impossible to specify which parallels should be examined (Lehrman, 1974).

However some social scientists take too extreme a view on this issue. For example Harré and Secord (1972) argue that, whilst the behaviour of both animals and man may be goal-directed, implying that animals can monitor their own behaviour, only man can monitor his own monitoring. Thus a man can not only try to carry out a task, continuously monitoring his success, but he can also assess the extent to which he is trying. This, coupled with the power of speech, means that we can plan ahead, talk about what we will do or did, and take care that we do what we intended. They therefore argue that explanations of human behaviour must be based on an actor-based understanding of situations. Contrasting analysis of human behaviour in terms of people as agents, with analysis in terms of people as patients whose behaviour is passively determined by circumstances, whilst half-heartedly admitting that both may be necessary, they put all their money on the former and discard the latter. Surely a more logical conclusion would be to admit that more than one tool is necessary.

And some ethological tools are likely to be useful to the social scientist. Methodologically, the descriptive techniques used by ethologists are now fairly sophisticated, and are being put to use by developmental psychologists, anthropologists, psychiatrists, and others. Comparative studies, if used not with an implication that people are just like animals, but to provide principles whose applicability to the human case can be assessed, can be a fruitful source of ideas and data: we shall meet some examples later. Indeed animal data are sometimes useful not because animals are like man, but just because they are different: the relative simplicity of the animal case may help in the refining of explanatory concepts (e.g., p. 210), or in disentangling the interaction of cultural and biological factors (e.g., pp. 242–3). Indeed the very fact that animals lack verbal language and culture as we know it can perhaps be turned to good advantage. Understanding of the influence of language on man's cognitive abilities or culture, or the influence of cultural factors on human relationships or social structure, may be enhanced by comparison with non-man, where such influences are absent or minimal. And the diversity of animal species can be utilized if we compare aspects of human structure and behaviour with a range of animal species, seeing where man 'fits': just as, by comparing our teeth with those of a range of animal species we can draw conclusions about the diet to which man was originally adapted, so can behavioural comparisons throw light on other aspects of our nature. Some even argue that similarities between human and animal behaviour can be instructive in the absence of any similarities of mechanism. For example Eibl Eibesfeldt (1979) suggests that analogies in greeting rituals between human and non-human throw light on the forces involved in their elaboration. Studies of a range of animal species permit the elaboration of principles whose applicability to the human case can be assessed (e.g., pp. 231–6). And it must be remembered that some of the basic scientific issues are surprisingly similar. For example, the ethological distinction between the four whys of causation, ontogeny, function and evolution finds a partial parallel in Thibaut and Kelley's (1959, p. 126) discussion of 'social norms'.

> Norms . . . may be described in terms of the social processes or mechanisms they involve . . ., in terms of their immediate effects . . . or . . . in terms of their more distal consequences or functions. Unless these different modes of description are carefully distinguished, misunderstandings may develop . . .

Of course, while ethology can contribute to the human social sciences, the ethologist cannot solve the problems of human social behaviour on his own. While some techniques devised for recording fish behaviour are helpful for nursery school children, children are not fish, and further techniques are necessary for the problems posed by children's use of language, fantasy play, role-taking skills and moral decisions. An amalgam of techniques, concepts and theories appropriate to the problem being tackled is essential. For these and other reasons I have a personal distrust of the increasing use of the term 'Human Ethology' to demarcate a new discipline. It implies an ethology which has cast off its comparative roots, and is bobbing about on the surface of the stream having refused a psychological anchor. But as I hope to show, if the ethologist is armed with humility his contribution can be considerable (see also Lockard, 1980).

(ii) Levels of analysis

Because of his biological background, the ethologist must feel that understanding within the social sciences requires a descriptive base. For that to be achieved, an absolute requirement is clear-headedness about the levels of complexity involved. It is useful to distinguish at least four levels – social behaviour, interactions, relationships and social structure – each of which involves properties that are simply not relevant to the level below.

To describe an interaction, it is necessary to specify what the individuals are doing together, and how they are doing it. They may for instance be fighting, but fighting ritualistically or viciously; one might be kissing the other, but kissing passionately or perfunctorily. And some terms used to describe interactions would not be relevant to individuals on their own – you can converse or compete only in interaction with another (real or imagined) individual.

A relationship involves a series of interactions between two individuals who are known to each other. To describe a relationship at the behavioural level it is necessary to specify not only the content and quality of the constituent interactions, but also their absolute and relative frequencies and how they are patterned in time. (Other aspects of relationships are considered in chapter 13.) A relationship may be multiplex (involving interactions of diverse types) or uniplex, controlling or permissive – properties inapplicable to, or at least carrying a rather different meaning from, isolated interactions.

Description of the structure of a group involves description of the constituent dyadic (and higher order) relationships within it, and also description of how those relationships are patterned. Thus the relationships could be arranged linearly, hierarchically, in a network and so on, and any such arrangement could be dense or loose – properties not applicable to relationships in isolation.

All that has been said so far could refer only to behaviour.

But in the human case it is clearly necessary to come to terms with the affective/cognitive concomitants of social interactions and relationships, and as knowledge advances the same may apply to other species. What is perceived to happen in an interaction may matter more than what actually happened: if you cough whilst I am talking, much may depend on whether I perceive the cough as an attempt to interrupt me. Interactions and relationships are evaluated by the participants, and their judgements affect their future behaviour. And relationships can endure in the absence of interactions. Thus it is necessary to come to terms not only with objective behaviour, but with the subjective phenomena related to it.

Thus the study of social phenomena involves discriminating and analysing several levels of complexity (interaction, relationships, social structure), each with its own emergent properties, and also coming to grips with both behaviour and affective/cognitive phenomena. We shall return to these issues later (chapter 13): here let us consider the processes actually involved in the study of social behaviour. An example, referring to a hypothetical group of monkeys containing three types of relationship (mother–infant, male–female, and peer–peer), is shown in fig. 28.

What we observe is the behaviour of individuals, usually in interaction with each other. From observations of a number of particular instances of particular sorts of interaction in one dyad, as represented by the rectangles marked 1, 2, 3, 4 or 5 in fig. 28, we can make generalizations about those sorts of interactions in that dyad (6, 7, etc.). Comparable generalizations about other dyads (rectangles behind 6, 7, etc.) permit generalizations about the several sorts of interactions (8, etc.) valid for a range of dyads. From descriptions of their interactions over time, we can abstract a description of the relationship between two individuals (9, 10, 11). Each relationship will involve interactions of a number of types. Generalizations about relationships of each type (12, 13, 14) may come from data on individual dyadic relationships.

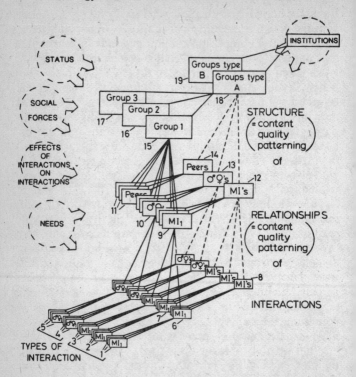

fig. 28.   Diagrammatic representation of the relations between interactions, relationships and social structure. Interactions, relationships and social structure are shown as rectangles on three levels, with successive stages of abstraction from left to right. The discontinuous circles represent some of the principles necessary to explain patterning at each level. Institutions, having a dual role, are shown in both a rectangle and a circle. In the specific instance of a non-human primate, the rectangles might represent:
  (1) Instances of grooming interactions between a mother A and infant B.
  (2) Instances of nursing interactions between A and B.
  (3) Instances of play between A and B.
  (4) Instances of grooming between female A and male C.
  (5) Instances of copulation between A and C.

(6) First stage abstraction – schematic grooming interactions between A and B. Abstractions of grooming interactions between other mother–infant pairs are shown behind, but the specific instances from which they were abstracted are not shown.

(7) First stage abstraction – schematic nursing interactions between A and B. Abstractions of nursing interactions of other mother–infant pairs are shown behind.

(8) Second stage abstraction – schematic grooming interactions between all mother–infant pairs in troop.

(9) Mother–infant relationship between A and B. Mother–infant relationships of other mother–infant pairs are shown behind (but connections to grooming, nursing, etc., interactions are not shown).

(10) Consort relationship between A and C. Other consort relationships are shown behind.

(11) Specific relationships of another type (e.g., peer–peer).

(12) (13) (14) Abstraction of mother–infant, consort and peer–peer relationships. These may depend on abstractions of the contributing interactions.

(15) Surface structure of troop containing A, B, C, etc.

(16) (17) Surface structures of other troops (contributing relationships not shown).

(18) Abstraction of structure of troops including that containing A, B, C, etc. This may depend on abstractions of mother–infant, etc., relationships.

(19) Abstraction of structure of a different set of troops (from another environment, species, etc.).

Rectangles labelled MI_1 refer to behaviour of dyad female A and her infant B. Rectangles labelled $\male\female_1$ refer to consort pair female A and male C. Rectangles labelled MIs, $\male\female$'s refer to generalizations about behaviour of mother–infant dyads and consort pairs respectively.

These relationships occur within a group. The 'surface structure' of the group (15, 16, 17) can be described in terms of the content, qualities and patterning of the constituent relationships (9–11). From the 'surface structures' of particular groups we may abstract a more general 'structure' (18, 19) which reflects those aspects of the content, qualities and patterning of relationships that show regularities across individuals and across societies, and neglects the peculiarities of individual ones. Of course neither 'surface structure' nor 'structure' implies a static entity, and they may include a temporal dimension.

All that has been said so far concerns the data level. We describe the individual interactions, and use also data about the relations between interactions to describe relationships, and data about the relations between relationships to describe structure. But we need also principles which will explain, in a causal or functional sense, the patterning that we observe at each level. An example from non-human primates may help.

In group-living monkeys, the females are usually arranged in a dominance order. Usually the dominant individual can 'boss', by a number of different criteria, all those below her; the second can boss all below her, and so on. Now monkeys spend much time grooming each other's fur. Two generalizations seem to be applicable to a considerable number of species: (a) high-ranking animals receive more grooming than others and (b) most grooming occurs between females of adjacent rank. There is, however, no consistent relationship between a female's rank and the amount of grooming she gives. Seyfarth (1977) has shown that these aspects of social structure can be understood in terms of a model incorporating two causal principles:

(a) A female's attractiveness to others is directly related to her rank.
(b) Access to preferred partners is restricted by competition.

Thus high-ranking females, meeting little or no competition, can interact with others of high rank. Middle-ranking females, who meet competition for those of high rank, must compromise by interacting with middle-ranking females. Low-ranking animals, meeting competition from all above them, must make do with other low-ranking animals. Thus the model, based on principles of individual behaviour which can be simulated on a computer, duplicates the observed properties of social structure. The principles are not expressed in pure form in the surface structure, which depends on their interaction. The value of the model is enhanced by the fact that attractiveness of high rank also explains other types of interaction in the troop, and can be understood in terms of (short-term) functions. The latter point depends on a presumed causal effect of A grooming B on the probability of B forming a coalition with A against a third party subsequently – a presumption in keeping with the data.

In the same way, it is necessary to search for principles that will help to explain the patterning of interactions in human inter-personal relationships, and the patterning of relationships in societies. In this search we are moving from data, or abstractions from data, to the language of explanation, and just as we explain feeding behaviour in terms of motivational concepts (see p. 48), so may the explanatory principles we use employ concepts not present in the data language.

In practice the principles necessary for understanding the patterning of interactions within relationships can be classified into three inter-related groups:

(a) Principles concerned with the natures or needs of individuals. Individuals have different needs, and will form relationships that go some way towards meeting those needs. The relative frequency and patterning of the interactions within the relationship will be affected by the needs of the participants.

(b) Principles concerned with the effects of interactions on interactions. For instance if A confides in B, B may be more (or less) likely subsequently to confide in A. A variety of issues studied by social psychologists are relevant here – for instance balance, dissonance and attribution theories; learning and exchange theories; and principles of positive and negative feedback (see e.g., Hinde, 1979).

(c) Principles concerned with social influences on the dyad. A's relationship with B is likely to be affected by B's relationship with C, and by the social norms and expectations that A and B have acquired from other members of their culture.

No special significance is attached to these three categories – they are merely a convenient way for classifying the principles that seem useful. The important point is that understanding requires both a descriptive base and a set of principles to explain the patterning of the data. Each such principle, or each explanatory concept, may have a limited area of applicability specifiable in terms of the descriptive base.

In the same way the patterning of relationships within a group requires a set of principles for its understanding. In non-human primates principles concerned with the nature of individuals (e.g., propensities to form relationships within or between age/sex classes), principles concerned with blood relationship or some correlate such as familiarity, and principles concerned with status (dominance/subordinance) have proved useful. In the human case, both for relationships and social structure, social norms and institutions are also of major importance. Thus the patterning and quality of interactions within a marital relationship is to be understood in terms of the norms applicable to the institution of marriage within the society. (In practice social scientists often use the concept of institution in two ways – as a description of what people do, and to refer to determinants of their behaviour. For that reason it has been given the symbols of both data language and theory language in fig. 28, but it is important that the usages should be clearly demarcated. Likewise in this book social structure is used to refer to something abstracted from data on behaviour, and not to a conceptualized or idealized pattern of relationships.) Anthropologists may note that the scheme suggested in fig. 28 comes close to that of Barth (1973, p. 10).

It will be apparent that these organizational principles interact with each other. They must also, at each level, be compatible with principles at finer levels (i.e., relationship, interaction, behaviour, physiology) of analysis. And they must be compatible with principles concerned with behavioural functions. For instance, a principle concerned with the relative tendencies of males and females to continue associating with their mothers may not only contribute towards an understanding of differences in the causal bases of the behaviour of males and females, but must also be compatible with principles concerned with the adaptive consequences for males and for females of maintaining or breaking matrilineal ties. It is here that the issues of individual and inclusive fitness become crucial (see pp. 146–51). Fitness depends on the appropriateness of behaviour to current circumstances, and thus both on propensities to respond and on selecting between alternative modes of responding according to the circumstances. Whilst natural selection operates through the actual behaviour displayed, it can act to enhance a *propensity* that *sometimes* produces functionless or even deleterious behaviour provided that its costs (in terms of inclusive fitness) are outweighed by the beneficial consequences produced by that propensity in other circumstances. The principle that it pays a female monkey to be attracted to high-ranking animals on average (p. 208) does not mean that it always will: some high-ranking individuals are selfish despots. A functional approach thus does not depend on proving that every act has functional consequences, but focuses on the extent to which the benefits of displaying particular propensities outweigh their costs. These issues will be discussed in more detail in chapter 15.

13. Social Psychology

Contact between ethologists and sociologists has been minimal. Contact with social psychologists has not been much stronger, but there seems no reason why liaison should not increase markedly in the next few years. We may consider two contexts where it has begun.

(i) Non-verbal communication

In spite of Darwin's (1872) lead, the scientific study of non-verbal communication remained almost in abeyance for nearly 100 years. In the late forties, Tinbergen's (1948) work on social releasers opened the way for ethological studies of communication. As discussed in chapter 2 (pp. 35–42) he showed that much social communication depends on selective responsiveness to signals emitted by another individual. These signals may involve any of the sensory modalities, and may have been elaborated in evolution to make them more effective in influencing the behaviour of another individual ('ritualization' – see chapter 5). Often the signals involve both a morphological structure, such as red breast feathers, and a behavioural component, such as a posture by which the structure is displayed. The evolution of signals is usually accompanied by a concomitant evolution of responsiveness to them (chapters 5 and 6). Many of the signals studied by ethologists are given in conflict situations – that is, when the signalling individual, or 'actor', has tendencies to behave in ways incompatible with each other (see chapter 2, pp. 65–70).

Some of these generalizations can be extended to aspects

of human communication. Many human expressive movements, such as smiling and crying, are found in all human cultures. This at least indicates that their development in the individual is independent of cultural differences, and suggests that they can be regarded as species-characteristic fixed action patterns comparable to those of non-human species.

As a more specific example, Lorenz (1950b) suggested that mothers respond selectively to certain features characteristic of babies, such as their bulging foreheads and uncoordinated gait – features that have been exploited by cartoonists. Not only has this received some experimental support (Gardner and Wallach, 1965; Sternglanz, Gray and Murakami, 1977; see also Hess, 1970), but there is also evidence that responsiveness to these stimulus features increases in girls around the age of puberty, and in boys a year or two later (Fullard and Reiling, 1976). Of course, as the latter authors point out, such evidence does not prove that biological factors are crucial in the development of responsiveness. But there seems little doubt that the baby's smile and cry qualify as social releasers (see pp. 35–6): their special effectiveness must surely be the consequence of selection for signalling effectiveness by elaboration of the movement pattern.

In the case of the smile, some interesting suggestions concerning its probable phyletic origin have been made. On the basis of evidence drawn from a wide variety of sources, van Hooff (1972) suggested that smiling and laughter vary along at least two dimensions, namely those of friendliness and playfulness. A full smile denotes the former, a full laugh the latter (fig. 29). He suggests that this continuum may be derived from two distinct facial expressions in non-human primates. First, many species have a 'play face', often accompanied by vocalizations, which seems to signify 'What I do is only in play, and not serious'. Second, many species have a 'fear grin' or 'silent bared teeth' display, sometimes accompanied by vocalizations. This is usually given by a frightened animal to a superior, when it seems to signify 'I

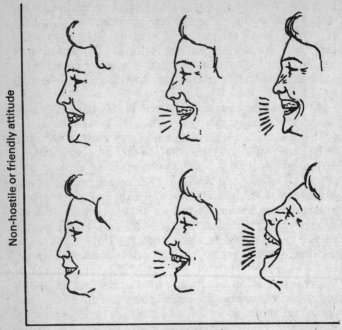

fig. 29. Two of the dimensions of variation of the smile–laugh continuum. From bottom to top there is increased baring of the teeth. From left to right there is increased mouth opening and vocalization. (From van Hooff, 1972.)

am harmless, and you need not attack me', but in some cases is also used by superiors to inferiors, when it seems to mean 'Don't be afraid, I will not attack you'. In the chimpanzee this display exists in three fairly distinct types, one being primarily friendly, one submissive, and one soothing in function. A possible course of evolution, illustrated by modern forms, is shown in fig. 30. In man the grin of terror remains as a rather separate entity. Van Hooff's suggestion has come in for some criticism, chiefly on the grounds that it does not account for all instances of smiling, and especially not for non-social smiles (e.g., Vine, 1973). However van Hooff specifically stated that the dimensions in fig. 29 were unlikely to be the only ones involved. Furthermore a hypothesis about the evolution of the movement patterns of smiling and laughter would not be expected to produce explanations for all the contexts in which they appear in man, and is compatible with the complexities in development and in contextual factors reviewed by later writers (e.g., Sroufe and Waters, 1976). And it does introduce a note of caution concerning unitary explanations, such as that in terms of tension release postulated by the latter authors.

Few detailed comparisons of other aspects of non-verbal communication between non-human primates and man seem to have been made so far. Resemblances between, for instance, infant tantrums and those shown by young monkeys (Jay, 1962; Hinde *et al.*, 1964; Chance and Jones, 1974), or between adult threat, greeting and reconciliation behaviour and those of chimpanzees (van Lawick-Goodall, 1968; de Waal and Roosmalen, 1979) suggest that a rich field awaits the investigator.

Independently of the ethologists, studies of human non-verbal communication were initiated by a number of other workers (e.g., La Barre, 1947; Birdwhistell, 1963, 1967, 1970; Argyle, 1967; Sebeok, 1977). Some of the earlier discussions between ethologists and social scientists on these issues involved deep differences of opinion on both sides, in part because rather extreme views were taken. For instance Eibl Eibesfeldt (1972), a pupil of Lorenz, studied cross-culturally movement patterns such as smiling and crying, and more complex entities, such as the patterns used in greeting and flirting. Impressed by the similarities, he argued that most expressive gestures were characteristic of the human species and developed with minimal cultural influence, though he conceded that some, like the eyebrow flash, had acquired different meanings, or were accentuated to different extents, or were used in different ways, in different cultures. On the other hand some social psychologists and anthropologists,

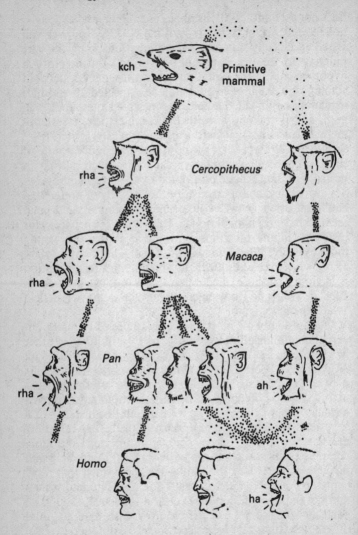

impressed by the complexity of human non-verbal communication and by its cultural diversity, held that concepts derived from the study of animal behaviour could contribute nothing to the understanding of human communication (e.g., Birdwhistell, l.c.; Leach, 1972).

Fortunately a more balanced view now prevails. On the one hand, certain movement patterns (e.g., smiling and crying) and syndromes of behaviour (e.g., anger, flirting) are similar between cultures. In most cases not only the motor patterns themselves but also the motivational bases of the movements and their interpretation by the reactor are pan-cultural. However the latter are more labile than the movement patterns. Indeed there may be cultural differences not only in the antecedents of a particular signal, but also in the extent to which it is amplified, suppressed or neutralized, and in the importance placed on it by the observer. Similarities between cultures occur especially with signals that concern personal or emotional characteristics. At the other extreme, some non-verbal signals, especially those closely dependent on verbal language, are specific to particular cultures. Much of the progress in this previously confused field is due to the conceptually sophisticated cross-cultural studies of Ekman (1977) and of Ekman and Friesen (1969, 1975), who carefully classified the various types of non-verbal signals, and described the extent to which each is pan-cultural and the nature of such cultural differences as occur. Those which have a pan-cultural basis are mostly 'affect' displays. Other categories of signal movement, such as the 'emblems' which can substitute for words, and signals

fig. 30. The phylogenetic development of laughter and smiling as suggested by homologues in existing members of the phyletic scale leading to *Homo*. On the left is the speciation of silent bared-teeth display and the bared-teeth scream display. The former, initially a submissive, later also a friendly response, seems to converge with the relaxed open-mouthed display (on the right), a signal of play. (From van Hooff, 1972.)

which illustrate and regulate verbal interchanges, are usually culturally specific and individually learned.

There are however some ways in which the very power of the sign stimulus and social releaser concepts in lower vertebrates led ethologists to neglect aspects of the communicatory process. For instance studies of the dramatic signals used in threat and courtship displays led to neglect of the trivial and often idiosyncratic movements which are often also important in communication. Slight nuances of posture, and seemingly trivial movements of hands or eyes, may yet be powerful regulators of social intercourse (e.g., Simpson, 1973). Whilst infant research first focused on the smile and cry, many other aspects of infant behaviour affect the mother (e.g., Stern, 1977).

Again, social releasers were often identified or assessed by the immediate response, often a fixed action pattern, of the reacting individual. This tended to obscure the fact that the effects of some signals are cumulative: for instance a male bird's courtship may produce a gradual change in the endocrine state of the female.

The social releaser approach also led to an underestimation of the communicatory significance of contextual factors. In their earlier writings Lorenz and Tinbergen spoke of social releasers as more or less automatically eliciting particular responses, 'as a key opens a lock'. But W. J. Smith (e.g., 1965, 1977) has pointed out that the effect of a particular signal varies with the context. He refers to the common factor in all the states of the communicator in the situations in which the signal is given, together with any identificatory information it may carry, as the 'message'. Its 'meaning' depends also on the context and can be deduced from the response of the recipient. Thus

Message plus Context = Meaning

For example a particular bird vocalization coming from another male might elicit an aggressive response from a territory-owning male, but the same vocalization coming from a fledgling would elicit feeding from its parent. A similar distinction had in fact been made by the linguist Bloomfield in the 1930s, but had been quite missed by ethologists. The importance of this distinction for studies of, for instance, the ability of mothers to differentiate between the different cries of their babies will be apparent.

As an extension of this issue, it now seems possible that the meaning of some bird vocalizations depends on the context of other calls in which they occur (Beer, 1976). This is however still a far cry from the layers of meaning imposed on many human gestures and expressive movements by the context of the ritual or institution in which they are embedded (e.g., Luckmann, 1979; Harré, 1979).

A final issue to be mentioned in connection with the social releaser approach concerns the extent to which signals actually convey valid information about the state of the signaller. Somewhat simplifying the situation, comparative evidence showed how the evolutionary processes of ritualization enhanced the effectiveness of signal movements (chapter 5). Since each species often has a repertoire of (e.g.) threat displays, or one variable display, each variant being followed by different probabilities of attacking the rival, fleeing or staying put, it seemed possible that the postures conveyed information about the internal state of the signaller. But there are circumstances in which it would not be in an individual's interests to impart such information. In a competitive situation, for instance, an individual that was certainly going to attack or to flee would do best to do so immediately, without signalling his intention beforehand. In general there are some circumstances in which it pays to be honest (e.g., Clutton-Brock and Albon, 1979), and others in which selection will favour those who are somewhat vague about their intentions, and yet others where it is advantageous to deceive or manipulate the other individual (Dawkins and Krebs, 1979). So far as threat postures go, it has been suggested that many are given in situations of uncertainty, when what the signaller will do next depends in part on what the other individual does. They thus convey only conditional information about what the signalling individual will do next – information of the type 'If you approach, I will attack you' (Hinde, 1981). So far these ideas have not been applied to human communication, but it would certainly be profitable to do so. In so far as non-verbal communication is not merely a matter of the expression of the emotions, but of negotiation between individuals, the title of Darwin's (1872) book has biased research.

(ii) The study of interpersonal relationships

The history of the study of social behaviour of animals in general, and especially that of primate groups, has involved increasing realization of the complexity of the subject matter. For instance monkey groups were at one time treated as collections of individuals. Gradually the importance of relationships between specific individuals – mother and offspring, male and female, female and sister, became apparent. More recently still it has been shown that triadic interactions, involving a coalition between two animals against a third, may be important. And it is now clear that some aspects of the dynamics of monkey groups involve the assessment by one animal of the relationship between two others: whether a low-ranking male hamadryas baboon attempts to take over a rival's female depends in part on how he assesses her attraction to her current mate (Backmann and Kummer, 1980).

Ethologists thus turned to the human social sciences' literature for guidance on how to study inter-personal relationships. However, most social psychological texts move from aspects of the social behaviour of individuals (attribution, attraction, social influence, etc.) to aspects of group structure and dynamics, with a neglect of long-term dyadic relationships. And whilst in related disciplines, such as psychiatry, much fascinating material is available, much of it is concerned either with case studies of relationships as seen by one of the participants, or with attempts to establish one theoretical or explanatory paradigm at the expense of another, with little attempt at integration. It seems, in fact, that there is no integrated science of human inter-personal relationships. Of the many possible reasons for this, one seems paramount – the lack of an adequate descriptive base. This may be an area in which ethologists, trained to appreciate the importance of selective description and classification in forming a basis for their science, could make some contribution. Accordingly an attempt has been made to provide a descriptive framework, and to indicate how it could help in the building of a science or sub-science of inter-personal relationships (Hinde, 1979).

The approach depends on the views that a relationship involves a series of interactions in time between two participants known to each other; that each interaction may be affected by past interactions and perhaps by expectations of future ones, and that the affective/cognitive concomitants of interactions are as important as the behavioural ones (see p. 205). Furthermore it is assumed that a science of inter-personal relationships must come to terms with dialectics of two types (fig. 31). First, every relationship is influenced by, and influences, the personalities of the participants. Influences of relationships on personality are perhaps most marked early in life, but continue in some degree with later relationships. There is thus a continuing dialectic between relationships and personality. Second, each relationship is influenced by the nexus of other relationships in which it is embedded, and by the social norms and expectations derived by the participants from their social group(s). Since the group is constituted by the dyadic (and higher order) relationships within it, and since norms are transmitted and/or transmuted through the agency of those relationships, there is also a continuing dialectic between relationships and the social group.

But the basis of a science of relationships must be descriptive. Description is inevitably selective and can never be entirely objective, but it is possible to specify eight categories of dimensions – that is, to classify the sorts of

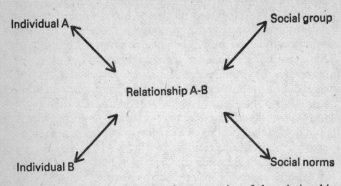

fig. 31. The dialectics between the properties of the relationship between A and B, and their individual characteristics on the one hand; and between the relationship and the social group in which it is placed, and the social norms operating therein, on the other. (From Hinde, 1979.)

dimensions likely to be useful for describing relationships into eight groups (Hinde, 1979):

(a) Content of interactions. This concerns what the participants do together and may distinguish relationships of different socially-recognized types (e.g., teacher–pupil from mother–child) as well as different relationships of the same type.

(b) Diversity of interactions. The diversity of things people do together may affect the dynamics of their relationship.

(c) Qualities of interactions. Description of any interaction demands specification not only of what the participants were doing together, but also how they were doing it. A mother may pick a baby up roughly or tenderly, a bath time may be a mutually enjoyable occasion or a fight. In general, four types of data have been used – the intensity (speed, amplitude, etc.) of movement, the verbal and non-verbal signals accompanying the interaction, and the degree of co-ordination ('meshing') between the participants.

(d) Relative frequency and patterning of interactions. The consequences of particular interactions may depend not so much on their frequency, as on their frequency in relation to interactions of other types. Several different issues are involved here, including correlations between interactions of different types (e.g., a mother must display several different types of behaviour before we ascribe 'maternal warmth' to a mother–child relationship); ratios of the frequency of one activity relative to that of others (e.g., help given to help solicited); relative frequencies of heterologous interactions (e.g., a controlling mother *both* often scolds her child for some sorts of behaviour *and* praises him for others) and the sequencing of interactions.

(e) Reciprocity vs complementarity. Interactions in which the two partners do the same thing, either simultaneously or in turn, can be described as reciprocal. Interactions in which they do different but related things can be described as complementary. Relationships in which all interactions are reciprocal are relatively rare, though relationships between peers may approach this condition. Relationships in which all interactions are complementary are common, especially in hierarchically structured organizations like armies and businesses. In close personal relationships there may be complex patterns of reciprocity and complementarity, with idiosyncratic patterns of imbalance.

(f) Intimacy. This refers to the extent to which the participants in a relationship reveal themselves to each other.

(g) Inter-personal perception. Here we are concerned with the extent to which each partner in a relationship sees the other as he or she really is (important for behavioural meshing); perceives the other to resemble him/herself (i.e., understands him/her); perceives the other as perceiving him/her as he/she perceives him/herself (i.e., feels understood); and perceives the other as close to his/her ideal partner in a relationship of the type specified (i.e., feels satisfied).

(h) Commitment. This refers to the extent to which the

partners either accept their relationship as continuing indefinitely or direct their behaviour towards ensuring its continuance or towards optimizing its properties. Commitment towards continuity of the relationship is not necessarily associated with a concern about the nature of its properties, or vice versa. Commitment may arise in the course of a relationship (endogenous) or be inevitably imposed by accident of birth or outside forces (exogenous). Belief in the partner's commitment to the relationship may be as important as commitment by each partner individually: for example freedom for personal growth within a relationship may demand flexibility in that relationship, and thus perceived commitment to continuity by the partner.

Whether these categories of dimensions do in fact embrace all the dimensions important for understanding the dynamics of relationships is a matter for future research to decide. In a more extended discussion elsewhere (Hinde, 1979) it has been argued that they facilitate the application of the four groups of principles most potentially valuable for understanding how relationships work – namely those derived from studies of social and other extra-dyadic influences, cultural norms, etc.; those derived from theories of dissonance, balance (e.g., Heider, 1958; Newcomb, 1961, 1971) and attribution (Kelley, 1971); those derived from theories of exchange and interdependence (e.g., Kelley, 1979; Walster, Berscheid and Walster, 1978); and those derived from systems theories and considerations of positive and negative feedback. For example, balance theory would predict that a mother would love a father more if he loves the baby that she loves. But it would also predict that, if Jack loves Jill and John loves Jill, Jack will love John: this is not necessarily the case. Thus if balance theory is to be useful, its limits of applicability must be specified by linking it to a method for describing relationships. Again, exchange theories hold that the course of a relationship is determined by the profits obtained or expected from the interactions. But this poses formidable problems: the value of the words 'I love you' depend on who says them and in what sort of relationship. Furthermore what the participants see as fair exchange (equality; equity, i.e., to each according to what he has contributed; or to each according to his needs) depends on the type of relationship. Such issues demand that theory be coupled to a system for describing relationships.

In conclusion, there are of course many problems in social psychology about which the classical ethological approach has nothing to say. But the examples discussed above indicate that, if he comes with humility and is prepared to marry his techniques with those in the field, the ethologist has much to contribute.

14. Developmental Psychology

Developmental psychology already had a long history of descriptive studies before ethology really started. However the importance attached to these disappeared in the 1940s and 1950s, partly because they had paved the way for more detailed studies of particular aspects of child development, but partly also because some of them made uncritical use of ill-defined descriptive categories (see p. 234). In recent years a close relationship has grown up between some ethologists and some students of child development (Hinde, in press, a and b), and many of the matters discussed in chapter 3 are proving to be of common interest. Two landmarks in the growth of that relationship have been Bowlby's (e.g., 1969) use of ethological concepts in his theoretical treatment of the mother–child relationship, and the use of ethological methods by Blurton Jones (1972b) and his colleagues to study child behaviour. The following paragraphs review these and some other examples of the application of ethological methods, concepts or data to the study of child development.

(i) Bowlby and attachment theory

John Bowlby, a London psychoanalyst, has been unusual amongst psychoanalysts in his willingness to consider the ideas and findings of disciplines remote from his own. His 'attachment theory' incorporated elements from a number of sources, including Piagetian theory, information-processing approaches to cognition, and systems theory. But the ethological contribution was central, and it is with that that we shall be primarily concerned here.

Bowlby saw the parallels between some of the findings from imprinting studies (see p. 193), and aspects of the human mother–child relationship. Just as a chick will initially follow any from amongst a wide range of objects provided they are presented within a certain sensitive period, but then responds selectively only to ones resembling that to which it has been exposed, so also do the stimuli effective for many of a baby's responses become narrowed by experience. For example a baby's feeding responses can be elicited by artificial stimuli, such as those provided by a bottle, but once a baby has been fed from a bottle for a while, it is far from easy to get it to feed from the breast.

Bowlby pointed out that the human baby, just like a chick, is equipped with a number of responses which mediate interaction with the parent. He focused especially on those that produce or enhance proximity between parent and baby – both those which act on the caregiver, like smiling and crying, and those by which the infant contacts or approaches the caregiver, like grasping and locomotion. His belief in the importance of infant–mother contact and proximity received support from the demonstration by Harlow, an experimental psychologist, of the importance to infant monkeys of contact comfort with the mother (Harlow and Zimmerman, 1959). In part as a reaction to the emphases on feeding by psychoanalysts and on primary drive reduction by learning theorists, Bowlby deliberately played down the importance of nutritive responses in the attachment of infant to mother.

There was of course no suggestion that the early development of the mother–baby relationship was just like the parent–offspring relationship in other species. Rather Bowlby made use of aspects of parent–offspring relationships that were common to a wide range of species, and suggested that they were likely to be important also in man. In particular he pointed out that natural selection must have favoured mechanisms that promoted parent–offspring proximity in our 'environment of evolutionary adaptedness'

– that is, the environment in which the relevant characteristics of the human species evolved: infant survival would have depended on it.

The degree of proximity to the caregiver demanded by the infant varies with time. Bowlby saw it as influenced both by factors internal (e.g., fatigue) and external (e.g., danger) to the infant, as well as changing with age. He described the changes as involving changes in the 'set-goal' of the attachment behaviour.

In very young babies, the several responses contributing to proximity seem to have considerable independence from each other. But Bowlby suggested that, at about the middle of the first year, the attachment behaviour becomes integrated in a manner which can best be described as involving a hierarchically-organized self-correcting system. Here he had in mind a 'behaviour system' very similar to those studied by the ethologists (see pp. 76–9), but with due regard to the infant's expanding cognitive capacities. He suggested that, as the infant comes to direct the various types of attachment behaviour to one or a small number of attachment figures, the attachment behaviour system becomes modified to incorporate 'models' of those figures, models which enable the infant to direct its behaviour in accordance with that of the other.

It is important to be clear about the terms used in discussions of attachment. 'Attachment behaviour' refers to a number of different types of behaviour contributing to proximity to the parent. It thus refers to *data* about behaviour. 'Attachment behaviour system' lies in the *theory* language, and refers to a control system postulated as integrating the various types of attachment behaviour. 'Attachment' is an aspect of the enduring relationship between infant and attachment figure. 'Attachment' is thus a *data* term, and is inferred from the attachment behaviour of the infant in interaction with the parent. The concept of attachment has been criticized, by psychologists who misperceived it as an intervening variable (see pp. 48–9), on the grounds that the various types of attachment *behaviour* were not highly correlated with each other. In practice the several types of attachment behaviour may be alternatives to each other, or change with age (e.g., Sroufe and Waters, 1977) so that correlations are not necessarily to be expected.

The concept of attachment has also been misused as referring to a hypothesized internal mechanism. This involves confusion between data and theory language, and could lead to the 'instinct fallacy' of postulating a mechanism essentially isomorphous with the behaviour, and then using that as an explanation of the behaviour. In any case, the concept of 'attachment behaviour system' is already available in the theory language, and does not suffer from that danger because it refers to postulated control systems that determine the *relations between* different kinds of behaviour.

Although a child's attachment to a caregiver cannot be assessed by counting the frequencies or durations of attachment behaviour, a means of categorizing it has been devised by Ainsworth (Ainsworth *et al.*, 1978; Ainsworth, 1979). This 'strange situation' technique involves a series of eight brief episodes staged in a standard order in a laboratory playroom, and used especially with 1–2-year-olds. In each episode the child may be with its mother and/or a stranger, or alone. The crucial data are ratings of the child's behaviour to adults in each episode and especially at reunion. On that basis the infants are assigned to one of three major categories, divided into eight sub-categories. Categorization has proved reliable from 12–18 months in most samples. Studies of babies at home during the course of the first year, and in a variety of situations at later ages, have shown considerable relation to the Strange Situation categories, and indicate that the technique taps enduring aspects of the parent–child relationship (e.g., Parkes and Stevenson-Hinde, eds., in press).

Attachment theory has led to considerable controversy amongst child developmentalists. A theory with such important practical implications has inevitably been affected by the current social climate: both its acceptance by some, and the criticisms to which it has been subjected by others, were affected by current views on the importance of the family and the growing recognition of women's rights in society as a whole. Bowlby's emphasis on the central importance of one 'monotropic' relationship with a parent figure is still controversial, though here again there has been misunderstanding: Bowlby was referring primarily to relationships or aspects of relationships providing 'felt security' to the infant, and never denied the possible importance of relationships of other kinds. The earlier implication that *babies* could be categorized by the Strange Situation technique is now clearly erroneous, for they may fall into different categories when assessed with mother and with father (Main and Weston, in press): the procedure assesses certain aspects of the parent-infant relationship from the infant's point of view. Focus on the mother–child relationship by attachment theorists has been associated with a neglect of father–child and child–sibling relationships, which also may have important influences on personality development: this however merely implies that there are further problems ahead.

Such issues are, of course, characteristic of those that are liable to arise with any new approach to a problem important both theoretically and practically, and in no way diminish the importance of attachment theory's contribution.

That contribution depends in part on the use Bowlby made of ethological issues of function and evolution. For example, the so-called irrational fears of childhood – fears of being alone, or of the dark – make good sense when considered in the context of our 'environment of evolutionary adaptedness'; for infant monkeys and apes, proximity to mother is crucial for survival. It is therefore important that, as attachment theory develops, it should assimilate some more recent trends in evolutionary theory. For example, we have seen that behavioural adaptations are liable to involve flexible or alternative behavioural strategies to meet the demands of diverse situations (p. 115). Thus

whilst the Bowlby and Ainsworth emphasis on the importance of maternal sensitivity to infant needs is indisputable, it
must not conceal the need for both mother and infant to vary
their strategies for interacting in accordance with the total
social situation (Hinde, in press; Main, in press). Again,
since it is adaptive for mothers to promote the independence
of their infants before the age at which the infants would
otherwise assume independence, some degree of conflict
between parent and offspring is inevitable (Trivers, 1974).
Presumably infants are adapted to cope with this, thriving
best with mothers who show some degree of rejection: in that
case maternal rejection is adaptive for both mother and
infant.

These more controversial issues have been mentioned here
because they provide further illustration of the issues that
arise when disciplines meet. Attachment theorists, primed in
part by ethological ideas, espoused views which were
outside, and seemed contrary to, current approaches in both
developmental psychology and psychiatry. Those already in
the field looked askance at the intruders, questioning the
relevance of the animal data and misunderstanding some
of the points being made. Happily a rapprochement is now
well under way, with the main tenets of the attachment
theorists being assimilated and discussion continuing over
the details.

(ii) The effects of temporary separations between mother and infant

The issues here arise in part from the work of Bowlby and
other attachment theorists, though Spitz (e.g., 1950) was
also an important influence in the USA. In the immediate
post 1939–45 war period, the amount of visiting by parents
to children's wards in hospitals was often severely restricted.
It was held that the children were so upset when the parents
left at the end of visiting time that it would be better if they
did not visit at all. This view was contested by Bowlby (e.g.,

1951) and by Spitz (e.g., 1950), who held that the long-term effects of not seeing their parents would be much more severe and important than the temporary upsets at the end of visiting hours.

The evidence was largely retrospective: for example a number of Bowlby's patients who had behaviour problems in adolescence turned out to have had periods of separation from their parents when young. Direct evidence was of course difficult to obtain, since experiments with human subjects were ethically impossible. Accordingly experiments with monkeys were initiated, and data involving temporary mother–infant, infant–infant and adult-adult separations are now available (Mineka and Suomi, 1978; Hinde and McGinnis, 1977).

In general, the immediate response of infant monkeys to maternal separation turned out to be very similar to that of human children. There is first marked 'protest' (vocalization, searching behaviour, etc.), followed by 'despair' (reduced locomotor activity, sitting in a hunched depressed posture, etc.). Children often also demonstrate 'detachment' by responding to their parents as though they were strangers on reunion, but this rarely occurs in monkeys.

Several issues emerged from the monkey experiments which are likely to be important in the human case. First, there were marked individual differences in the immediate sequelae of a temporary (e.g., six to fourteen days) separation experience. Many factors have been shown to affect these outcome measures. For instance the way the separation was carried out – mother removed and infant left in its home cage for the duration of the separation or vice versa – affects both the behaviour of the infant during separation and the longer-term outcome (see below). Sex plays a part, males being affected slightly more than females. But the most important issue seems to be that the effects of a separation experience on the infant operate at least mainly through their effects on the mother–infant relationship. Thus infants are more affected if they have a tensionful relationship (as assessed by objective criteria) with their mothers beforehand, and they are more affected the longer the separation. A number of variables that affect the mother–infant relationship also affect the outcome.

A second point is that long-term effects of a separation experience can be picked up: in tests of responsiveness to mildly stressful situations carried out six months or even two years later, previously separated monkeys may differ from controls. But the presence of an effect depends on the nature of the separation experience (see above) and on a number of other factors.

The finding that separation may, but need not, have long-term sequelae has since been confirmed in man. Males who had separation experiences in early childhood may be more likely to show a variety of behaviour disorders in adolescence, but the effect appears only in those coming from psychosocially-disadvantaged backgrounds (Douglas, 1975; Quinton and Rutter, 1976). Females may be affected in other ways, such as in showing a greater susceptibility to reactive depression (Brown *et al.*, 1975).

Two aspects of the use of generalizations from monkey to man in these studies are of interest. One is that the effect of a separation experience may vary with the species of monkey. Thus separation by removal of the mother from a group of bonnet macaques causes much less distress to the infant than it does in rhesus or pigtail macaques. The difference is probably related to differences in the social structures of the species concerned. Thus there are dangers in the use of an animal model, dangers which are exacerbated by the diversity of human societies. But if we use not one animal model but several, and if we study in each case the factors that affect the response to separation, we may find *principles* which are applicable to man. If we were to find that in all species the effects of a separation experience were ameliorated by contact with adult females other than the mother during the separation period, we might ask whether the same was true in man. Or if we found in each species that the effects varied with the social structure of the group, we might look for similar relations in man.

The second aspect concerns the level of abstraction at which we search for principles valid for both monkey and man. Studies of mother–infant separation in group-living rhesus monkeys indicate that the effects are more marked if the mother is removed and the infant left at home than vice versa. The opposite is probably true for man. But with monkeys, removal of the mother has more profound effects than removal of the infant because, for reasons which need not be discussed here, the mother–infant relationship is more disturbed in that case. As we have seen, the effects of the separation are likely to be more severe, the more disturbed the mother–infant relationship. It is this generalization, rather than the findings at the data level, that is likely to apply to man.

(iii) Studies of nursery school children by Blurton Jones and colleagues

Another important influence from ethology, though opposed in some respects to the attachment theorists, came from the work of Blurton Jones (e.g., 1972 a and b), a former student of Tinbergen. He has consistently argued that, in building a scientific study of social behaviour, we must be able to test and if necessary reject our everyday categorizations of behaviour. Laying particular emphasis on the need for objective description in terms of behavioural elements, he eschewed the uncritical use of more global concepts such as 'aggression', 'attachment' and 'anxiety'. One example comes from his studies of nursery school children. Factor analyses and other evidence indicated that, of the seemingly aggressive behaviour elements shown by the children, rough-and-tumble play was not positively related to such items as frown, hit, push and take-tug-grab, although it seemed to resemble them in many ways.

Blurton Jones's introduction to the volume he edited in 1972 was a masterly statement of the current ethological view of studies in child development, and provided powerful arguments for the use of an ethological approach. As the dust has settled it has, I believe, become apparent that he overstated his case on some issues. For example, in criticizing rating scales he neglected the contexts in which they are useful; in deploring the use of interview techniques as a means of finding out about child behaviour he overlooked the fact that what a mother feels about her child may be, for some purposes, as important as what she actually does with it; and, as discussed above, in arguing against the 'attachment' concept he seems to have overrated the power of factor analysis. These issues are mentioned only because Blurton Jones's work has so clearly been of pioneering importance in this field, and they are of interest because they, and comparable overstatements by the more traditional child developmentalists, are another example of the frictions that may first arise when representatives of different backgrounds meet over a common problem, and which pave the way for fruitful co-operation (see Blurton Jones and Woodson, 1979, for a more recent statement of his position).

(iv) Comparative Studies

Blurton Jones (e.g., 1972c) has also made a strong case for using comparative data on a range of species to provide principles whose applicability to man can then be assessed. An example is provided by studies of suckling behaviour. Whilst the young of some mammals spend the greater part of the day attached to the nipple, in other species they are suckled only once a day, or even less often. Comparative study shows that the frequency of suckling is inversely related to the protein content of the milk. Human milk has a low protein content, suggesting that neonates should be nursed at intervals shorter than the four-hourly feeds common in many maternity hospitals (Blurton Jones, 1972c). Breast milk differs from bottle milk in its protein concentration, and comparisons between breast-

and bottle-fed babies confirm this view (Bernal, 1972).

Perhaps these examples demonstrate that in some ways the present relationship between ethology and developmental psychology is both more interesting and more exciting than that between ethology and any other discipline. Whilst some of the earlier contacts involved rather uninspiring attempts to apply uncritically to children methods and concepts devised for work with animals, a real integration is now in progress. Ethologists are using their traditional techniques alongside those more suited to the psychological complexity of the subject matter, and there is a two-way exchange at the conceptual level – an exchange which still involves mutual suspicion, but also a willingness to learn.

15.   Anthropology

(i) Some historical issues

Ethology's contacts with anthropology came first with physical anthropology. This was due in part to an accident of history: C. R. Carpenter's pioneering studies of primate natural history must have been partly responsible for the realization by a physical anthropologist, S. Washburn, that man's evolution could not be traced simply by comparing the skeletons of fossil and living material, but required also functional interpretation. This orientation led Washburn, and later also the archaeologist Louis Leakey, to sponsor field work on living monkeys and apes. They felt that a knowledge of the relations between the structure of modern non-human primates and their way of life were essential for two purposes – interpreting the fossil evidence about man's evolution from his primate forebears, and deducing from that evidence early man's probable way of life. Washburn sponsored work on monkeys (e.g., De Vore, 1963), whilst Leakey initiated studies of the great apes (e.g., van Lawick-Goodall, 1968; Fossey, 1979; Galdikas, 1979). Whilst Washburn's functional approach brought him into contact with ethologists (see e.g., Roe and Simpson, 1958), neither Washburn nor Leakey were themselves much influenced by them. But the field workers that they sponsored came to work closely with ethologists and behavioural ecologists. De Vore (e.g., 1963), for instance, carried out some of the early field work on baboons, and subsequently sponsored a major anthropological study of the Kalahari bushmen: whilst at first thinking somewhat loosely about function (see chapter 4), he apparently suffered a Pauline conversion on the road to Nairobi and became an ardent advocate of individual selection (e.g., Popp and De Vore, 1979).

Another important issue has been the contribution of Japanese anthropologists to primatology. Japan is one of the very few educationally advanced countries with its own population of non-human primates. After the Second World War Japanese scientists 'started to exploit local resources: one aspect of this was the initiation of studies of the Japanese macaque. The work has been developed by several generations of Japanese primatologists, who have worked also in many other countries.

As a result of these enterprises, during the last fifteen years field primatology has emerged from a stage in which valuable data could be collected by walking through the forest with notebook and pencil, to one in which the natural history of many species is known, specific problems of behaviour and ecology can be tackled in depth, and cross-species comparisons are fertile (e.g., Clutton-Brock, 1977). In this work anthropologists and biologists have participated, and it is often not obvious which is which.

One unexpected by-product of this work has concerned the very definition of man. Evolution of man from ape-like ancestors must have involved a continuous series of changes, of which the fossil record provides only discontinuous fragments. There is thus inevitably a degree of arbitrariness in deciding which fossil specimens should be regarded as human. At one time evidence of association with prepared tools was regarded as an important criterion. However the value of this was called into question when it was found that chimpanzees not only use tools, as do many other species, but sometimes prepare tools before using them. To be specific, chimpanzees forage for termites by poking pieces of grass into the holes in termite nests. Termites cling to the grass stem when it is withdrawn, and can then be eaten. But beyond that chimpanzees may also prepare grass stems, by removing superfluous leaves, at a distance from a termite mound, and then carry them to the mound and use them (van Lawick-Goodall, 1971). More recent evidence indicates that forms of tool-using are apparently culturally trans-mitted within chimpanzee communities (McGrew *et al.*, in press).

The growth of knowledge about non-human primates led to the view that it might be profitable to search for a possible model of man's ancestors among present-day non-human primates. Some argued that the chimpanzee is closer to man than any other species, so we should focus our attention on chimpanzees. Others believed that early hominid social structures are unlikely to have resembled that of chimpanzees, and that the savannah-living baboon is a better model. Yet others suggested that the pygmy chimpanzee *Pan paniscus,* which is said to have some neotenous characters, should be studied. But as we have seen, the use of animal models for understanding human behaviour is full of dangers. Some species resemble man in some ways, and others in others: none is all that close. Indeed, for some purposes a non-primate model could be more appropriate than a primate one (e.g., Schaller and Lowther, 1969). The characters of each species form an adaptive complex (see pp. 105–6) which hinders the use of any one as a model for man.

However this does not mean that data from non-human species cannot be useful to both physical and social anthropologists. There are at least two other interrelated ways in which they can be used. One is to exploit the relative simplicity of non-human primates to throw light on the complexity of man: this is discussed in the next section. Another is to study a range of species and assess whether principles that emerge are applicable to the human case. One example, discussed below, involves the application of the concept of the adaptive complex (see pp. 105–6) to throw light on the probable social behaviour of early man. Another, discussed in the final section, is the role of kin selection theory (p. 146) in bringing the question of how far social systems can be interpreted in functional terms, an issue which had been dismissed as involving disreputable social Darwinism, once more to the fore.

(ii) The study of social structure

That the cultures and social structures to be found in human societies are diverse and complex is a truism. However non-human primate social behaviour is also diverse and not lacking in complexity. It may contain lessons for the study of social structure in man.

Some non-human primates live singly, some in monogamous pairs, and some in groups, troops or bands of varying

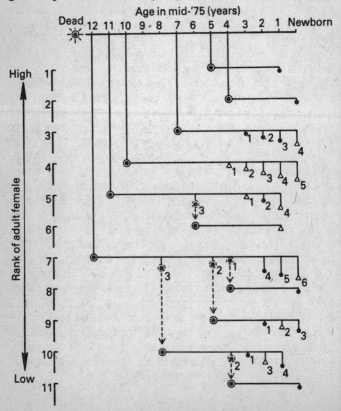

types. Amongst the latter, social interchanges may be dyadic, involving individual preferences and long-term relationships, and there may be coalitions (e.g., Stammbach, 1978; de Waal, 1978) in triadic or higher order interactions (Kummer *et al.,* 1974; de Waal, 1977). Most troop-living species can be called matrifocal, but this conceals considerable complexity. For example in rhesus macaques the troop is based on subgroups of related females (fig. 32). Each of these involves a matriarch and her daughters. The daughters are arranged in a dominance order in inverse order of age. Their daughters are likewise arranged in inverse order of age. This comes about by each young female rising above her elder sisters when three to four years old, probably with the mother's help. The matrilines are also arranged in a sequence, each animal in one matriline being superordinated to all those in another. The adult males have for the most

fig. 32.   The social structure of rhesus macaques: rank relationships within one matriline of group J., Cayo Santiago, in mid-1975. Age reads horizontally, the eldest individuals being to the left of the diagram. Rank reads vertically. The female from whom the matriline originated is shown at the top left hand corner, but was dead at the time to which the diagram refers. The figures indicate the rank relationships between siblings within families. The discontinuous arrows lead from the ranking of a particular adult female amongst her maternal siblings to her ranking amongst the adult females.

Key

•   non-adult female
△   non-adult male
◉   the position of a female now adult, amongst her maternal sibs: the same individual female is connected by a discontinuous arrow to her position as an adult female with respect to other adult females.
◎   adult female
     Solid vertical and horizontal lines indicate descent. (From Datta, 1981)

part immigrated from other troops, and have a somewhat independent social structure (Sade, 1972; Datta, 1980). Of course even this does not indicate the full range of complexity of social structure to be found in non-human primates, and practically every field study concerned with social structure reveals fresh subtleties. Furthermore each species has a characteristic range of social structures: within that range considerable variations occur, perhaps with ecological correlates.

If any relations are to be found between the anthropological material on human social behaviour and structure, and the ethological material on non-human primates, they will certainly not lie in comparisons between any particular human group and any particular primate species. It is even unlikely that they will come through comparisons between conjectures about a supposedly primitive human type of social structure and any particular primate group. Rather they will come through comparison of principles abstracted from the study of diverse primate species with comparable principles derived from studies of our own.

Such comparisons are likely to be interesting not because human societies are like non-human ones, but precisely because they are not. One difficulty in evaluating the effects of cultural factors on human relationships or social structures is that all are influenced by them in some way. It is possible to search for features of relationships or of social structure that are common to all societies, and then to attempt to find explanatory principles that are pan-cultural. What we find will then at least be independent of cultural differences. But a further step is to compare human relationships with relationships in which cultural factors play at least an incomparably smaller part, or human social structure with social structures in which institutions are absent. If complexities of the type described above are present in species which lack institutions, and whose powers of communication are so vastly smaller than our own, an additional perspective is added to the role of cultural factors in the human case.

Such data on the social structure of non-human primates are accumulating rapidly, and the abstraction of principles requires some means of ordering the material. One possible tool to that end has already been discussed in chapter 12 (fig. 28). In studies of non-human primates principles concerned with dominance/subordinance, with blood relationship, and with differences between age/sex categories have all proved useful in understanding social structure. It is also becoming apparent that principles concerned with investment in inter-individual relationships in the (perhaps unconscious) expectation of future rewards are also necessary. Grooming, which seems to be an analogue of expressions of social approval or social acceptance in human societies (Hinde and Stevenson-Hinde, 1976), can be seen as a token of this investment. Thus the elements of social exchange are present well below the human level.

As an example, young female baboons tend to direct their grooming towards the more dominant adult females in the troop, and young males to the more subordinate ones. This can be seen as an appropriate investment in each case. The young females will stay in the troop and may later be aided by dominant females: young males will later leave the troop, but in the meantime practice in sexual behaviour is important for them, and the only females they can mount without interference from dominant males are the sub-ordinate ones (Cheney, 1978). This raises further problems: why should grooming be an investment aiding future co-operation? Possibly the mere enhancement of familiarity by proximity is important, for chimpanzees are more likely to give aid to the more familiar of two individuals (de Waal, 1978). And the propensity to give aid to familiar individuals is compatible with the requirements of inclusive fitness because, at least amongst female monkeys, the more familiar individuals are more likely to be genetic relatives (Chapais, pers. comm.). In this way the action of selection on the propensities underlying behaviour can be surmised, and causal and functional understanding become integrated.

Of course in understanding human social structure

principles concerned with institutionalization and culturally-defined goals are paramount. But this does not mean that principles of the other types are not also important. Differences between individuals of different age/sex classes, some aspects of blood relatedness and principles of dominance/subordinance clearly also affect human culturally-specific patterns. And, as we shall see later, human institutions may be not unrelated to behavioural propensities of biological significance.

It has often been argued that what we see in non-human forms is simply the result of inherent species-characteristic behaviour by individuals, whereas human institutions are the product of individual experience within a specific culture. But this neglects the importance of predispositions to learn (chapter 11, pp. 188–92), which can lead to local 'proto-cultures' independently of genetic change even in animals. Thus we saw earlier how particular motor patterns and learning propensities have led to the formation of local habits of opening milk bottles by tits (fig. 19) as well as, on occasion, to behaviour apparently profitless and costly to the individual (pp. 106–8). In birds, local variation in vocal dialects is also well known (e.g., Slater and Ince, 1979) and learning by example to respond to predators seems to be so powerful in some species (e.g., Curio *et al.,* 1978) that the possibility for cultural differentiation is clearly present. Local food-seeking proto-cultures are well known in monkeys (e.g., Kawai, 1963) and apes (McGrew *et al.,* in press). Thus cultural diversity also has its origin in non-human forms.

(iii) Speculations about early human social organization

A more specific issue concerns the probable nature of the social behaviour of early man. Here the concept of the adaptive complex (pp. 105–6) can be of value. The great apes and man show marked inter-species differences in sexual dimorphism, and in various aspects of reproductive physiology and behaviour. In the great apes the various characteristics of structure and behaviour are inter-related in ways adaptive to their environments. Man's physical structure is well known, but direct evidence about the social behaviour of early man is lacking. However for man too physical structure and behaviour presumably once formed an adaptive complex. Thus comparisons with the great apes permit speculations about his early social behaviour.

Consider first the social structure of the apes. The basic presumption is that individuals form relationships when, and to the extent that, it is to their long-term advantage to do so (Kummer, 1978). Amongst the apes, gibbons and siamang are monogamous and live in family groups on defended territories; orang-utan males and females live mostly alone and largely independently; and gorilla live in small groups of females dominated by one adult male, sometimes with one or two additional males. Chimpanzee females live on individual undefended home ranges within a territory which is defended by a group of related males. In a stimulating paper Wrangham (1979; see also Wrangham, 1980) has argued that these differences can be understood in terms of a network of functional requirements (fig. 33). First, the females' strategies have been determined by their nutritional needs and the distribution of food. As vegetarians sometimes exploiting locally available fruits, their optimal strategy should be to minimize competition and to forage alone. This is the case in the orang-utans and usually in chimpanzees. That female gorilla live in groups thus requires further explanation, though their diet of relatively dispersed and abundant food must involve little inter-female competition and thus may permit group living. Chimpanzee females do not defend feeding territories because the distance travelled daily is too small to permit them to visit the boundaries of their home range sufficiently frequently, and it would presumably be energetically uneconomic for them to do so.

Second, males compete primarily for females. Since they may not be able accurately to predict female fertility, their best strategy might be to stay with as many females for as

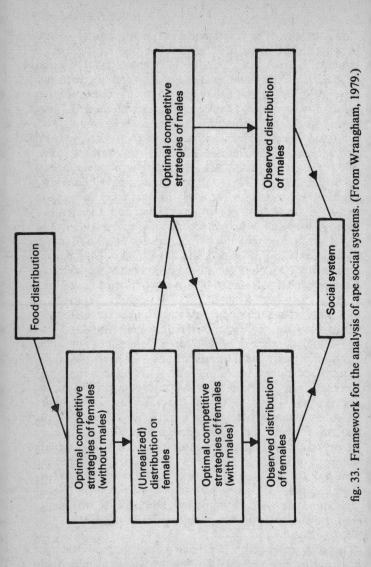

fig. 33. Framework for the analysis of ape social systems. (From Wrangham, 1979.)

long as possible. This however is potentially incompatible with the females' strategy of foraging alone. The actual social structure depends, Wrangham suggests, on how this conflict is resolved. In the gibbons, monogamy is maintained partly because females attack other females. Females tolerate the proximity of, and thus competition for food with, their mates in part because the male reduces the female's burden of territorial defence by taking on most of that responsibility himself.

There is a selective advantage to females in choosing a dominant male, because he can protect them most effectively from harassment by other males. For that reason, and because competition over food is unimportant for them, gorilla females tolerate the presence of other females. Gorilla groups do in fact depend much more on female-male bonds than on female-female bonds, and in this respect are quite unlike macaque and baboon troops (Harcourt and Stewart, 1979). In orang-utans, which are largely frugivorous, food competition is important and renders permanent consort-ships impracticable for both sexes: however the social organization of this species is not yet well understood.

Wrangham considers that the costs of locomotion are lower for chimpanzees than for orang-utans, and it is this that enables chimpanzee males to patrol and defend a large (group) territory, whereas orang-utan males do not. Also their food permits social foraging for some of the time, though not when food is scarce. Co-operation between chimpanzee males may be to the advantage of each individual both through his enhanced individual reproductive success, and by virtue of the fact that the members of the group are related (see pp. 146–51). The females benefit by the co-operation between local males, because it reduces harassment by unfamiliar males. It is thus in their interests to aid that co-operation. They therefore advertise their receptivity by large sexual swellings and are ready to mate promiscuously unless coerced to do otherwise by a male.

Wrangham's scheme, summarized only briefly here, would not receive universal acceptance. As he emphasizes, it minimizes for example the importance of predator pressure as an ultimate cause of group life (see e.g., Alexander, 1974; Clutton-Brock and Harvey, 1976). But it does show the sort of way in which the differences between the social structures of relatively closely related species could be understood.

Now in general sexual dimorphism in fighting ability, which usually means in size, is associated with polygyny or serial monogamy. This is so because, if the sex ratio is initially equal, the males will compete for females. As correlates of this, males usually mature more slowly than females, and suffer greater mortality. The greater variance in the reproductive potential of males means that only the production of very healthy males is likely to be a sound parental investment, for a less healthy male is likely to provide no grandchildren. For that reason very young males (i.e., foetuses) are more likely than females to be discarded, but healthy male offspring are likely to be favoured over females. These correlations hold in a wide range of mammals (Alexander *et al.*, 1979).

A relation between sexual dimorphism and polygyny is also to be found in the great apes, with the possible exception of the orang-utan (Clutton-Brock and Harvey, 1977; Short, 1979). Human sexual dimorphism is about the same as that of the chimpanzee, though less than that of the gorilla, indicating that early man had at least a strong tendency to polygyny (or to serial monogamy). This is in keeping with the general trend of marriage systems in existing societies. Although polyandry does occur, it is rare and probably related to rather unusual ecological circumstances (Murdock, 1949; Crook, 1980). Furthermore, amongst human societies sexual dimorphism is greater in those that are polygynous, and in those where monogamy is imposed by rule or law (and which were thus probably relatively recently polygynous), than in those societies in which monogamy can be ascribed to ecological factors making it unprofitable for a man to have more than one wife (Alexander and Noonan 1979; Alexander *et al.*, 1979).

Short (1979) has summarized further data showing how

the reproductive anatomy and physiology of the great apes can be related to their sexual behaviour. Thus in the sexually dimorphic gorilla the dominant male does virtually all the mating. Copulation is infrequent: since it is initiated by the female, and nearly always involves the dominant male, there has been no need for conspicuous external genitalia for use in display.

Orang-utan males and females live separately and alone (except for the female's offspring). There is marked sexual dimorphism, but little is known in detail about their sexual behaviour. External genitalia are small.

Chimpanzee mating is initiated by the male and occurs either when a male and female go off 'on safari' alone for some hours or days, or in 'gang bangs' when a number of males mate an oestrous female in succession. The male has a conspicuous penis which is used in precopulatory display, and oestrus is advertised by conspicuous genital swellings in the female. The frequency of mating and the promiscuity of the female have placed a premium on competition between sperm: the males have very large testes.

In man the testes are relatively small, and one study suggests that semen volume and sperm density decrease if copulation occurs more frequently than once every two to three days. This is compatible with absence of sperm competition in a polygynous or serially monogamous system. The penis is enormous relative to body size, which suggests adaptation to enhance male attractiveness either visually or in intercourse, though adaptation to changes in the vagina consequent upon the adoption of an upright gait may also have played a part (A. F. Dixson, pers. comm.). The female's secondary sexual characteristics, especially the breasts, also show a remarkable development. These facts could suggest promiscuity, but the relative frequency of intercourse, as compared for instance with the gorilla, coupled with the suppression of behavioural oestrus, are in harmony with the view that copulation has been adapted in both sexes to maintain a pair bond under conditions in which paternal investment in the offspring is at a premium.

A similar conclusion is reached by Alexander and Noonan (1979). They emphasize especially the concealment of ovulation and the conspicuousness of female orgasm in man. Both, they suggest, are related to the importance to the female that the male should play a part in parental care. If a male cannot tell when a female ovulates, he must tend her more or less continuously to be sure he sires her offspring. And if the female displays orgasm as an indication of sexual satisfaction, the male may be more confident that she will not seek sexual satisfaction elsewhere. It may be noted, however, that conspicuous female orgasm does occur in at least some other primates (Goldfoot *et al.*, 1980).

In general, therefore, the comparative anatomical and physiological evidence indicates that man was primitively polygynous or serially monogamous, with males competing for females.

In virtually all animals, emigration by at least one sex guards against in-breeding. In most (but not all) non-human primates it is the males which leave the natal group, but in at least some apes and in human societies movement of females is more common. It may be supposed that in the human primitive condition their movement came to be regulated by the males. If property exchange between harems was related to an exchange of daughters, the family structure would be preserved as a unit of descent and alliance with other families would form, those other families also coming thereby to contain related individuals. Further discussion of these issues can be found in Crook (1980).

(iv) Human social structure

In the previous section we saw how application of the comparative method can yield evidence about the sort of social life to which early man was adapted. The assumption has been that early man's physical, behavioural and social characteristics formed a co-adapted complex, comparable to those discussed for animals in chapter 7 (pp. 137–41). The question now arises, how far can the diverse social systems and social customs displayed by human societies be interpreted as adaptive to local conditions? Discussions on this issue are at an exciting and interesting stage – a stage at which, as could be predicted from what we have seen already, proponents of both reactionary and radical viewpoints are prone to overstatement, but which nevertheless shows promise for a balanced and integrated view in the future. Here we shall focus primarily on the possible usefulness of ethological/ecological ideas for anthropology, though we shall conclude that ultimately this approach in no way pre-empts, and must indeed be seen only as a possible new source for understanding of, the traditional concerns of anthropology.

Our starting point can be the functionalist view that each culture involves a series of customs, beliefs and values which are interdependent, so that the significance of each aspect of the structure depends in some measure on others (e.g., Malinowski, 1929; Radcliffe-Brown, 1922; cf. pp. 137–41). This does not mean that each society is to be seen as a wholly integrated totality, but rather as the 'provisionally stable' consequence of interactions between parts which can be seen as reproducing themselves until such time as the internal or external dynamics of the system require a gradual or a sudden change in the system (Godelier, 1974).

But while it is agreed that the different aspects of a culture form a more or less integrated whole, opinion has been divided over the extent to which human cultures are constrained by ecological factors. Once the excesses of the early social Darwinists were rejected, most anthropologists accepted the cultures of the societies they were studying as given, focusing either on the natures of, or mutual influences between, their several aspects, or relating them to the ways in which their participants perceived the world (e.g., Lévi-Strauss, 1962; Leach, 1961, 1972). There has however been a continuing minority who have maintained a functional approach, attempting to relate cultures to environmental factors. Their work, which can properly be compared with the developments due to Lack, Crook and others in behavioural ecology (see pp. 137–42), had much earlier roots (e.g., Radcliffe-Brown, 1922; White, 1949), but flowered somewhat later (e.g., Harris, 1968, 1974; Rappaport, 1968; Vayda, 1969).

First we may consider some examples of correlations between social structure and environmental factors. One that provides both cross-cultural and some historical perspective is provided by Maitland-Bradfield's (1973) work on the peoples of West Africa south of the Sahara. In the savannah areas these peoples live in small scattered communities of extended families, farming the rather poor soil. The social structure is patrilineal, with the men working the land. Their labour is adjusted to maximizing production during the short rainy season and to storing food. Over-cultivation results in deterioration of the land and the settlements are forced to move every few years. Since the settlements are dispersed, co-operation between them is slight.

The forest people combine simple agriculture by the women with hunting and gathering in the uncultivated land. The small scattered compact villages, surrounded by gardens carved out of the forest, are suited to the poor soil and the need for fallow periods to permit soil recuperation. In both forest and savannah dependence on agriculture has led to inheritance of property from one generation to the next down lineages which have their foci in plots of land.

In the savannah, organization of the society into age-sets provides a basis for co-operation between individuals over such tasks as clearing the trees, or in aggression in offence or defence. This cuts across the lineages, providing both a set of warriors and a group of elders who facilitate the settling of disputes. In the forests, where settlements are denser and the families are more interdependent, organization depends on secret societies which also cut across the lineages and provide powerful social sanctions. Social exclusion is a severe penalty and an effective deterrent. In both forest and savannah the social structure results in a reduction in the probability of conflict between lineages and provides a means of population control when a region reaches its carrying capacity. Whether these consequences can be seen as biological functions in a strict sense (see p. 103) is a matter we shall return to in a moment.

Another example is provided by the !Kung Bushmen, who live in a semi-arid area where water is at a premium. Their selection of food appears to follow four categories of criteria – taste, supposed nutritive value, abundance, and ease of availability. The bushmen stay in the same site for so long as it is possible for them to find the food and water that they need within walking distance. The necessity for moving thus varies with the season: in the driest seasons the groups must be within reach of the four permanent water holes, but at other times of year food and water are to be found close together. Since they lack the technology of finding underground water, their movements are determined by the availability of food-near-water (Lee, 1966). Their social organization is thus constrained by their environment. Even the spacing of births is related to the costs to the women of carrying children whilst gathering food or fetching water (Lee and De Vore, 1968; Blurton Jones and Sibly, 1978).

However two issues to do with this approach must be mentioned. The first concerns where the lines are to be drawn. To some anthropologists the diversity of cultures, including that of cultures in closely similar environments, is such that the notion that the differences between them could be regarded as adaptations is patently absurd. Others argue that cultural change has often been so rapid that it could not be accounted for by the known mechanisms of natural selection. Harris and the ecological anthropologists, on the other hand, although often focusing on nutritional requirements to the neglect of other aspects of biology (Chagnon, pers. comm.), sought to build 'a corpus of theory equally capable of explaining the most generalized features of universal history and the most exotic specialities of particular cultures' (Harris, 1974). But neither extreme view is necessary. The broad features of a culture must be compatible with its ecological constraints – otherwise it would not be there. Yet more than one cultural pattern could satisfy a given set of constraints (p. 121), and explanations of the differences in detail between cultures could be sought elsewhere.

A second issue with the approach of the ecological anthropologists concerns the mechanisms by which adaptation to ecological constraints is seen to be achieved. Whilst often successful in demonstrating that the broad outlines, and in some cases even the details, of social systems meet ecological requirements, they are in difficulty over the mechanisms by which social change occurs. What provokes a change in a social system? Who exactly is the beneficiary? So long as the emphasis is on benefits to the group – reducing conflict, preventing overpopulation or environmental degradation – the mechanism implied must be one of group selection. We have seen that this is unlikely to be important in animals (p. 144), and whilst the requirements for group selection to operate may sometimes be met in man (e.g., Alexander, 1974; Lewontin, 1970; Wilson, 1975), empirical studies have failed to provide evidence for group level adaptations to control population (Bates and Lees, 1979). Indeed some characteristics, such as the accumulation of cattle by the members of nomadic pastoral societies in western and eastern Africa, involve a high risk of destroying, by overgrazing, the conditions necessary for the culture to continue.

In the event, the approach of the ecological anthropologists, like the early attempts of the behavioural ecologists to relate animal social systems to ecological factors, is being superseded by a more powerful approach involving selection acting on the individual and the principle of inclusive fitness (see chapter 7). Focus on the reproductive properties of individuals permits a new view which does not necessarily invalidate the earlier findings that the characteristics of a culture may have consequences beneficial for the group (see pp. 252–3), but sees at least some of those consequences as by-products of the effects of selection on individual propensities, and provides a potentially more detailed insight into cultural dynamics. In some cases, as in the nomadic pastoralists just mentioned, the beneficial effects of cultural characteristics for individuals provide an explanation for their potentially disastrous consequences for the group as a whole. Possessing a large herd of cattle provides the owner with a greater chance of ensuring that the herd will reproduce and survive droughts and epizootic diseases, even though it results in environmental degradation.

On this view, culture and cultural change depend on behaviour of individuals which, although guided in the short term by immediate motivational satisfactions, has been shaped by natural selection in such a manner that in the long term it contributes to their inclusive fitness. Thus it is argued that what we consciously evaluate as desirable is to be equated with what is on average biologically optimal for us as individuals (Irons, 1979a and b; Alexander, 1979; Crook, 1980). In accordance with the considerations advanced in chapter 7, individuals may be expected to act selfishly to further their own fitness, or to further the fitness of relatives, and to show altruism to non-related others when, and only when, the probable benefits outweigh the probable costs. As one example, Irons (1979b) supports his view that in most human societies the conscious goals which people set themselves relate to achievements that make biological success more probable, by data from the Turkmen of Persia, who measure social success by accumulation of wealth. The evidence shows a positive association between wealth and inclusive fitness which appears not to be due solely to the immediate effects of wealth on individual health and survival.

If selection operates on individuals, we would expect individuals to accept and to perpetuate aspects of culture that contribute to their own fitness, and indeed to produce innovations to that end. An individual selectionist approach thus entails the view that individuals are not passively moulded by the culture into which they are born, but actively select from their experiences so as either to re-create or to renovate their culture. We have already encountered a similar issue in discussing how individuals both affect, and are affected by, their inter-personal relationships (p. 221). In the same way individuals are to be seen as moulding and moulded by the society in which they live. There must be an active dialectic between the individuals within a culture and the customs, norms, beliefs and values that constitute that culture. And that dialectic must be mediated by relationships with other individuals – individuals who are also in part self-interested and may attempt to impose ways of behaviour that are more in their own interests than anyone else's.

Of course this would not mean that *all* cultural characteristics and all cultural changes are brought about by individuals acting in ways conducive to their own inclusive fitness (Alexander, 1979). Some changes are imposed by external forces, such as climatic changes. Others are the indirect effects of human activities which, though perhaps beneficial to some individuals in the short term, are not necessarily so in the longer term: resource depletion and over-population are examples. Thus the environmental degradation produced by the cattle herds of nomadic pastoralists (see above) can produce a trend towards agriculture and a different type of social organization. Furthermore there is no implication that a given culture will promote the good of all its members all the time: historical inertia may involve the continuation of characteristics long after they have ceased to be useful to anyone. The Yakuts, when driven back by the Mongols towards the subarctic regions of Siberia, persisted in their attempts to preserve a horse-oriented culture in an environment unsuited to it, until they eventually imitated the reindeer breeders around them (Godelier, 1974). In any case, individuals may be mistaken in their innovations or selections from the existing culture.

Nor do attempts to interpret cultural differences in terms of the inclusive fitness of individuals imply that all individuals are able to act as they would wish all the time. Competition for scarce resources is present at least from time to time in all human societies. Conflict even between parent and child is, as we have seen, almost inevitable. Social hierarchies may be maintained by those who profit from them at the expense of those who do not; parents may impose on children. So if natural selection has operated to produce individuals who support cultural characteristics which favour the inclusive fitness of some individuals at the expense of others, it must also have favoured tendencies in the latter to cheat the system to further their own ends. Sociologists who see social systems as products of propensities within individuals produced by natural selection to favour the inclusive fitness of those individuals also see attempts to evade cultural constraints, to cuckold husbands, manipulate children and cheat the lawmakers, as coming from the same source.

In fact the view that selection acts to promote individual inclusive fitness can encompass a number of aspects of both the co-operation and the hostility between individuals that characterize all human societies. Early man's cognitive abilities would have enabled him, even better than his non-human ancestors, to further his own ends, to regulate inbreeding vs outbreeding, to distribute his aid differentially to his blood relatives or to those who would be likely to reciprocate. And if we accept that individuals are more likely to learn some things rather than others (pp. 188–92), and that the constraints and predispositions that determine what they learn have been shaped by natural selection through their effects on inclusive fitness, then certain rather general characteristics of human societies become readily comprehensible (e.g., Wilson, 1978). For example many characteristics of human marriage systems can be understood in terms of inclusive fitness given a basically polygynous tendency (see pp. 249–50). In the great majority of societies males control the exchange of women by kinship systems. The double standard about virginity on marriage and adultery during marriage can be related to the fact that a woman must know that her child is hers, but a man can be cuckolded. The generally older age of men on marriage may be related to reproductive potential: a young virgin has greater reproductive potential than an older woman, but an older man may have greater protective expertise to offer.

Considerations of inclusive fitness would predict that the affiliations of individuals should be guided by considerations of genetic relatedness. Evidence for the validity of such a view in a particular case comes from Chagnon's work with the Yanamamö Indians in South America. Chagnon and Bugos (1979) analysed a film of an axe-fight in a Yanamamö village, and were able to show that genetic relatedness correlated highly with aiding in the fight. That is not to say that the data were completely accounted for in terms of relatedness, and Chagnon and Bugos point out that affinity and alliance (see below) also operated. But the case is of unusual interest because of the detail with which the degrees of genetic relatedness were known, and because, since all the individuals on each side came from the same group, the pattern of aiding could not be explained in terms of propinquity (see also Hames, 1979).

Most human societies are of course organized along lines which do not correspond precisely with degrees of genetic relatedness. Each has its own way of classifying kin, with the nature of the categories used, and the extent to which they correspond with biological relatedness, differing between societies (Goody, 1973). The kinship categories invariably constrain the behaviour of individuals – most particularly by specifying who can and who cannot be married. Observation of the rules of kinship within any one society is an essentially moral matter, and appears at first sight to be independent of any considerations of economic, political or biological reward (Fortes, 1969). Indeed some anthropologists have argued that their essentially moral nature, their very independence from immediate material ends, may facilitate cultural change in adaptation to changing circumstances in a way which would not be possible if society was organized around material goals (Bloch, 1973).

However a different view is now possible, for there is evidence that kinship classifications can in fact be interpreted at least partially as compatible with considerations of individual inclusive fitness. Chagnon's (1979) work again provides a particular example. He has shown that many aspects of the social structure of the Yanamamö Indians can be seen as the outcome of competition for women amongst the males. The hostility and display amongst the males ultimately involves women, and lineages involve coalitions of related males aiding each other in the competition for females. Lineages form intermarrying pairs, and supply each other reciprocally with mates. Such pairs of lineages form the bases of most villages, and both intervillage warfare and the fissioning of villages result from inter-male competition.

In general sociobiologists are accumulating data suggesting that kin classificatory systems may indeed be adaptive in providing an optimal balance between the requirements of inclusive fitness for individuals to propagate their own or their blood relative's genes, and the necessity for avoiding excessive inbreeding (Alexander, 1977). Whilst this balance may depend in part on biological mechanisms (p. 130; Bischof, 1975), cultural ones may be superimposed. Since Hamilton's theory of inclusive fitness suggests that the extent to which individuals should favour their genetic relatives should vary with the potential cost to their own inclusive fitness, the degree and pattern of altruism to be expected is likely to vary with ecological factors. The optimal pattern of differential investment between kin and non-kin, and between inbreeding versus outbreeding, must therefore be expected to vary between societies, and could provide a basis for some of the observed diversity in kinship classifications (Fox, 1979).

Such a view has received considerable opposition, much of which has centred round the limited extent to which kinship categories do in fact correspond to genetic relationships (e.g., Sahlins, 1977). While in some cases the existence and importance of a close relation between kinship classification and genealogical relatedness has been demonstrated (e.g., Chagnon, pers. comm.), in other instances the degree of coincidence is quite small. However it can be shown theoretically that kin selection could operate even in the latter cases (Lewontin, 1970; Schulman, 1978).

Anyway there is no implication that kinship systems are determined only by considerations of inclusive breeding success. Other issues may also be important, and some of these may have an ecological basis. For example in Australia the kinship systems apparently became increasingly complex, with a gradual increase in the number of divisions and subdivisions, as one penetrates further into the interior. It has been suggested that this was related to the greater aridity of the environment, which enforces greater mobility over larger areas, greater spatial separation between groups, greater risk of catastrophes from drought or famine, and thus greater need for access to the territories of neighbouring groups (Yengoyan, in Lee and De Vore, 1968). Thus in general the kinship system can be seen as regulating many aspects of social, as well as sexual, intercourse.

Even the practice of infanticide, often regarded as a group-level adaptation for controlling population, can at least sometimes be explained as a device for enhancing individual inclusive fitness. It would be advantageous for women to vary the sex ratio of their offspring if (a) male reproductive success has a higher variance than that of females, as in polygynous and serially monogamous populations, and (b) if females could predict whether their children would lie nearer the higher or lower end of the variance. A woman whose offspring were likely to have high reproductive success would have more grandchildren if she had mostly boys, but a woman whose offspring were likely to have low reproductive success would do better to make sure of having a few grandchildren by having mostly girls (Trivers and Willard, 1973; Alexander, 1974). This would clearly be a reasonable line of argument if females could vary the sex ratio of their offspring by differential mortality of zygotes, but it has also been extended to infanticide with the suggestion that female infanticide should be more common amongst the more successful sections of the population. This prediction would apply most particularly to societies which are stratified and where the children tend to acquire their parents' status. Where these conditions are fulfilled

Dickemann (1979) in fact found female infanticide pre-
dominantly in the higher social strata. In a masterly survey
she showed that a number of cultural traits are compatible
with a model based on male competition for mates. Male
reproductive success is greatest at the top of the social
hierarchy and, in keeping with the above predictions, the
relative success of males over females is augmented by a
greater incidence of preferential female infanticide, suicide
and celibacy in the higher strata. Middle and upper class
families compete for the high status grooms, transferring
their females up the hierarchy by means of a dowry. By
contrast at the bottom of the scale, where women have
greater reproductive expectations than men, males compete
for the purchase of brides. If polygyny and female infanticide
in the upper classes produce a marked shortage of women
lower down, competition for women in the lower strata
becomes intense. However male infanticide is not practised,
perhaps because the males may assist economically in
various ways, and thus facilitate the rearing of female
offspring (Irons, 1979b). Dickemann's model is supported
by data from a wide range of societies in India, China and
Europe.

In this sort of way many characteristics of human societies
including the incest taboo, war, altruism within groups, male
and female reproductive strategies, kinship and descent
systems, and even legal and ethical systems can at least be
tackled from a sociobiological perspective. In the exciting
ferment of ideas that at present characterizes the application
of these ideas, there are inevitably differences of opinion,
even amongst sociobiologically-oriented anthropologists.
Durham (e.g., 1979), for instance, taking the view that
biological and cultural evolution co-exist, argues that
individual human beings, by virtue of certain 'biases', allow
those cultural influences that 'past experience and some
degree of prediction suggest to be most advantageous for
personal inclusive fitness'. These biases, which enable
individuals to produce innovations or select cultural
practices which best enhance their inclusive fitness, are not

very clearly described by Durham. They are said to include the greater provision of 'satisfaction' by some alternatives than others, the acquisition of particular alternatives rather than others in the processes of socialization, and predispositions to learn in some ways rather than in others. He goes on to argue that 'there need be no genetic basis to the selected aspects of phenotype' (p. 53), but in doing so forgets that all his 'biases' must depend on the sort of brains that individuals have – brains that have presumably been shaped by natural selection to produce behavioural propensities conducive to individual inclusive fitness. It is thus difficult to understand the sharp distinction that Durham makes between his position and the more straightforward sociobiological stance of Irons and Alexander. The latter would agree that cultural change must be understood 'without presuming a genetic basis or predisposition for any *specific* adaptive form' (Durham, 1979, p. 57, my italics), but would insist on the necessity for presuming a genetic basis for the behavioural propensities that gave rise to the particular form. In insisting that 'there need be no genetic basis to the selected aspects of phenotype' (p. 53) Durham is simply failing to specify the ultimate origins of his 'biases'.

Dawkins (1976b) who, it may be remembered (p. 144), sees the genes as the essential replicators in natural selection, postulates analogous units of cultural transmission called 'memes'. 'Examples of memes are tunes, ideas, catch-phrases, clothes fashions, ways of making pots or building arches. Just as genes propagate themselves in the gene pool by leaping from body to body via sperm or eggs, so memes propogate themselves in the memepool by leaping from brain to brain via a process which, in the broad sense, can be called imitation' (Dawkins, 1976b, p. 206). On this view cultural evolution involves selection between memes which exploit their cultural environment to their own advantage. The crucial question behind this colourful picture is 'What makes for success amongst memes?' Dawkins suggests that the survival value of 'memes' depends in part on their psychological appeal. He acknowledges that this means appeal to brains that have been shaped by natural selection, but dismisses the possibility that natural selection could influence the course of cultural evolution on the hypothetical view that evolution based on natural selection is not the only type conceivable. That may well be so, but such cultural evolution can involve only selection between memes that have equal (or zero) influence on the inclusive fitness of the brains which assess their 'appeal'.

But the controversies amongst those who are trying to apply the principles of individual selection and inclusive fitness to human societies are as nothing compared with their exchanges with anthropologists of a different persuasion. Inevitably, it would seem, each side overstates its case, and to an outsider the sharp differences of opinion expressed by the protagonists are not always easy to comprehend. No one could seriously hold either the view that *all* aspects of culture are closely connected with the capacities of individuals (or genes) to reproduce themselves, or the view that *all* are totally unrelated. Neither the view that evolutionary biology offers the *best* route to understanding human behaviour (Irons, 1970c, p. 507), nor the view that it is useless, is likely to predominate in the long run. It is thus crucially important to maintain a broad perspective, with a proper balance between functional and causal/developmental approaches. A proper integration of the four whys (pp. 19–20) is as necessary for anthropology as for ethology, though the balance between them is likely to be very different.

It is clear that natural and cultural evolution can to some extent proceed independently (e.g., Boyd and Richerson, in press). Many everyday actions whose immediate consequences lie in the context of the particular institutions of a culture are very far removed from any effects on inclusive fitness, and their long-term effects on fitness may be minimal. They may nevertheless depend on propensities selected in another context to promote individual fitness. There is plenty of scope for cultural change and cultural elaboration, and for selection between 'memes', within the constraints set by considerations of inclusive fitness. Thus the interesting issues now concern not whether a sociobiological approach to anthropological problems is worth exploring, but how far it can be taken. Which aspects of human culture are to be seen as adaptations promoting the inclusive fitness of individuals, and which as by-products of propensities originally adapted to that end, but themselves of negligible cost or benefit to anyone? How heavy is the inertial force of history?

Over such questions the sociobiologists have an unfair advantage: they can provide compelling evidence for adaptation in particular instances, whereas the reactionary anthropologist cannot prove his null hypothesis. But correlations between characteristics of societies and beneficial outcomes can never in themselves demonstrate that the diversity of human social systems is to be understood solely in terms of the inclusive fitness of their members. Three points must be emphasized here. First, beneficial consequences are not enough to establish the operation of selection pressures (pp. 102–4). Second, and closely related to that, it is one thing to argue that many cultural practices meet a human need or even contribute to inclusive fitness, but quite another to show why they take particular forms in particular cultures. For instance mourning and other cultural practices surrounding death may ameliorate the loss and promote a healthy outcome for the bereaved, but the actual practices of mourning differ dramatically between cultures (e.g., Gorer, 1973). The extent of variation can be interpreted on the view that each culture selects for emphasis particular aspects of the range of experiences of bereaved individuals (Bowlby, 1980), but the basis for such a selection remains to be explained.

The third point has been mentioned several times already. Only a proportion, and perhaps only a small proportion, of the differences between cultures is likely to be explicable as the direct result of selection. Even in animals, abilities and propensities adaptive in some contexts may be deleterious in others (pp. 107–8). Likewise many cultural characteristics have minimal effects on the inclusive fitness of individuals, but may still be comprehensible in terms of psychological propensities which have been selected for contributions to inclusive fitness in other contexts. And only manipulation by others or the misdirection of otherwise adaptive propensities can account for the production of celibate priests or overworked executives too tired to make love to their wives or to play with their children. Thus it is only a first step for the sociobiological anthropologist to show that the benefits for individuals of selected cultural *characteristics* exceed the costs: in the longer term he must aim to show that the benefits of the underlying *propensities* exceed the costs over all occasions they are exhibited.

Understanding how social systems work will require an understanding of how inter-personal relationships are affected by and constitute the social nexus, how they are influenced by, transmit and transmute social norms. It requires understanding of the interplay between fidelity and cuckoldry, selfishness and devotion, adherence to law and cheating. It will require understanding of how culturally imposed beliefs about mobility between social groups affects within group conformity and attitudes to members of other groups and thus social structure (Tajfel, 1978). Whilst a sociobiological approach to social structures may well pay dividends, it in no way diminishes the need for other routes of anthropological and sociopsychological inquiry. In so far as the sociobiologist is concerned with groups and sub-groups within societies, he must examine the psychological processes on which they depend and the terms in which they are rationalized. Thus the sociobiological approach may be a powerful tool, but it can do no more than supplement the more traditional endeavours of social anthropologists.

16. Psychiatry

Ethology's contributions to psychiatry are necessarily limited by the differences in cognitive complexity between animals and man. Nevertheless, they are not absent. First we may consider two examples of conceptual contributions, both of which refer to issues discussed already in previous chapters.

The first concerns the use of energy models of motivation. Lorenz's psychohydraulic model of motivation (see pp. 183–4) had much in common with the Freudian one, and in the early fifties psychoanalysts were often to be found at ethological meetings, attracted to the new discipline in part for that reason. However such models soon came to be rejected by most ethologists (e.g., Hinde, 1960), and their arguments have had some influence on the less traditionally-minded psychoanalysts. This has been especially important in considerations of the bases of aggression: proponents of energy models, believing that man's propensity to aggression depends on endogenous sources of motivation, must seek the solution in the harmless discharge of the aggressive energy through other channels – in sublimation and/or redirection (e.g., Lorenz, 1966). Rejection of energy models, on the other hand, leads to a search for the causes of aggression amongst the ontogenetic, predisposing and precipitating factors (see fig. 14) acting on the individual concerned (e.g., de Wit and Hartup, 1974).

A second important conceptual contribution concerns the Bowlby/Ainsworth model of attachment, as discussed in chapter 14 (pp. 226–30). In so far as psychopathological states have their roots in the processes of early development, understanding of those processes is crucial to the psychiatrist. Bowlby's sponsorship of an interest in what babies and children actually do, interpreted in terms of the requirements of an 'environment of evolutionary adaptedness' and with recognition of the infant's gradually increasing cognitive abilities, has paved the way for new understanding of the dynamics of development: this in turn is beginning to throw light on some aspects of child psychopathology (e.g., Bowlby, 1980). In particular studies of the short- and long-term consequences of rearing monkeys in various degrees of social deprivation (Suomi and Harlow, 1978a), and of temporary separation between mother and infant (chapter 14; Suomi and Harlow, 1975, 1977), is providing hard data on the manner in which early experience, and especially early social relationships, affects adult personality. Furthermore, work on attachment is beginning to throw light on some aspects of adult relationships. Bowlby (e.g., 1969) used the term 'attachment' to refer to relationships between one individual and another perceived as stronger or wiser than himself, irrespective of their age: it is of course possible for two individuals to be attached each to the other in this way. With this extension, recognition that the child's response to separation from its attachment figure is natural and in many circumstances adaptive throws light also on apparently irrational anxiety and fear in adulthood, on responses to separation from loved others and on bereavement (Parkes, 1972; Bowlby, 1980; Parkes and Stevenson-Hinde, in press).

A related issue concerns the relevance of ethological data on the behaviour of animals in conflict situations to certain childhood disorders. For example Tinbergen and Tinbergen (1972) have suggested that ethological methods for the analysis of motivational conflicts can be applied to the study of childhood autism, which they regard as a consequence of approach/avoidance conflicts exacerbated by timidity in the child or unsociable behaviour in the adult (see also Hutt and Ounstead, 1966; Richer, 1976). Whilst these views have not met with general acceptance amongst child psychiatrists, the disagreements stem at least in part from matters of definition – of whether the children studied by the Tinbergens were

really autistic, or on a continuum of 'the isolation
syndrome'.

An understanding of the dynamics of non-verbal communication, supposedly crucial in this last case, has many
other applications in human psychopathology – for instance
in the behaviour of schizophrenics, and in analysing the
course of the psychiatric interview (Rioch and Weinstein,
1964; Gottschalk and Auerbach, 1966). As we have seen in
chapter 13 (pp. 212–19), ethology has made a considerable
contribution here.

Animal experiments have of course been crucial in the
development of psychotherapeutic drugs, and animal
models are now making modest contributions to the
understanding of a number of aspects of human psychopathology (e.g., Suomi, in press). Such contributions have a long
history (e.g., Masserman, 1943; Pavlov, 1955), but are now
coming to have an increasing ethological contribution. The
use of rhesus monkeys to study the consequences of
mother–infant separation has already been mentioned. A
specific suggestion for the treatment of socially deprived
individuals came from a related series of experiments with
rhesus monkeys. In studies designed to assess the influences
of rearing under a variety of conditions on behavioural
development, Harlow and his colleagues found that young
monkeys reared in conditions of social deprivation displayed
gross deficits in many aspects of social behaviour and many
idiosyncratic movement stereotypes never seen in normally
reared individuals. Attempts to rehabilitate such animals
were initially unsuccessful. However Suomi and Harlow
(1972) reasoned that it might be helpful to cage the deprived
monkeys with other individuals who would promote
physical contact without threatening them with aggression
or complex play interactions. Three-month-old 'therapists'
were used with six-month social isolates, and significant
rehabilitation of the latter was achieved. Subsequently the
same technique was applied to the rehabilitation of human
children reared under conditions of social deprivation with
considerable success (Furman *et al.*, 1979).

As another example, Seligman (1975) and his colleagues found that dogs treated with inescapable electric shock subsequently showed diminished learning capacity in comparable situations, and many symptoms of depression. This led to the suggestion that depression in man might involve comparable experiences in its aetiology, a suggestion which has led to a great deal of research on 'learned helplessness' and has thrown light on a number of aspects of human depressive illness. Of course this does not mean that depression can be understood solely in terms of exogenous factors: metabolic factors are also important, and here again animal models have been valuable (Kraemer and McKinney, 1979).

Of course, animals can provide only *models* for human psychopathology, but they may serve to highlight issues clouded by the complexity of the human case, and they certainly provide opportunities for an experimental approach totally unacceptable with human subjects. It goes without saying that such experiments must be conducted only when clearly justified by their potential for alleviating human suffering, and then with compassion. And it is important that it is the principles derived from such experiments, rather than direct parallels between animals and man, that are most productive: often the value of an animal model lies in the differences between animal and man as much as in the similarities.

Whilst ethology thus has a number of areas of contact with psychiatry, and books on ethology and psychiatry are beginning to proliferate (e.g., White, 1974; McGuire and Fairbanks, 1977), it would be wrong to pretend that the common ground is extensive. The psychiatrists' proper concern with subjective experience inevitably constrains what traditional ethology has to offer. But if interdisciplinary barriers can be discarded the indirect contribution of ethology, mediated by developmental, social, psychological and experimental psychology, will also be considerable.

PART IV
Conclusion

17. Epilogue

In these chapters we have seen that ethology has common ground with diverse other sciences. Those discussed do not exhaust the possibilities – genetics, veterinary studies, and much else could have been included. There are also inter-relations between those other sciences – between behavioural endocrinology and neurophysiology, between anthropology and psychiatry, and so on. Science is to be seen as a multi-dimensional web, with each discipline influencing many others in many ways.

The relations between ethology and other sciences are of diverse types. In a number of cases, true union has occurred. It no longer makes sense to discuss the differences between ethologists and comparative psychologists, or between ethologists and behavioural ecologists. In other cases steps in that direction have been taken. With both experimental and developmental psychology, for example, common ground has been recognized and a degree of mutual respect achieved. And the importance of an adequate ethological base for many investigations in behavioural endocrinology and neurophysiology has been clearly established.

The situation is different yet again with the human social sciences. For the reasons I have given, I believe that ethologists entering the social sciences with circumspection have a considerable contribution to make. This comes in large measure from the questions asked – from recognition of the distinctions between, and the relations amongst, the four whys. Except in the case of specific animal models used to study human physiological processes or disorders, contributions from direct comparisons between particular animal species and man are likely to be rare. The animal data will be valuable, but primarily when used as a basis for the abstraction of principles or the refining of concepts whose validity in the human case can subsequently be assessed. This is especially likely to be the case when the animal data involve comparisons between species. And ethological techniques will be useful when used in combination with others designed for the peculiarly human aspects of human behaviour.

I would like especially to emphasize the way in which the early contacts between disciplines are often accompanied by hostile posturing. We have seen how the intense antagonism between many comparative psychologists and many ethologists has now disappeared completely. There was also at one time a good deal of posturing between ethologists and child developmentalists, and that also has pretty well disappeared. In these cases the ethologists have been as much to blame as anyone – they were incredibly naive about learning theory, and some have been pretty brash about child development. I hope that the curious posturing displayed by the sociobiologists – and here the ethologists are not to blame – is to be seen in the same light, and will pave the way for mutual endeavours.

To change key for one moment, although I have chosen to emphasize the contribution of ethology to other disciplines, I could have put the emphasis differently, and spoken of missed opportunities. How *could* ethologists have taken so long to come to terms with experimental studies of learning? Why did we have to wait for W. J. Smith, when the distinction between message and meaning had been made by Bloomfield in the 1930s? Ethologists could have made major contributions to understanding the roles of human mother and infant in interaction if they had been quicker off the mark. I might have argued that the ethologists' contribution could have been greater if they had taken more trouble to keep up with related sciences.

Where does this leave us with respect to the vexed question, raised in chapter 1, of the definition of ethology? The evidence shows, I think, that discussion about this *must* be unsatisfactory. No definition must be allowed to constrain the growth of the subject. Our attitude to ethology must be one that promotes these liaisons with other disciplines, and if that makes the task of defining ethology about as easy as describing the shape of *Amoeba*, so be it. After all, ethologists are not so insecure that they need to signpost their boundaries, threaten to invade the territories of others, or fear cannibalization. Over the years the nature of the behavioural sciences will change, and the boundaries between their subdivisions will change. Strict territorial demarcation is undesirable.

However for the moment it is convenient to have a label which adequately distinguishes at least some of the courses, text books and the like that we would call ethological from those that we would not. If a tight definition is not desirable, perhaps it is best to say no more than that ethology involves attempts to tackle, from a descriptive base, the four inter-related questions about behaviour discussed by Tinbergen – namely the questions of immediate causation, development, function and evolution. *Of course* this leaves the boundaries vague, but that will facilitate progress.

Glossary

Altruism In everyday speech, this implies providing benefits to another at a cost to oneself. In biology, the benefits and costs are measured in terms of reproductive success. Thus an altruistic act confers a reproductive advantage to another at the cost of immediate personal reproductive loss. (N.B. it is sometimes argued that the immediate personal reproductive loss may involve a long-term reproductive gain through kin selection (q.v.)).

Ambivalent Tending to behave in two or more incompatible ways at the same time.

Androgen Any substance with the biological action of the male sex hormone in vertebrates.

Attribution The process of ascribing causation to events. Attribution theory is concerned with the bases on which individuals make attributions.

Autonomic Nervous System That part of the nervous system of vertebrates that supplies the gut, blood vessels, etc., as opposed to the skeletal muscles.

Autoshape The shaping of an operant response through a classical conditioning procedure.

Balance theories Theories concerned with the relation between the attitudes and perceptions of one person towards another person and an object.

Character Any property (of structure or behaviour) of an organism or population chosen for study.

Classical Conditioning A procedure which involves the pairing of an 'unconditioned stimulus', which already elicits a response, with a (to be) 'conditioned stimulus', which does not initially elicit that response. After one or more pairings the conditioned stimulus, even if presented on its own, comes to elicit a response closely similar to that initially elicited only by the unconditioned stimulus.

Cost In biology this usually refers to a decrement in probable reproductive success resulting from engaging in a particular activity.

Cryptic Conducive to concealment.

Cyclicity Recurrence with a more or less regular period.

Demography The study of population structure.

Density dependence The dependence of a character of a population on the size of that population. Used here to refer to an increase in mortality rate with increase in population size.

Dimorphism Existing in two forms. (Sexual dimorphism refers to a difference between male and female.)

Diploid Refers to cell nuclei which have the chromosomes in homologous pairs.

Dissonance Lack of consistency between the attitudes and/or beliefs of an individual.

Dyad Two individuals in relationship with each other (includes a 'pair', which usually has a sexual connotation).

Ecology Study of the relations between animals and plants to each other and to their physical environment.

Effector Organ, cell, limb, etc., by means of which an animal acts.

Endocrine system System of glands producing hormones (q.v.).

Endocrinology The study of hormones (q.v.), their production and effects.

Endogenous Generated from within the organism.

Enzyme A protein which promotes chemical reactions.

Erbkoordination Term used by the early ethologists to refer to that aspect of a stereotyped species-characteristic movement that, though elicited by external stimuli, is not subsequently guided by them.

Exchange and Interdependence Theories Theories of interpersonal behaviour involving the view that such behaviour depends on the rewards or expectations of rewards consequent upon it. Interdependence theories stress the effects of each individual within a dyadic relationship on the other.

Exogenous Generated from outside the organism.

Exposure Learning Changes in behaviour that result from an individual being exposed to an object or situation, under circumstances in which no consistent response apart from investigatory or exploratory behaviour is elicited by that situation, and with no obvious reward.

Exteroceptor A sense organ which responds to changes originating outside the body.

Feedback Used here to refer to consequences of behaviour which serve to augment (positive) or diminish (negative feedback) that behaviour.

Fitness The contribution to the next generation of one individual or genotype relative to that of others.

Frugivorous Feeding on fruit.

Ganglion Distinguishable group of nerve cell bodies.

Genotype The genetic constitution of an organism, usually specified in relation to given characters.

Glans penis The sensitive tip of the penis.

Gonadectomy Removal of the gonads.

Gonadotrophins Hormones released from the pituitary gland that affect the development or activity of the gonads.

Habituation Reduction in response to a stimulus consequent upon its repeated or continuous presentation (sometimes subsumed within exposure learning).

Haploid Refers to cell nuclei which have only one member of each pair of homologous chromosomes.

Hardware The parts of which a computer is made (contrast Software). Used here to refer to the neuromuscular machinery underlying behaviour.

Hemispheres The two halves of part of the forebrain especially developed in higher vertebrates.

Homeostasis Maintenance of a constant state.

Hormone A substance produced in minute quantities in one

part of an organism and affecting visceral or somatic activity (including behaviour) by action elsewhere.

Hypothalamus Part of the brain of vertebrates lying just behind the forebrain.

Hypothalamus-pituitary-gonad system The nervous and endocrine system concerned with the secretion and regulation of sex hormones.

Instar Stage in the development of an insect.

Institution A type of relationship or pattern of relationships characteristic of a given society. Thus marriage is an institution, husband and wife are roles (q.v.); the monarchy is an institution, the king and subjects roles.

Laterality Used here to refer to a difference in function between left and right sides of the nervous system.

LH Luteinizing hormone: a gonadotrophin (q.v.).

Metamorphosis Period of rapid transformation from one form to another in the course of development.

Neocortex Evolutionarily the most recent part of the brain.

Neonate A newborn.

Neoteny Development in which immature characteristics persist until later than in related forms.

Neural Concerned with the nervous system.

Neuroendocrinology The study of the relations between the neural and endocrine systems.

Neuronal Concerned with nerve cells.

Norm Shared expectations about how individuals will or should behave.

Oestrogen A female sex hormone.

Oestrus The state of sexual heat or receptivity: applied only to females.

Ontogeny The course of individual development (contrast Phylogeny).

Operant conditioning A procedure in which an operant response (q.v.) is followed on a proportion of occasions by a reinforcer (q.v.).

Operant response A response which acts on the environment

to produce an event which affects the subsequent probability of that response (see Reinforcer).

Ovulation The release of a ripe egg from an ovarian follicle.

Phenotype The observed characteristics of an organism after development has proceeded (contrast genotype).

Pheromone A substance used in chemical communication between individuals within a species.

Phylogeny The evolutionary history or relationships of a particular organism or group of organisms (contrast Ontogeny).

Pituitary Gland An endocrine gland situated below the brain and responsible, amongst other things, for the production of gonadotrophins (q.v.).

Plasma The blood, other than the corpuscles.

Polygyny The tendency of one male to mate with two or more females.

Population Biology The study of the properties of populations of organisms – i.e. of groups of individuals living together in a limited area.

Progesterone A female sex hormone.

Prolactin A hormone released by the pituitary gland.

Proprioceptor A sense organ which detects changes inside the body, especially those consequent upon the movement of skeletal muscles.

Pseudopodium Temporary protrusion of a cell wall associated with flowing movements of the cell fluids.

Radiation (Adaptive) The evolution from one form of a range of forms suited to different ways of life.

Reinforcer When a response is predictably followed by an event, and the occurrence of that event can be shown to increase the future probability of that response, the event is termed a reinforcer.

Reticular Activating System A system in the brain-stem, activity in which is related to the state of arousal of the organism.

RNA Ribonucleic acid. A long chain compound which plays an essential part in protein synthesis.

Role Used by anthropologists to refer to the rights and

duties imposed on the incumbents of certain positions within a society, and rather more widely by social psychologists (see Institution).

Selection – natural The differential contribution of young to the next generation by individuals of different genetic constitution.

  group The differential contribution of young to the next generation by groups of individuals differing in genetic constitution.

  kin A more general case of individual selection due to individuals influencing the survival or reproduction of others who possess the same genes by common descent.

Sequelae Events that follow a given event.

Sibling Used here to refer to a brother or sister.

Software The programs that govern the operation of a computer. Used here to refer to the relations between the parts of the neuromuscular machinery that determine the patterning of behaviour.

Somatic Used to contrast body cells to germ cells or (here) the skeletal-muscular apparatus to the viscera.

Squab A newly-hatched pigeon.

Steroid A category of hormones including the sex hormones.

Synapse The region in which activity in one nerve cell affects that in another.

Systems theory The study of the inter-relations between sets of operators, applicable to mechanical devices, organisms or parts of organisms.

Testosterone Male sex hormone of vertebrates.

Toxicosis The consequences of ingesting poison.

Transmitter Used here to refer to a chemical substance released by a nerve cell and causing activity in another cell.

Ungulate A hoofed animal.

Zygote A fertilized ovum before cleavage.

References

Ainsworth, M. D. S., Blehar, M. C., Waters, E. and Wall, S. (1978). *Patterns of Attachment*. Erlbaum, Hillsdale, N. J.

Ainsworth, M. D. S. (1979). Attachment as related to mother-infant interaction. *Adv. Study Behav. 9*, 2–52.

Alcock, J. (1975). *Animal Behavior*. Sinauer, Sunderland, Mass.

Alexander, R. D. (1974). The evolution of social behavior. *Ann. Rev. Ecol. & Systematics 5*, 325–83.

Alexander, R. D. (1977). Natural selection and the analysis of human sociality. In *Changing scenes in the natural sciences, 1776–1976*. (Goulden, C. E., ed.) The Academy, Philadelphia.

Alexander, R. D. (1979). Evolution and culture. In Chagnon and Irons.

Alexander, R. D., Hoogland, J. L., Howard, R. D., Noonan, K. M. and Sherman, P. W. (1979). Sexual dimorphisms and breeding systems in pinnipeds, ungulates, primates and humans. In Chagnon and Irons.

Alexander, R. D. and Noonan, K. M. (1979). Concealment of ovulation, parental care and human social evolution. In Chagnon and Irons.

Alexander, R. D. and Sherman, P. W. (1977). Local mate competition and parental investment in social insects. *Science, 196*, 494–500.

Amsel, A. and Stanton, M. (1980). The ontogeny of phylogeny of the paradoxical reward effects. *Adv. Study Behav., 11*, 227–75.

Andrew, R. J. (1972). The information potentially available in mammal displays. In Hinde.

Andrew, R. J. (1974). Arousal and the causation of behaviour. *Behaviour 51*, 135–65.

Andrew, R. J. (1976). Attentional processes and animal behaviour. In Bateson and Hinde.

Andrewartha, H. G. and Birch, L. C. (1954). *The Distribution and Abundance of Animals*. Chicago University Press.

Argyle, M. (1967). *The Psychology of Interpersonal Behaviour* Penguin, Harmondsworth.

Backmann, C. and Kummer, H. (1980). Male assessment of female choice in Hamadryas baboons. *Behav. Ecol. and Sociobiol. 6*, 315–22.

Baerends, G. P. (1941). Fortpflanzungsverhalten und Orientierung der Grabwespe *(Ammophilia campestris)*. *Jur. Tijdschr Ent., 84*, 68–275.

Baerends, G. P. (1975). An evaluation of the conflict hypothesis as an explanatory principle for the evolution of displays. In Baerends, Beer and Manning.

Baerends, G. P. (1976). The functional organization of behaviour. *Anim. Behav. 24*, 726–38.

Baerends, G. P., and Baerends van Roon, J. M. (1950). An introduction to the study of the ethology of cichlid fishes. *Behaviour Suppl. 1*, 1–242.

Baerends, G. P., Beer, C. and Manning, A. (eds.) (1975). *Function and Evolution in Behaviour*. Oxford.

Baerends, G. P., Brouwer, R., and Waterbolk, H. Tj. (1955). Ethological studies on *Lebistes reticulatus* (Peters): I. An analysis of the male courtship pattern. *Behaviour 8*, 249–334.

Baerends, G. P. and Drent, R. H. (1970). The herring gull and its egg. *Behav., Suppl. 17*, 1–312.

Baerends, G. P. and Kruijt, J. P. (1973). Stimulus selection. In Hinde and Stevenson-Hinde.

Barlow, G. W. (1977). Modal action patterns. In *How Animals Communicate*. (Sebeok, T. A., ed.) Indiana University Press.

Barlow, H. B. (1961). The coding of sensory messages. In Thorpe and Zangwill.

Barrett, P. and Bateson, P. P. G. (1978). The development of play in cats. *Behaviour 66*, 106–20.

Barth, F. (1973). Descent and marriage reconsidered. In Goody.

Bates, D. G. and Lees, S. H. (1979). The myth of population regulation. In Chagnon and Irons.

Bateson, P. P. G. (1964). Effect of similarity between rearing and testing conditions on chicks' following and avoidance responses. *J. Comp. Physiol. Psychol. 57*, 100–3.

Bateson, P. P. G. (1966). The characteristics and context of imprinting. *Biol. Rev., 41*, 177–220.

Bateson, P. P. G. (1973a). Internal influences on early learning in birds. In Hinde and Stevenson-Hinde.

Bateson, P. P. G. (1973b). Preferences for familiarity and novelty: a model for the simultaneous development of both. *J. Theor. Biol. 41*, 249–59.

Bateson, P. P. G. (1974). Specific and non-specific brain events associated with learning. *Biochem. Soc. Trans. 2*, 189–93.

Bateson, P. P. G. (1976a). Specificity and the origins of behavior. *Adv. Study Behav. 6*, 1–20.

Bateson, P. P. G. (1976b). Rules and reciprocity in behavioural development. In Bateson and Hinde.

Bateson, P. P. G. (1978a). How does behaviour develop? In *Perspectives in Ethology*. (Bateson, P. P. G. and Klopfer, P. H., eds.) Plenum, New York.

Bateson, P. P. G. (1978b). Early experience and sexual preferences. In *Biological Determinants of Sexual Behaviour*. (Hutchison, J. B., ed.) Wiley, London.

Bateson, P. P. G. (1978c). Sexual imprinting and optimal outbreeding. *Nature 273*, 659–60.

Bateson, P. P. G. (1979). How do sensitive periods arise and what are they for? *Anim. Behav. 27*, 470–86.

Bateson, P. P. G. (1981). Ontogeny of behaviour. *Brit. Med. Bull. 37*, No. 2, 159–64.

Bateson, P. P. G. and Hinde, R. A. (eds.) (1976). *Growing Points in Ethology*. Cambridge University Press.

Bateson, P. P. G., Horn, G. and McCabe, B. J. (1977). Imprinting and the incorporation of uracil in the chick brain: a radio-autographic study. *J. Physiol. 275*, 70.

Bateson, P. P. G. and Reese, E. P. (1969). The reinforcing properties of conspicuous stimuli in an imprinting situation. *Anim. Behav. 17*, 692–9.

Bateson, P. P. G., Rose, S. P. R. and Horn, G. (1973). Experience and plasticity in the central nervous system. *Science 181*, 506–14

Beach, F. A. (1976). Sexual attractivity, proceptivity and receptivity in female mammals. *Hormones and Behavior 7*, 105–38.

Beach, F. A., and Levinson, G. (1950). Effects of androgen on the glans penis and mating behavior of castrated male rats. *J. exp. Zool. 114*, 159–68.

Beer, C. G. (1963). Incubation and nest-building behaviour of black-headed gulls: IV. Nest-building in the laying and incubation periods. *Behaviour 21*, 155–76.

Beer, C. G. (1975). Was Professor Lehrman an ethologist? *Anim. Behav. 23*, 957–64.

Beer, C. (1976). Some complexities in the communication behavior of gulls. *Ann. N.Y. Acad. Sci. 280*, 413–32.

Bentley, D. R. and Hoy, R. R. (1970). Postembryonic development of adult motor patterns in crickets: a neural analysis. *Science, N.Y. 170*, 1409–11.

Bernal, J. (1972). Crying during the first 10 days of life, and maternal responses. *Dev. Med. Child Neurol. 14*, 362–72.

Bernstein, I. S., Rose, R. M. and Gordon, T. P. (1977). Behavioral and hormonal responses of male rhesus monkeys introduced to females in the breeding and non-breeding seasons. *Anim. Behav. 25*, 609–14.

Bertalanffy, L. von (1968). *General System Theory*. Braziller, New York.

Birdwhistell, R. L. (1963). The kinesis level in the investigation of the emotions. In *Expressions of the Emotions in Man*. (Knapp, P. H., ed.) Int. Univ. Press, New York.

Birdwhistell, R. L. (1967). Communication without words. In *L'Aventure Humaine*. (Alexandre, P., ed.) Soc. d'Etudes Littéraires et Art, Paris.

Birdwhistell, R. (1970). *Kinesics and Content*. University of Philadelphia Press.

Birkhead, T. R. (1978). Behavioural adaptations to high density nesting in the common guillemot. *Anim. Behav. 26*, 321–31.

Bischoff, N. (1975). Comparative ethology of incest avoidance. In *Biosocial Anthropology*. (Fox, R., ed.) Malaby, London.

Bloch, M. (1973). The long term and the short term: the economic and political significance of the morality of kinship. In Goody.

Bloomfield, L. (1933). *Language*. Holt, Rinehart and Winston, New York.

Blurton Jones, N. G. (1968). Observations and experiments on causation of threat displays of the great tit *(Parus major)*. *Anim. Behav. Monogr. 1*, 2.

Blurton Jones, N. (1972a). *Ethological Studies of Child Behaviour*. Cambridge University Press.

Blurton Jones, N. (1972b). Characteristics of ethological studies of human behaviour. In Blurton Jones (1972a).

Blurton Jones, N. (1972c). Comparative aspects of mother–child contact. In Blurton Jones (1972a).

Blurton Jones, N. and Sibly, R. M. (1978). Testing adaptiveness of culturally determined behaviour. *Sym. Soc. Human Biol. 18*, 135–57.

Blurton Jones, N. G. and Woodson, R. H. (1979). Describing behavior: the ethologist's perspective. In *Social Interaction Analysis*. (Lamb, M. E., Suomi, S. J. and Stephenson, G. R., eds.) University of Wisconsin Press.

Bolles, R. C. (1967). *Theory of Motivation*. Harper & Row, New York.

Bowlby, J. (1951). *Maternal Care and Mental Health*. H.M.S.O., London.

Bowlby, J. (1969). *Attachment and Loss, Vol. 1. Attachment*. Hogarth, London.

Bowlby, J. (1973). *Attachment and Loss, Vol. 2. Separation*. Hogarth, London.

Bowlby, J. (1980). *Attachment and Loss, Vol. 3. Loss*. Hogarth, London.

Boyd, R. and Richerson, P. J. (in press). Sociobiology, culture and economic theory. *J. Econ. Behav. and Organization*.

Bradley, P., Horn, G. and Bateson, P. (1981). Imprinting: an electron microscopic study of chick hyperstriatum ventrale. *Exper. Brain. Res. 41*, 115–20.

Breland, K. and Breland, M. (1961). The misbehavior of organisms. *Am. Psychol. 16*, 681–4.

Brockmann, H. J. (1980). The control of nest depth in a digger wasp. *Anim. Behav. 28*, 426–45.

Brown, G. W., Bhrolchain, M. N. and Harris, T. (1975). Social class and psychiatric disturbance among women in an urban population. *Sociology 9*, 225–54.

Brown, J. L. (1964). The evolution of diversity in avian territorial systems. *Wilson Bull. 76*, 160–9.

Brown, J. L. (1975). *The Evolution of Behavior*. Norton, New York.

Brown, R. E. and McFarland, D. J. (1979). Interaction of hunger and sexual motivation in the male rat: a time-sharing approach. *Anim. Behav. 27*, 887–96.

Brown, W. L. and Wilson, E. O. (1956). Character displacement. *Syst. Zool. 5*, 49–64.

Bruner, J. (1978). Learning how to do things with words. In *Human Growth and Development*. (Bruner, J. S. and Gartlan, A., eds.) Clarendon Press, Oxford.

Buckley, P. A. and Buckley, F. G. (1972). Individual egg and chick recognition by adult royal terns. *Anim. Behav. 20*, 457–62.

Burley, R. A. (1980). Precopulatory and copulatory behaviour in relation to stages of the oestrous cycle in the female Mongolian gerbil. *Behav. 72*, 211–41.

Chagnon, N. A. (1979). Mate competition, favouring close kin, and village fissioning among the Yanomamö Indians. In Chagnon and Irons.

Chagnon, N. A. and Burgos, P. E. (1979). Kin selection and conflict: an analysis of a Yanomamö Axe fight. In Chagnon and Irons.

Chagnon, N. A. and Irons, W. (eds.) (1979). *Evolutionary Biology and Human Social Behaviour: an anthropological Perspective.* Duxbury Press, North Scituate, Mass.

Chance, M. R. A. and Jones, E. (1974). A protracted startle response to maternal rejection in infants of *Macaca fascicularis. Folia Primat. 22,* 218–36.

Cheney, D. (1978). Interactions of immature male and female baboons with adult females. *Anim. Behav. 26,* 389–408.

Cheney, D. R. and Seyfarth, R. M. (1981). Selective forces affecting the predator alarm calls of vervet monkeys. *Behaviour 76,* 25–61.

Cheng, M. F. (1977). Egg fertility and prolactin as determinants of reproductive re-cycling in doves. *Hormones and Behavior 9,* 85–98.

Clarke, A. M. and Clarke, A. D. B. (1976). *Early Experience: Myth and Evidence.* Open Books, London.

Clarke, J. R. (1953). The effect of fighting on the adrenals, thymus and spleen of the vole *(Microtus agrestis). J. Endocr. 9,* 114–26.

Clutton-Brock, T. H. (ed.) (1977). *Primate Ecology.* Academic Press, New York.

Clutton-Brock, T. and Albon, S. D. (1979). The roaring of red deer and the evolution of honest advertisement. *Behaviour 69,* 145–70.

Clutton-Brock, T. H. and Harvey, P. (1976). Evolutionary rules and primate societies. In Bateson and Hinde.

Clutton-Brock, T. H. and Harvey, P. H. (1977). Primate ecology and social organization. *J. Zool., London 183,* 1–39.

Clutton-Brock, T. H. and Harvey, P. H. (1978). Mammals, resources and reproductive strategies. *Nature 273,* 191–5.

Cohen, S. and McFarland, D. (1979). Time-sharing as a mechanism for the control of behaviour sequences during the courtship of the three-spined stickleback. *Anim. Behav. 27,* 270–83.

Collier, G. H. and Rovee-Collier, C. K. (1980). A comparative analysis of optimal foraging behavior: laboratory simulations. In *Foraging Behavior.* (Kamil, A. C. and Sargent, T., eds.) Garland Press, New York.

Cott, H. B. (1940). *Adaptive Coloration in Animals.* Methuen, London.

Crook, J. H. (1964). The evolution of social organization and visual communication in the weaver birds *(Ploceinae). Behaviour Suppl. 10,*1–178.

Crook, J. H. (1980). *The Evolution of Human Consciousness.* Clarendon, Oxford.

Cullen, E. (1957). Adaptations in the kittiwake to cliff-nesting. *Ibis* 99, 275–302.

Cullen, J. M. (1959). Behaviour as a help in taxonomy. *Systematics Assn. Publ. No. 3*, 131–40.

Curio, E. (1975). The functional organization of anti-predator behaviour in the pied flycatcher. A study of avian visual perception. *Anim. Behav. 23*, 1–115.

Curio, E. (1978). The adaptive significance of avian mobbing. *Zeits. f. Tierpsychol. 48*, 175–83.

Curio, E., Ernst, U. and Vieth, W. (1978). The adaptive significance of avian mobbing II. *Zeits f. Tierpsychol. 48*, 184–202.

Darwin, C. R. (1859). *The Origin of Species by Means of Natural Selection*. Murray, London.

Darwin, C. (1872). *The Expression of the Emotions in Man and the Animals*. Murray, London.

Datta, S. (1981). The dynamics of dominance in rhesus females. Ph.D. Thesis, Cambridge.

Davies, N. B. (1977). Prey selection and the search strategy of the spotted flycatcher. *Anim. Behav. 25*, 1016–33.

Davies, N. B. and Houston, A. I. (1981). Owners and satellites: the economics of territory defence in pied wagtails. *J. Anim. Ecol. 50*.

Davis, J. (1957). Comparative foraging behavior of the spotted and brown towhees. *Auk 74*, 129–66.

Davis, W. J. and Ayers, J. L. (1972). Locomotion: control of positive feedback optokinetic responses. *Sciences, N.Y. 177*, 183–5.

Dawkins, M. (1971). Perceptual changes in chicks: another look at the 'search image' concept. *Anim. Behav. 19*, 566–74.

Dawkins, R. (1976a). Hierarchical organization: a candidate principle for ethology. In Bateson and Hinde.

Dawkins, R. (1976b). *The Selfish Gene*. Oxford University Press.

Dawkins, R. (1979). Twelve misunderstandings of kin selection. *Zeits f. Tierpsychol. 51*, 184–200.

Dawkins, R. (1980). Good strategy or evolutionary stable strategy? In *Sociobiology: beyond nature and nurture*. (Barlow, G. and Silverberg, eds.)

Dawkins, R. and Krebs, J. R. (1979). Animal signals. In Krebs and Davies.

Dell, P. C. (1958). Some basic mechanisms of the translation of bodily needs into behaviour. In *Ciba Foundation Symposium* on the 'Neurological Basis of Behaviour'. (Wolstenholme, G. E. W. and O'Connor, C. M., eds.) Boston.

Denenberg, V. H. (1979). Paradigms and paradoxes in the study of behavioural development. In *Origins of the infant's social responsiveness*. (Thoman, E. B., ed.) Erlbaum, Hillsdale, N.J.

De Vore, I. (1963). Mother-infant relations in free-ranging baboons. In *Maternal Behavior in Mammals*. (Rheingold, H., ed.) Wiley, New York.

Dewsbury, D. A. (1978). What is (was?) the 'Fixed Action Pattern'? *Anim. Behav. 26,* 310–11.

Dickemann, M. (1979). Female infanticide, reproductive strategies, and social stratification: a preliminary model. In Chagnon and Irons.

Dill, L. M. (1974). The escape response of the zebra danio (*Brachydanio rerio*). I. The stimulus for escape. *Anim. Behav. 22,* 711–22.

Douglas, J. W. B. (1975). Early hospital admissions and later disturbances of behaviour and learning. *Develop. Med. Child Neurol. 17,* 456–80.

Duncan, I. J. H. and Hughes, B. O. (1972). Free and operant feeding in domestic fowls. *Anim. Behav. 20,* 775–7.

Dunn, J. (1976). How far do early differences in mother–child relations affect later development? In Bateson and Hinde.

Durham, W. H. (1979). Towards a co-evolutionary theory of human biology and culture. In Chagnon and Irons.

Ehrhardt, A. A. and Meyer-Bahlberg, H. F. L. (1979). Psychosexual development. In *Sex Hormones and Behavior. Ciba Foundation Symp. 62,* 41–58.

Eibl Eibesfeldt, I. (1972). Similarities and differences between cultures in expressive movements. In Hinde.

Eibl Eibesfeldt, I. (1975). *Ethology*. Holt, Rinehart, New York.

Eibl Eibesfeldt, I. (1979). Ritual and ritualization from a biological perspective. In *Human Ethology*. (Cranach, M. von *et al.*, eds.) Cambridge University Press.

Einarsen, A. S. (1945). Some factors affecting ring-necked pheasant population density. *Murrelet 26,* 39–44.

Ekman, P. (1977). Biological and cultural contributions to body and facial movement. In *Anthropology of the Body*. (Blacking, J., ed.) A.S.A. Monograph 15, Academic Press, London.

Ekman, P. and Friesen, W. V. (1969). The repertoire of non-verbal behaviour: categories, origins, usage and coding. *Semiotica, 1,* 49–98.

Ekman, P. and Friesen, W. V. (1975). *Unmasking the Face*. Prentice-Hall, New Jersey.

Elton, C. (1927). *Animal Ecology*. Sidgwick & Jackson, London.

Emlen, S. T. and Oring, L. W. (1977). Ecology, sexual selection and the evolution of mating systems. *Science 197*, 215–23.

Erickson, C. J. and Zenone, P. G. (1978). Aggressive courtship as a means of avoiding cuckoldry. *Anim. Behav. 26*, 307–8.

Fabricius, E. and Boyd, M. (1954). Experiments on the following reactions of ducklings. *Wildfowl Trust Ann. Rep., 1952–3*, 84–9.

Falk, J. L. (1971). The nature and determinants of adjunctive behaviour. *Physiol. Behav. 6*, 577–88.

Feder, H. H., Story, A., Goodwin, D. and Reboulleau, C. (1977). Testosterone and '5 alpha-dihydrotestosterone' levels in peripheral plasma of male and female ring doves during the reproductive cycle. *Biol. Reprod. 16*, 666–77.

Fentress, J. C. (1976). Dynamic boundaries of patterned behaviour: interaction and self organization. In Bateson and Hinde.

Fentress, J. C. (1980). How can behavior be studied from a neuroethological perspective? In *Information Processing in the Nervous System*. (Pinsker, H. M. and Willis, W. D. Jr., eds.) Raven Press, New York.

Fentress, J. and Stillwell, F. (1973). Grammar of a movement sequence in inbred mice. *Nature 244*, 52–3.

Fisher, R. A. (1958). *The Genetical Theory of Natural Selection*. Dover, New York.

Ford, E. B. (1956). *Moths*. Collins, London.

Fortes, M. (1969). *Kinship and the Social Order*. Aldine, Chicago.

Fossey, D. (1979). Development of the mountain gorilla. In Hamburg and McCown. Benjamin/Cummings, Menlo Park, California.

Fox, R. (1979). Kinship categories as natural categories. In Chagnon and Irons.

Friedman, M. B. (1977). Interactions between visual and vocal courtship stimuli in the neuroendocrine response of female doves. *J. Comp. Physiol. Psychol. 91*,1408–16.

Fullard, W. and Reiling, A. M. (1976). An investigation of Lorenz's 'babyishness'. *Child Development 47*, 1191–3.

Furman, R., Rahe, D. F. and Hartup, W. W. (1979). Rehabilitation of socially-withdrawn children through mixed-age and same-age socialization. *Child Development 50*, 915–22.

Galdikas, B. M. F. (1979). Orang-utan adaptation at Tanjung Puting Reserve: mating and ecology. In Hamburg and McCown.

Gardner, B. T. and Wallach, L. (1965). Shapes of figures identified as a baby's head. *Percept. Motor Skills, 20*, 135–42.

Gibson, E. J. and Walk, R. D. (1956). The effect of prolonged exposure to visually presented patterns on learning to discriminate them. *J. Comp. Physiol. Psychol. 49*, 239–42.

Glickman, S. E. and Schiff, B. B. (1967). A biological theory of reinforcement. *Psychol. Rev. 74*, 81–109.

Godelier, M. (1974). Anthropology and biology: towards a new form of co-operation. *Int. Soc. Sci. J. 26*, 611–35.

Goldfoot, D. A., Westerborg-van Loon, H., Groeneveld, W. and Koos Slob, A. (1980). Behavioural and physiological evidence of sexual climax in the female stump-tailed macaque. *Science, 208*, 1477–8.

Goldman, B. D. (1978). Developmental influences of hormones on neuroendocrine mechanisms of sexual behaviour. In Hutchison.

Goody, J. (ed.) (1973). *The Character of Kinship*. Cambridge University Press.

Gorer, G. (1973). Death, grief and mourning in Britain. In *The Child in his Family: the Impact of Disease and Death*. (Anthony, E. J. and Koupernik, C., eds.) Wiley, New York.

Gottlieb, G. (1976). The roles of experience in the development of behavior and the nervous system. In *Studies on the Development of Behavior and the Nervous System, 3*. (Gottlieb, G., ed.) Academic Press, New York.

Gottschalk, L. A. and Auerbach, A. H. (eds.) (1966). *Methods of Research in Psychotherapy*. Appleton-Century-Crofts, New York.

Gould, S. J. and Lewontin, R. C. (1979). The spandrels of San Marco and the Panglossian paradigm: a critique of the adaptionist programme. *Proc. Roy. Soc. B. 205*, 581–98.

Goy, R. W. (1979). Sexual compatability in rhesus monkeys. In *Sex, Hormones and Behavior. Ciba Foundation Symp. 62*, 209–20.

Grafan, A. (1979). The hawk-dove game played between relatives. *Anim. Behav. 27*, 905–7.

Gray, J. and Lissmann, H. W. (1946). The co-ordination of limb movements in the amphibia. *J. exp. Biol. 23*, 133–42.

Green, R. (1979). Sex-dimorphic behaviour development in the human. In *Sex, hormones and behaviour. Ciba Foundation Symp. 62*, 59–80.

Hailman, J. P. (1967). The ontogeny of an instinct. *Behaviour Suppl.* 15.

Haldane, J. B. S. (1932). *The Causes of Evolution*. Longmans Green, London.

Halliday, T. R. (1976). The libidinous newt. An analysis of

variations in the sexual behaviour of the smooth newt. *Anim. Behav. 24.* 398–414.

Halliday, T. R. and Sweatman, H. P. A. (1976). To breathe or not to breathe; the newt's problem. *Anim. Behav. 24,* 551–61.

Hamburg, D. A. and McCown, E. R. (eds.) (1979). *The Great Apes.* Benjamin/Cummings, Menlo Park, California.

Hames, R. B. (1979). Relatedness and interaction among the Ye' Kwana: a preliminary analysis. In Chagnon and Irons.

Hamilton, W. D. (1964). The genetical theory of social behaviour. *J. Theor. Biol. 7,* 1–52.

Harcourt, S. and Stewart, K. (1979). Social relationships between adult male and female mountain gorilla in the wild. *Anim. Behav. 27,* 325–42.

Harlow, H. F. and Zimmermann, R. R. (1959). Affectional responses in the infant monkey. *Science 130,* 421–32.

Harré, R. (1979). Comments. In *Human Ethology.* (Cranach, M. von, *et al.,* eds.) Cambridge University Press.

Harré, R. and Secord, P. F. (1972). *The Explanation of Social Behaviour.* Oxford University Press.

Harris, G. W. (1955). *Neural Control of the Pituitary Gland.* Arnold, London.

Harris, G. W., Michael, R. P. and Scott, P. P. (1958). Neurological site of action of stilboestrol in eliciting sexual behaviour. *Ciba Foundation Symp.* on the *Neurological Basis of Behaviour.* Churchill, London.

Harris, M. (1968). *The rise of anthropological theory.* Cromwell, New York.

Harris, M. (1974). *Cows, Pigs, Wars and Witches.* Fontana, London.

Hart, M't. (1978). A study of a short term behaviour cycle: creeping through in the three-spined stickleback. *Behaviour 67,* 1–66.

Hartley, P. H. T. (1953). An ecological study of the feeding habits of the English titmice. *J. Anim. Ecol. 22,* 261–88.

Hassenstein, B. (1961). Wie sehen Insekten Bewegungen? *Naturwiss 48,* 207–14.

Hausfater, G. (1975). Dominance and reproduction in baboons: a quantitative analysis. *Contributions to Primatology 7,* 1–150.

Heider, F. (1958). *The Psychology of Interpersonal Relations.* Wiley, New York.

Heller, R. and Milinski, M. (1979). Optimal foraging of sticklebacks on swarming prey. *Anim. Behav. 27,* 1127–41.

Herbert, J. (1978). Neuro-hormonal integration of sexual behaviour in female primates. In Hutchison.

Hershkowitz, M. and Samuel, D. (1973). The retention of learning during metamorphosis of the crested newt *(Triturus cristatus)*. *Anim. Behav. 21*, 83–5.

Hess, E. H. (1959). Natural preferences of chicks and ducklings for objects of different colours. *Psych. Rep. 2*, 477–83.

Hess, E. H. (1970). Ethology and developmental psychology. In *Carmichael's Manual of Child Psychology*. (Mussen, P. H., ed.) Wiley, New York.

Hess, W. R. (1943). Das Zwischenhirn als Koordinationsorgan. *Helv. Physiol. Acta 1*, 549–65.

Hinde, R. A. (1953a). The conflict between drives in the courtship and copulation of the Chaffinch. *Behaviour 5*, 1–31.

Hinde, R. A. (1953b). Appetitive behaviour, consummatory act, and the hierarchical organization of behaviour – with special reference to the Great Tit *(Parus major)*. *Behaviour 5*, 189–224.

Hinde, R. A. (1953c). A possible explanation of paper-tearing behaviour in birds. *Brit. Birds 46*, 21–3.

Hinde, R. A. (1956). The biological significance of the territories of birds. *Ibis 98*, 340–69.

Hinde, R. A. (1959a). Some recent trends in ethology. In Koch.

Hinde, R. A. (1959b). Some factors influencing sexual and aggressive behaviour in male Chaffinches. *Bird Study 6*, 112–22.

Hinde, R. A. (1959c). Behaviour and speciation in birds and lower vertebrates. *Biol. Rev. 34*, 85–128.

Hinde, R. A. (1960). Energy models of motivation. *Sym. Soc. exp. Biol. 14*, 199–213.

Hinde, R. A. (1961). The establishment of parent-offspring relations in birds, with some mammalian analogies. In Thorpe and Zangwill.

Hinde, R. A. (1962). Some aspects of the imprinting problem. *Sym. Zool. Soc. Lond. 8*, 129–38.

Hinde, R. A. (1965). Interaction of internal and external factors in integration of canary reproduction. In *Sex and Behavior*. (Beach, F. A., ed.) Wiley, New York.

Hinde, R. A. (1970). *Animal Behaviour: a synthesis of ethology and comparative psychology*. (2nd ed.). McGraw-Hill, New York.

Hinde, R.A. (1972). Aggression. In *Biology and the Human Social Sciences*. (Pringle, J. W. S., ed.) Clarendon, Oxford.

Hinde, R. A. (ed.) (1972). *Non-verbal Communication*. Cambridge University Press, London.

Hinde, R. A. (1974). *The Biological Bases of Human Social Behaviour*. McGraw-Hill, New York.

Hinde, R. A. (1975). The concept of function. In Baerends, Beer and Manning.

Hinde, R. A. (1979). *Towards Understanding Relationships*. Academic Press, London.

Hinde, R. A. (1981). Animal signals: ethological and games theory approaches are not incompatible. *Anim. Behav. 29*, 535–42.

Hinde, R. A. (in press a). Attachment: conceptual and biological considerations. In *The Place of Attachment in Human Behaviour*. (Parkes, C. and Stevenson-Hinde, J., eds.)

Hinde, R. A. (in press b). Ethological contributions to the study of child development. In *Manual of Child Psychology*. (Mussen, P., Campos, J. J. and Haith, M. M. eds.)

Hinde, R. A. and Fisher, J. (1951). Further observations on the opening of milk bottles by birds. *Brit. Birds 44*, 393–6.

Hinde, R. A. and McGinnis, L. (1977). Some factors influencing the effects of temporary mother-infant separation – some experiments with rhesus monkeys. *Psychol. Med. 7*, 197–212.

Hinde, R. A., Rowell, T. E. and Spencer-Booth, Y. (1964). Behaviour of socially living rhesus monkeys in their first six months. *Proc. Zool. Soc. London, 143*, 609–49.

Hinde, R. A. and Steel, E. A. (1966). Integration of the reproductive behaviour of female canaries. *Symp. Soc. Exp. Biol. 20*, 401–26.

Hinde, R. A. and Steel, E. A. (1972). Reinforcing events in the integration of canary nest-building. *Anim. Behav. 20*, 514–25.

Hinde, R. A. and Steel, E. (1978). The influence of daylength and male vocalizations on the estrogen-dependent behavior of female canaries and budgerigars. *Adv. Study Behav. 8*, 40–74.

Hinde, R. A. and Stevenson, J. G. (1969). Integration of response sequences. *Adv. Study Behav. 2*, 267–96.

Hinde, R. A. and Stevenson, J. G. (1970). Goals and response control. In *Development and Evolution of Behaviour, 1*. (Aronson, L. R., Tobach, E., Rosenblatt, J. S. and Lehrman, D. S., eds.) Freeman, New York.

Hinde, R. A. and Stevenson-Hinde, J. (eds.) (1973). *Constraints on Learning: Limitations and Predispositions*. Academic Press, London.

Hinde, R. A. and Stevenson-Hinde, J. (1976). Towards understanding relationships: dynamic stability. In Bateson and Hinde.

Hogan, J. A. and Bols, R. J. (1980). Priming of aggressive motivation in Betta splendens. *Anim. Behav. 28*, 135–42.

Hogan, J. A., Kruijt, A. J. P. and Frijlink, J. H. (1975)

'Supernormality' in a learning situation. *Zeits f. Tierpsychol. 38,* 212–18.

Holst, E. von, and Mittelstaedt, H. (1950). Das Reafferenzprinzip. *Naturwiss. 37,* 464–76.

Holst, E. von, and Saint Paul, U. von (1963). On the functional organization of drives. *Anim. Behav. 11,* 1–20, translated from *Naturwiss. 18,* 409–22.

Hooff, J. A. R. A. M. von (1972). A comparative approach to the phylogeny of laughter and smiling. In Hinde.

Horn, G. (1979). Imprinting – in search of neural mechanisms. *Trends in Neurosciences* September, 1979, 219–22.

Horn, G. and Hinde, R. A. (eds.) (1970). *Short-term Processes in Neural Activity and Behaviour.* Cambridge University Press.

Horridge, G. A. and Sandeman, D. C. (1964). Nervous control of optokinetic responses in the crab, *Carcinus. Proc. Roy. Soc. B, 161,* 216–46.

Houston, A. and McFarland, D. (1976). On the measurement of motivational variables. *Anim. Behav. 24,* 459–75.

Huber, F. (1978). The insect nervous system and insect behaviour. *Anim. Behav. 26,* 969–81.

Huntingford, F. A. (1976a). An investigation of the territorial behaviour of the three-spined stickleback using principal components analysis. *Anim. Behav. 24,* 822–34.

Huntingford, F. A. (1976b). The relationship between inter- and intra-specific aggression. *Anim. Behav. 24,* 485–97.

Hutchison, J. B. (1978). Hypothalamic regulation of male sexual responsiveness to androgen. In Hutchison.

Hutchison, J. B. (ed.) (1978). *Biological Determination of Sexual Behaviour.* Wiley, Chichester.

Hutchison, J. B. and Lovari, S. (1976). Effects of male aggressiveness in behavioural transitions in the reproductive cycle of the barbary dove. *Behaviour 59,* 296–318.

Hutt, C. and Ounstead, C. (1966). The biological significance of gaze aversion with particular reference to the syndrome of infantile autism. *Behav. Science 11,* 346–56.

Huxley, J. S. (1942). *Evolution, the Modern Synthesis.* Allen and Unwin, London.

Immelmann, K., Piltz, A. and Sossinka, R. (1977). Experimental investigation of the function of mouth markings in nestlings of the Zebra finch. *Zeits. f. Tierpsychol. 45,* 210–18.

Irons, W. (1979a). Natural selection, adaptation and human social behaviour. In Chagnon and Irons.

Irons, W. (1979b). Culture and biological success. In Chagnon and Irons.

Irons, W. (1979c). Editorial contribution. In Chagnon and Irons.

Jackson, D. D. (1959). Family interaction, family homeostasis and some implications for conjoint family psychotherapy. In *Individual and Familial Dynamics*. (Masserman, J. H., ed.) Grune & Stratton, New York.

James, H. (1959). Flicker: an unconditioned stimulus for imprinting. *Canad. J. Psychol. 13*, 59–67.

Jander, U. von. (1966). Untersuchungen zur Stammesgeschichte von Putzbewegungen von Tracheaten. *Zeits. f. Tierpsychol. 23*, 799–844.

Jarman, P. J. (1974). The social organization of antelope in relation to their ecology. *Behaviour 48*, 215–67.

Jaspars, J. M. F. and Leeuw, J. A. de (1980). Genetic-environment covariation in human behaviour genetics. In *Psychometrics for Educational Debate*. (Kamp, L. J. T. van der *et al.*, eds.) Wiley, Chichester.

Jay, P. C. (1962). Aspects of maternal behavior among langurs. *Ann. N.Y. Acad. Sci. 102*, 468–76.

Kandel, E. R. (1976). *Cellular Basis of Behavior*. Freeman, San Francisco.

Kandel, E. R. (1978). A cell-biological approach to learning. Grass Lecture Monogr. 1. *Soc. Neuroscience*, Bethesda.

Kawai, M. (1963). On the newly acquired behaviors of the natural troop of Japanese monkeys on Koshima Island. *Primates 4*, 113–15.

Kear, J. (1962). Food selection in finches with special reference to interspecific differences. *Proc. Zool. Soc. Lond. 138*, 163–204.

Kelley, H. H. (1971). *Attribution in Social Interaction*. General Learning Press, Morristown, N.J.

Kelley, H. H. (1979). *Personal Relationships*. Erlbaum, Hillsdale, N.J.

Keverne, E. B., Meller, R. E. and Martinez-Arias, A. M. (1978). Dominance, aggression and sexual behaviour in social groups of talapoin monkeys. In *Recent Advances in Primatology*. (Chivers, D. J. and Herbert, J. eds.). Vol. 1. Academic Press, London.

Kimble, G. A. (ed.) (1967). *Foundations of conditioning and learning*. Appleton-Century-Crofts, New York.

Kling, J. W. (1971). Learning: an introductory survey. In *Experimental Psychology*, 3rd edition. (Kling, J. W. and Riggs, L. A., eds.) Holt, Rinehart, New York.

Kling, J. W. and Stevenson, J. G. (1970). Habituation and extinction. In *Short-term Changes in Neural Activity and Behaviour*. (Horn, G. and Hinde, R. A., eds.) Cambridge University Press.

Klopfer, P. and Klopfer, M. (1977). Compensatory responses of goat mothers to their impaired young. *Anim. Behav. 25*, 286–91.

Knowlton, N. (1979). Reproductive synchrony, parental investment, and the evolutionary dynamics of sexual selection. *Anim. Behav. 27*, 1022–33.

Koch, S. (1954). Clark, L. Hull. In *Modern Learning Theory*. (Estes, W. *et al.*, eds.) Appleton-Century-Crofts, New York.

Koch, S. (ed.) (1959). *Psychology: a Study of a Science*. McGraw-Hill, New York.

Konorski, J. (1948). *Conditioned Reflexes and Neuron Organization*. Cambridge University Press.

Kortlandt, A. (1955). Aspects and prospects of the concept of instinct. *Arch neérl Zool. 11*, 155–284.

Kraemer, G. W. and McKinney, W. T. (1979). Interactions of pharmacological agents which alter biogenic amine metabolism and depression. *Journal of Affective Disorders 1*, 33–54.

Krebs, J. R. (1976). Review of E. O. Wilson's *Sociobiology*. *Anim. Behav. 24*, 709–10.

Krebs, J. R. (1978). Optimal foraging: decision rules for predators. In Krebs and Davies.

Krebs, J. R. and Davies, N. B. (eds.) (1978). *Behavioural Ecology*. Blackwell, Oxford.

Krebs, J. R., Kacelnik, A. and Taylor, P. J. (1978). Optimal sampling by foraging birds. *Nature 275*, 27–30.

Krebs, J. R., MacRoberts, M. H. and Cullen, J. M. (1972). Flocking and feeding in the great tit – an experimental study. *Ibis 114*, 507–30.

Krebs, J. R., Ryan, J. C. and Charnov, E. L. (1974). Hunting by expectation or by optimal foraging? *Anim. Behav. 22*, 953–64.

Kruijt, J. P. (1964). Ontogeny of social behaviour in Burmese red junglefowl *(Gallus gallus spadiceus* Bonnaterre). *Behaviour Suppl. 12*.

Kruuk, H. (1975). Functional aspects of social hunting by carnivores. In Baerends, Beer and Manning.

Kummer, H. (1978). On the value of social relationships to non-human primates: a heuristic scheme. *Social Sci. Information 17*, 687–705.

Kummer, H., Götz, W. and Angst, W. (1974). Triadic differentiation: an inhibitory process protecting pair bonds in baboons. *Behaviour 49*, 62–87.

La Barre, W. (1947). The cultural basis of emotions and gestures. *J. Pers. 16.*

Lack. D. (1939). The behaviour of the robin: I and II. *Proc. Zool. Soc. Lond. A 109*, 169–78.

Lack, D. (1947). *Darwin's Finches.* Cambridge University Press.

Lack, D. (1954). *The Natural Regulation of Animal Numbers.* Clarendon, Oxford.

Lack, D. (1966). *Population Studies of Birds.* Clarendon, Oxford.

Lack, D. (1968). *Ecological Adaptations for Breeding in Birds.* Methuen, London.

Lawick-Goodall, J. van (1968). The behaviour of free-living chimpanzees in the Gombe Stream Reserve. *Anim. Behav. Monogr. 1*, 3.

Lawick-Goodall, J. van (1971). *In the Shadow of Man.* Houghton Mifflin, Boston.

Leach, E. (1961). *Pul Elija, a Village in Ceylon: a Study of Land Tenure and Kinship.* Cambridge University Press.

Leach, E. (1972). The influences of cultural context on non-verbal communication in man. In Hinde.

Lee, R. B. and De Vore, I. (1968). *Man the Hunter.* Aldine-Atherton, Chicago.

Lehrman, D. S. (1953). A critique of Konrad Lorenz's theory of instinctive behaviour. *Quart. Rev. Biol. 28*, 337–63.

Lehrman, D. S. (1955). The physiological basis of parental feeding behaviour in the Ring Dove (*Streptopelia risoria*). *Behaviour 7*, 241–86.

Lehrman, D. S. (1970). Semantic and conceptual issues in the nature–nurture problem. In *Development and Evolution of Behaviour.* (Aronson, L. R. *et al.*, eds.) Freeman, San Francisco.

Lehrman, D. S. (1974). Can psychiatrists use ethology? In *Ethology and Psychiatry.* (White, N. F., ed.) University of Toronto.

Le Magnen, J. (1952). Les Phénomènes olfacto-sexuels chez le rat blanc. *Arch. Sci. Physiol. 6*, 295–331.

Lévi-Strauss, C. (1962). *La Penseé Sauvage.* Plon, Paris.

Lewontin, R. C. (1970). The units of selection. *Ann. Rev. Ecol. and Systematics 1*, 1–18.

Lewontin, R. C. (1975). Genetic aspects of intelligence. *Amer. Rev. Genetics 9*, 387–405.

Lindauer, M. (1975). Evolutionary aspects of orientation and learning. In Baerends, Beer and Manning.

Lockard, J. S. (1980). *The Evolution of Human Social Behaviour*. Elsevier, New York.

Logan, F. A. (1959). The Hull-Spence Approach. In Koch.

Lorenz, K. (1935). Der Kumpan in der Umwelt des Vogels. *J. f. Ornith. 83*, 137–213, 289–413.

Lorenz, K. (1937). Uber die Bildung des Instinktbegriffes. *Naturwiss 25*, 289–300, 307–18, 324–31.

Lorenz, K. (1941). Vergleichende Bewegungsstudien an Anatinen. *Suppl. J. Ornith. 89*, 194–294.

Lorenz, K. (1950a). The comparative method in studying innate behaviour patterns. *Sym. Soc. Exp. Biol. 4*, 221–68.

Lorenz, K. (1950b). Ganzheit und Teil in der tierischen und menschlichen Gemeinschaft. *Studium Generale* 3/9.

Lorenz, K. (1958). Methods of approach to the problems of behaviour. In *Studies in Animal and Human Behaviour*. (1970). Methuen, London.

Lorenz, K. (1965). *Evolution and Modification of Behavior*. University of Chicago.

Lorenz, K. (1966). *On Aggression*. Methuen, London.

Lorenz, K. (1970). *Studies in Animal and Human Behaviour*, Vols. 1 and 2. (Translated by R. Martin). Harvard University Press, Cambridge, Mass.

Lorenz, K. and Tinbergen, N. (1939). Taxis und Instinkthandlung in der Eirolbewegung der Graugans: I. *Z. Tierpsychol. 2*, 1–29.

Luckmann, T. (1979). Personal identity as an evolutionary and historical problem. In *Human Ethology*. (Cranach, M. von *et al.*, eds.) Cambridge University Press.

MacArthur, R. H. and Pianka, E. R. (1966). On the optimal use of a patchy environment. *Amer. Nat. 100*, 603–9.

Mackintosh, N. J. (1973). Stimulus selection: learning to ignore stimuli that predict no change in reinforcement. In Hinde and Stevenson-Hinde.

McCabe, B. J., Horn, G. and Bateson, P. P. G. (1981). Effects of restricted lesions of the chick forebrain on the acquisition of filial preferences during imprinting. *Brain Research, 205*, 29–37.

McCall, R. B. and Kagan, J. (1969). Individual differences in the infant's distribution of attention to stimulus discrepancy. *Devel. Psychol. 2*, 90–8.

McCleery, R. H. (1978). Optimal behaviour sequences and decision making. In Krebs and Davies.

McClintock, M. K. (in press). Simplicity from complexity: a

naturalistic approach to behavior and neuroendocrine function. In *Directions for Methodology of Social and Behavioral Science*. (Silberman, I., ed.) Jossey Bass, San Francisco.

MacDonnell, M. F., and Flynn, J. P. (1966). Control of sensory fields by stimulation of hypothalamus. *Science, 152*, 1406–8.

McFarland, D. (1966). On the causal and functional significance of displacement activities. *Zeits. f. Tierpsychol. 23*, 217–35.

McFarland, D. (1971). *Feedback Mechanisms in Animal Behaviour*. Academic Press, London.

McFarland, D. J. (1974a). Time-sharing as a behavioural phenomenon. *Adv. Study Behav. 5*, 201–25.

McFarland, D. (ed.) (1974b). *Motivational Control and Systems Analysis*. Academic Press, London.

McFarland, D. (1976). Form and function in the temporal organization of behaviour. In Bateson and Hinde.

McFarland, D. (1978). Hunger in interaction with other aspects of motivation. In *Hunger Models: Computable Theory of Feeding Control*. (Booth, D., ed.) Academic Press, London.

McFarland, D. and Sibly, R. (1972). Unitary drives revisited. *Anim. Behav. 20*, 548–63.

McFarland, D. J. and Sibly, R. M. (1975). The behavioural final common path. *Phil. Trans. Roy. Soc. London 27*, 265–93.

McGrew, W. C., Tutin, C. E. G. and Baldwin, P. J. (in press). Chimpanzees, tools and termites. Man.

McGuire, M. T. and Fairbanks, L. A. (1977). *Ethological Psychiatry*. Grune and Stratton, New York.

Maier, N. R. F. and Schneirla, T. C. (1935). *Principles of Animal Psychology*. McGraw-Hill, New York.

Main, M. (in press). Avoidance in the service of proximity. In *Behavioural Development: The Bielefeld Interdisciplinary Project, New York*. (Immelmann, K., Barlow, G., Main, M. and Petrinovitch, L., eds.) Cambridge University Press.

Main, M. and Weston, D. R. (in press). The independence of infant-mother and infant-father attachment relationships: security of attachment characterizes relationships, not infants. *Child Dev.*

Maitland-Bradfield, R. (1973). *A natural history of associations*. Duckworth, London.

Malinowski, B. (1929). *The Sexual Life of Savages*. Harcourt, Brace and World, New York.

Malthus, T. R. (1803). *An Essay on Population*. Murray, London.

Manning, A. (1979). *An Introduction to Animal Behaviour*, 3rd ed. Arnold, London.

Marler, P. (1955). Studies of fighting in chaffinches: (2) The effect on dominance relations of disguising females as males. *Brit. J. Anim. Behav. 3*, 137–46.

Marler, P. (1956a). Behaviour of the chaffinch (*Fringilla coelebs*). *Behaviour Suppl. 5*, 1–184.

Marler, P. (1956b). Studies of fighting in chaffinches: (3) Proximity as a cause of aggression. *Brit. J. Anim. Behav. 4*, 23–30.

Marler, P. and Mundinger, P. (1971). Vocal learning in birds. In *Ontogeny of Vertebrate Behavior*. (Moltz, H., ed.) Academic Press, New York.

Marshall, F. H. A. (1942). Exteroceptive factors in sexual periodicity. *Biol. Rev. 17*, 68–90.

Masserman, J. H. (1943). *Behavior and Neurosis*. Chicago.

Maynard Smith, J. (1964). Group selection and kin selection. *Nature 201*, 1145–7.

Maynard Smith, J. (1976a). Evolution and the theory of games. *Amer. Sci. 64*, 41–5.

Maynard Smith, J. (1976b). Group selection. *Quart. Rev. Biol. 51*, 277–83.

Maynard Smith, J. (1977). Parental investment: a prospective analysis. *Anim. Behav. 25*, 1–9.

Maynard Smith, J. (1978). In defence of models. *Anim. Behav. 26*, 632–3.

Maynard Smith, J. and Parker, G. A. (1976). The logic of asymmetric contests. *Anim. Behav. 24*, 159–75.

Maynard Smith, J. and Price, G. R. (1973). The logic of animal conflict. *Nature 246*, 15–18.

Mayr, E., Hinde, R. A. and Andrew, R. J. (1956). Die systematische Stellung der Gattung Fringilla. *J. f. Ornith. 97*, 258–73.

Michael, R. P. (1971). Neuroendocrine factors regulating primate behavior. In *Frontiers in Neuroendocrinology*. (Martini, L. and Ganong, W. F., eds.) Oxford University Press.

Michel, G. F. (1977). Experience and progesterone in ring dove incubation. *Anim. Behav. 25*, 281–5.

Miller, G. A., Galanter, E. and Pribram, K. H. (1960). *Plans and the Structure of Behavior*. Holt, Rinehart, New York.

Miller, N. E. (1959). Liberalization of basic S-R concepts: extensions to conflict, behavior, motivation and social learning. In Koch.

Mineka, S. and Suomi, S. J. (1978). Social separation in monkeys. *Psychol. Bull. 85*, 1376–1400.

Mittelstaedt, H. (1962). Control systems of orientation in insects. *Ann. Rev. Entomol. 7*, 177–98.

Moltz, H., and Stettner, L. J. (1961). The influence of patterned-light deprivation on the critical period for imprinting. *J. Comp. Physiol. Psychol. 54*, 279–83.

Moore, B. R. (1973). The role of directed Pavlovian reactions in simple instrumental learning in the pigeon. In Hinde and Stevenson-Hinde.

Morgan, M. J. (1974). Resistance to satiation. *Anim. Behav. 22*, 449–66.

Moruzzi, G. (1958). The functional significance of the ascending reticular system. *Arch. ital. Biol. 96*, 17–28.

Murdock, G. P. (1949). *Social Structure*. Macmillan, New York.

Murton, R. K. and Westwood, N. J. (1977). *Avian Breeding Cycles*. Clarendon, Oxford.

Nelson, J. B. (1975). Functional aspects of behaviour in the Sulidae. In Baerends, Beer and Manning.

Newcomb, T. M. (1961). *The Acquaintance Process*. Holt, Rinehart, New York.

Newcomb, T. M. (1971). Dyadic balance as a source of clues about interpersonal attraction. In *Theories of Attraction and Love*. (Murstein, B. I., ed.) Springer, New York.

Nice, M. M. (1943). Studies in the life-history of the song sparrow. *Trans. Linn. Soc. N.Y. 6*, 1–328.

Nicholson, A. J. (1933). The balance of animal populations. *J. Anim. Ecol. 2*, 132–78.

Noirot, E. (1964). Changes in responsiveness to young in the adult mouse: IV. The effect of an initial contact with a strong stimulus. *Anim. Behav. 12*, 442–5.

Noonan, K. M. (1978). Sex ratio of parental investment in colonies of the social wasp. *Polistes fuscatus. Science, 199*, 1354–6.

Northup, L. R. (1977). Temporal patterning of grooming in three lines of mice. *Behaviour 61*, 1–25.

Nottebohm, F. (1967). The role of sensory feedback in the development of avian vocalizations. *Proc. 14th Int. Ornith. Cong. Oxford.* 265–80. Blackwell, Oxford.

Nottebohm, F. (1971). Neural lateralization of vocal control in a passerine bird. I. Song. *J. Exp. Zool. 177*, 229–62.

Nottebohm, F. (1972). Neural lateralization of vocal control in a passerine bird. II. Subsong, and a theory of vocal learning. *J. Exp. Zool. 179*, 35–50.

Nottebohm, F. (1980). Brain pathways for vocal learning in birds.

A review of the first 10 years. *Progress in Psychobiol. and Physiol. Psychol.* Vol. 9, 85–124.

Nottebohm, F., Stokes, T. M. and Leonard, C. M. (1976). Central control of song in the canary. *J. Comp. Neurol. 165*, 457–86.

Orians, G. H. (1969). On the evolution of mating systems in birds and mammals. *Amer. Nat. 103*, 589–603.

Overton, W. F. and Reese, H. W. (1973). Models of development: methodological implications. In *Life-span Developmental Psychology: Methodological Issues.* (Nesselroade, J. R. and Reese, H. W., eds.) Academic Press, New York.

Packer, C. (1977). Reciprocal altruism in *Papio anubis. Nature 265*, 441–2.

Packer, C. (1979). Male dominance and reproductive activity in *Papio anubis. Anim. Behav. 27*, 37–45.

Pantin, C. F. A. (1950). Behaviour patterns in lower invertebrates. *Sym. Soc. exp. Biol. IV*, 175–95.

Park, T. (1961). An ecologist's view. *Bull. ecol. Soc. Amer. 42*, 4–10.

Parker, G. A. and MacNair, M. R. (1979). Models of parent-infant conflict. IV. Suppression: evolutionary retaliation by the parent. *Anim. Behav. 27*, 1210–35.

Parkes, C. M. (1972). *Bereavement: Studies of Grief in Adult Life.* Tavistock, London.

Parkes, C. M. and Stevenson-Hinde, J. (eds.) (in press). *The Place of Attachment in Human Behaviour.* Basic Books.

Patterson, I. J. (1965). Timing and spacing of broods in the black-headed gull, *Larus ridibundus. Ibis 107*, 433–59.

Pavlov, I. P. (1955). *Selected Works.* Central Books, London.

Plapinger, L. and McEwen, B. S. (1978). Gonadalsteroid – brain interactions in sexual differentiation. In Hutchison.

Popp, J. L. and De Vore, I. (1979). Aggressive competition and social dominance theory: synopsis. In Hamburg and McCown.

Pring-Mill, A. F. (1979). Tolerable feed-back a mechanism for behavioural change. *Anim. Behav. 27*, 226–36.

Pyke, G. H., Pulliam, H. R. and Charnov, E. L. (1977). Optimal foraging: a selective review of theory and tests. *Quart. Rev. Biol. 52*, 137–54.

Quinton, D. and Rutter, M. (1976). Early hospital admissions and later disturbances of behaviour: an attempted replication of Douglas's findings. *Devel. Med. Child. Neurol. 18*, 447–59.

Radcliffe-Brown, A. R. (1922). *The Andaman Islanders.* Cambridge University Press.

Rappaport, R. A. (1968). *Pigs for the Ancestors: Ritual in the*

Ecology of a New Guinea People. Yale University Press, New Haven.

Rasmussen, K. (1980). Consort behaviour and mate selection in yellow baboons (*Papio cynocephalus*). Ph.D. thesis, Cambridge University.

Razran, G. (1971). *Mind in Evolution*. Houghton Mifflin, Boston, Mass.

Revusky, St Garcia, J. (1970). Learned associations over long delays. In *Psychology of Learning and Motivation 4*, 1–83. (Bower, G. H., ed.) Academic Press, New York.

Rice, J. C. (1978). Effects of learning constraints and behavioural organization on the association of vocalizations and hunger in Burmese red junglefowl chicks. *Behaviour, 67,* 259–98.

Richard, G. (1979). Ontogenesis and phylogenesis: mutual constraints. *Adv. Study Behav. 9,* 229–78.

Richer, J. (1976). The social-avoidance behaviour of autistic children. *Anim. Behav. 24,* 898–906.

Rioch, D. McK. and Weinstein, E. A. (eds.) (1964). *Disorders of Communication*. Williams and Wilkins, Baltimore.

Roe, A. and Simpson, G. G. (eds.) (1958). *Behaviour and Evolution*. Yale University Press.

Roeder, K. D. (1935). An experimental analysis of the sexual behavior of the praying mantis. *Biol. Bull. 69,* 203–20.

Roeder, K. D. (1963). Ethology and neurophysiology. *Zeits f. Tierpsychol. 20,* 434–40.

Roeder, K. D. (1966). Auditory system of noctuid moths. *Science, 154,* 1515–21.

Roper, T. J. (1976). Self-sustaining activities and reinforcement in nest-building behaviour of mice. *Behaviour 59,* 40–58.

Roper, T. J. (1978). The effect of food deprivation on drinking and running in Mongolian gerbils. *Anim. Behav. 26,* 1264–72.

Rosenblatt, J. S. (1976). Review of Wilson's *Sociobiology*. *Anim. Behav. 24,* 713–15.

Rowan, W. (1926). On photoperiodism, reproductive periodicity, and the annual migration of birds and certain fishes. *Proc. Boston Soc. Nat. Hist. 38,* 147–89.

Rowell, C. H. F. (1961). Displacement grooming in the chaffinch. *Anim. Behav. 9,* 38–63.

Royama, T. (1970). Factors governing the hunting behaviour and selection of food by the great tit. *J. Anim. Ecol. 39,* 619–68.

Rozin, P. (1976). The evolution of intelligence and access to the cognitive unconscious. In *Progress in Psychobiology and*

Physiological Psychology. Vol. 6. (Sprague, J. M. and Epstein, A. N., eds.) Academic Press, New York.

Ruiter, L. de (1956). Countershading in caterpillars. *Arch. néerl Zool. 11*, 285–342.

Ryden, O. (1978). The significance of antecedent auditory experiences on later reactions to the 'seet' alarm-call in great tit nestlings. *Zeits. f. Tierpsychol. 47*, 396–409.

Sade, D. (1972). A longitudinal study of social behavior of rhesus monkeys. In *The Functional and Evolutionary Biology of Primates*. Aldine-Atherton, Chicago.

Sahlins, M. D. (1977). *The Use and Abuse of Biology*. Tavistock, London.

Sameroff, A. J. (1975). Early influences on development: fact or fancy? *Merrill-Palmer Quart. 21*, 267–94.

Sameroff, A. J. and Chandler, M. J. (1975). Reproductive risk and the continuum of caretaking causality. In *Review of Child Development Research, 4*. (Horowitz, F. D., Hetherington, M., Scair-Salapatck, S. and Sregal, G., eds.). University of Chicago Press.

Schaller, G. B. and Lowther, G. R. (1969). The relevance of carnivore behavior to the study of early hominids. *Southwestern J. Anthrop. 25*, 307–41.

Schneirla, T. C. (1940). Further studies on the army-ant behaviour pattern. *J. Comp. Psychol. 29*, 401–9.

Schneirla, T. C. (1966). Behavioural development and comparative psychology. *Quart. Rev. Biol. 41*, 283–302.

Schulman, S. R. (1978). Kin selection, reciprocal altruism, and the principle of maximization: a reply to Sahlins. *Quart. Rev. Biol. 53*.

Schutz, D. P. (1965). *Sensory Restriction*. Academic Press, New York.

Scott, J. P. and Marston, M. V. (1950). Critical periods affecting the development of normal and maladjustive social behavior of puppies. *J. genet. Psychol. 77*, 25–60.

Sebeok, T. (ed.) (1977). *How Animals Communicate*. Indiana University Press.

Sebeok, T. A. and Umiker-Sebeok, J. (eds.) (1980). *Speaking of Apes*. Plenum Press, New York.

Seitz, A. (1940–1). Die Paarbildung bei einigen Cichliden: I. *Z. Tierpsychol. 4*, 40–84.

Seligman, M. E. P. (1970). On generality of the laws of learning. *Psychol. Rev. 77*, 406–18.

Seligman, M. E. P. (1975). *Helplessness: On Depression, Development, and Death*. W. H. Freeman and Company, San Francisco.

Seligman, M. E. P. and Hager, J. L. (1972). *Biological Boundaries of Learning*. Appleton-Century-Crofts, New York.

Sevenster, P. (1961). A causal analysis of a displacement activity (Fanning in *Gasterosteus aculeatus* L.) *Behavior Suppl. 9*, 1–170.

Sevenster, P. (1973). Incompatibility of response and reward. In Hinde and Stevenson-Hinde.

Sevenster-Bol, A. C. A. (1962). On the causation of drive reduction after a consummatory act. *Arch. néerl. Zool. 15*, 175–236.

Seyfarth, R. (1976). Social relationships among adult female baboons. *Anim. Behav. 24*, 917–38.

Seyfarth, R. M. (1977). A model of social grooming among adult female monkeys. *J. Theor. Biol. 65*, 671–98.

Sherman, P. W. (1977). Nepotism and the evolution of alarm calls. *Science 197*, 1246–53.

Sherman, P. W. (in press). The limits of ground squirrel nepotism. In *Sociobiology: beyond nature-nurture?* (Barlow, G. W. and Silverberg, J., eds.) Westview Press, Boulder, Colorado.

Sherrington, C. S. (1906). *Integrative Action of the Nervous System*. Cambridge University Press.

Shettleworth, S. J. (1972). Constraints on learning. *Adv. Study Behav. 4*, 1–68.

Short, R. (1979). Sexual selection and its component parts, somatic and genital selection, as illustrated by man and the great apes. *Adv. Study Behav. 9*, 131–58.

Sibly, R. M. and McFarland, D. (1976). On the fitness of behaviour sequences. *Amer. Nat. 110*, 601–17.

Simpson, M. J. A. (1973). The social grooming of male chimpanzees. In *The Comparative Ecology and Behaviour of Primates*. (Crook, J. H. and Michael, R. P,, eds.) Academic Press, London.

Slater, P. J. B. (1976). Review of *Function and Evolution in Behaviour*. (Baerends, G. P. *et al.*, eds.) *Anim. Behav. 24*, 720.

Slater, P. J. B. (1978). A simple model for competition between behaviour patterns. *Behaviour 67*, 236–58.

Slater, P. J. B. and Ince, S. A. (1979). Cultural evolution in chaffinch song. *Behaviour 71*, 146–66.

Sluckin, W. and Salzen, E. A. (1961). Imprinting and perceptual learning. *Q. J. Exp. Psychol. 13*, 65–77.

Smith, D. G. (1979). Male singing ability and territorial integrity in red-winged Blackbirds. *Behaviour 68*, 192–206.

Smith, J. N. M. and Sweatman, H. P. (1974). Food searching behaviour of titmice in patchy environments. *Ecology 55*, 1216–32.

Smith, N. G. (1966). Adaptations to cliff-nesting in some arctic gulls (*Larus*). *Ibis 108*, 68–83.

Smith, W. J. (1965). Message, meaning and context in ethology. *Am. Nat. 99*, 405–9.

Smith, W. J. (1977). *The Behavior of Communicating*. Harvard Univ. Press, Cambridge, Mass.

Spencer-Booth, Y. and Hinde, R. A. (1967). The effects of separating rhesus monkey infants from their mothers for six days. *J. Child Psychol. Psychiatr. 7*, 179–97.

Spitz, R. A. (1950). Anxiety in infancy: a study of its manifestations in the first year of life. *Int. J. Psycho-Anal. 31*, 138–43.

Sroufe, L. A. and Waters, E. (1976). The ontogenesis of smiling and laughter: a perspective on the organization of development in infancy. *Psychol. Rev. 83*, 173–89.

Sroufe, L. A. and Waters, E. (1977). Attachment as an organizational Construct. *Child Development 48*, 1184–99.

Staddon, J. E. R. and Ayres, S. L. (1975). Sequential and temporal properties of behavior induced by a schedule of periodic food delivery. *Behaviour 54*, 26–59.

Stammbach, E. (1978). On social differential in groups of captive female hamadryas baboons. *Behaviour 67*, 322–38.

Steel, E. (1979). Male-female interaction throughout the oestrous cycle of the Syrian hamster (*Mesocricetus auratus*). *Anim. Behav. 27*, 919–29.

Steel, E. (1980). Changes in females' attractivity and proceptivity throughout the oestrous cycle of the Syrian hamster (*Mesocricetus auratus*). *Anim. Behav. 28*, 256–65.

Steimer, Th. and Hutchison, J. B. (1980). Aromatization of testosterone within a discrete hypothalamic area associated with the behavioural action of androgen in the male dove. *Brain Res. 192*, 586–91.

Stern, D. (1977). *The First Relationship: Infant and Mother*. Fontana/Open Books, London.

Sternglanz, S. H., Gray, J. L. and Murakami, M. (1977). Adult preferences for infantile facial features: an ethological approach. *Anim. Behav. 25*, 108–15.

Stevenson, J. G. (1966). Stimulus generalization: the ordering and spacing of test stimuli. *J. Exp. Anal. Behav. 9,* 457–68.

Stevenson-Hinde, J. G. (1972). Effects of early experience and testosterone on song as a reinforcer. *Anim. Behav. 20,* 430–5.

Stevenson-Hinde, J. (1973). Constraints on reinforcement. In Hinde and Stevenson-Hinde.

Stevenson-Hinde, J. and Roper, R. (1975). Individual differences in reinforcing effects of song. *Anim. Behav. 23,* 729–34.

Suomi, S. J. (in press). Animal models of human psychopathology: relevance for clinical psychology. In *Handbook of research methods in clinical psychology.* (Kendall, P. C. and Butcher, J. N., eds.) Wiley, New York.

Suomi, S. J. and Harlow, H. F. (1972). Social rehabilitation of isolate-reared monkeys. *Developmental Psychology 6,* 487–96.

Suomi, S. J. and Harlow, H. F. (1975). Effects of differential removal from group on social development of rhesus monkeys. *J. Child Psychol. Psychiatry 16,* 149–64.

Suomi, S. J. and Harlow, H. F. (1977). Production and alleviation of depressive behaviors in monkeys. In *Psychopathology: experimental models.* (Maser, J. and Seligman, M. E. P., eds.) Freeman, San Francisco.

Suomi, S. J. and Harlow, H. F. (1978a). Early experience and social development in rhesus monkeys. In *Social and Personality Development.* (Lamb, M., ed.) Holt, Rinehart, New York.

Suomi, S. J. and Harlow, H. F. (1978b). Early separation and behavioral maturation. In *Genetics, Environment and Intelligence.* (Oliverio, A., ed.) Elsevier, Amsterdam.

Sutherland, N. S. (1969). Shape discrimination in rat, octopus and goldfish. *J. Comp. Physiol. Psychol. 67,* 160–76.

Tajfel, H. (ed.) (1978). The psychological structure of intergroup relations. In *Differentiation between Social Groups.* Academic Press, London.

Terrace, H. S. (1968). Discrimination learning, the peak shift and behavioral contrast. *J. Exp. Anal. Behav. 11,* 727–41.

Thibaut, J. W. and Kelley, H. H. (1959). *The Social Psychology of Groups.* Wiley, New York.

Thomas, T. R. and Thomas, C. N. (1973). Mediation of mating induced increase in accessory reproductive organ size of male rats. *Physiol. Behav. 10,* 13–17.

Thorpe, W. H. (1961). *Bird Song.* Cambridge University Press.

Thorpe, W. H. (1963). *Learning and Instinct in Animals.* (1st ed. 1956). Methuen, London.

Thorpe, W. H. (1979). *The Origins and Rise of Ethology*. Heinemann, London.

Thorpe, W. H. and Jones, F. G. W. (1937). Olfactory conditioning and its relation to the problem of host selection. *Proc. Roy. Soc. Ser. B 124*, 56–81

Thorpe, W. H. and Zangwill, O. L. (eds.) (1961). *Current Problems in Animal Behaviour*. Cambridge University Press.

Tinbergen, E. A. and Tinbergen, N. (1972). Early childhood autism – an ethological approach. *Adv. in Ethology 10*.

Tinbergen, J. (1980). Foraging decisions in starlings. Thesis, Rijksuniversiteit te Groningen.

Tinbergen, L. (1960). The natural control of insects in pinewoods: I. Factors influencing the intensity of predation by song birds. *Arch. néerl. Zool. 13*, 265–343.

Tinbergen, N. (1939). The behavior of the Snow Bunting in spring. *Trans. Linn. Soc. N. 5.*

Tinbergen, N. (1942). An objectivistic study of the innate behaviour of animals. *Biblioth. Biother. 1*, 39–98.

Tinbergen, N. (1948). Social releasers and the experimental methods required for their study. *Wilson Bull. 60*, 6–51.

Tinbergen, N. (1951). *The Study of Instinct*. Oxford University Press.

Tinbergen, N. (1952). A note on the origin and evolution of threat display. *Ibis 94*, 160–2.

Tinbergen, N. (1953). *The Herring Gull's World*. Collins, London.

Tinbergen, N. (1958). Curious Naturalists. Country Life, London.

Tinbergen, N. (1963). On aims and methods of ethology. *Z. Tierpsychol. 20*, 410–33.

Tinbergen, N. (1967). Adaptive features of the black-headed gull *Larus ridibundus L. Proc. XIV Int. Orn. Cong.* 43–59.

Tinbergen, N., Impekoven, M. and Franck, D. (1967). An experiment on spacing-out as a defence against predation. *Behaviour 28*, 307–21.

Toates, F. M. and Archer, J. A. (1978). A comparative review of motivational systems using classical control theory. *Anim. Behav. 26*, 368–80.

Tolman, E. C. (1959). Principles of purposive behavior. In Koch,

Trivers, R. L. (1971). The evolution of reciprocal altruism. *Q. Rev. Biol. 46*, 35–57.

Trivers, R. L. (1972). Parental investment and sexual selection. In

Sexual Selection and the Descent of Man. (Campbell, B., ed.) Aldine, Chicago.

Trivers, R. L. (1974). Parent-offspring conflict. *Amer. Zool. 14,* 249–64.

Trivers, R. L. and Hare, H. (1976). Haplodiploidy and the evolution of the social insects. *Science 191,* 249–63.

Trivers, R. L. and Willard, D. E. (1973). Natural selection of parental ability to vary the sex ratio of offspring. *Science 179,* 90–2.

Tschanz, B. (1959). Zur Brutbiologie der Trottellumme *(Uria aalge aalge* Pont.). *Behaviour 14,* 1–100.

Tschanz, B. and Hirsbrunner-Scharf, M. (1975). Adaptations to colony life on cliff ledges. In Baerends, Beer and Manning.

Vayda, P. (1969). Expansion and warfare among swidden agriculturalists. *Amer. Anthrop. 63,* 346–58.

Vince, M. A. (1964). Use of the feet in feeding by the great tit *Parus major. Ibis, 106,* 508–29.

Vine, I. (1973). The role of facial visual signalling in early social development. In *Social Communication and Movement: Studies of Men and Chimpanzees.* (Cranach, M. von and Vine, I., eds.) Academic Press, London.

Waal, F. B. M. de (1977). The organization of agonistic relations within two captive groups of Java-monkeys. *Zeits f. Tierpsychol. 44,* 225–82.

Waal, F. B. M. de (1978). Exploitative and familiarity-dependent support strategies in a colony of semi-free-living chimpanzees. *Behaviour 66,* 268–312.

Waal, F. B. M. de and Roosmalen, A. van (1979). Reconciliation and consolation among chimpanzees. *Behav. Ecol. and Sociobiol. 5,* 55–66.

Walster, E., Walster, G. W. and Berscheid, E. (1978). *Equity Theory and Research.* Allyn and Bacon, Boston.

Washburn, S. L. (1963). Behavior and human evolution. In *Classification and Human Evolution.* (Washburn, S. L., ed.) Viking Fund Publ. Anthrop., New York.

Watzlawick, P., Beavin, J. H. and Jackson, D. D. (1967). *Pragmatics of Human Communication.* Norton, New York.

Wertheim, E. S. (1975). The science and typology of family systems. 2. Further theoretical and practical considerations. *Family Process 14,* 285–300.

White, L. A. (1949). *The Science of Culture.* Farrar, Straus and Giroux, New York.

White, N. F. (ed.) (1974). *Ethology and Psychiatry*. University of Toronto.

Williams, G. C. (1966). *Adaptation and Natural Selection*. Princeton University Press, N.J.

Wilson, E. O. (1975). *Sociobiology*. Harvard Univ. Press, Cambridge, Mass.

Wilson, E. O. (1976). Reply to reviewers of *Sociobiology*. *Anim. Behav. 24*, 716–18.

Wilson, E. O. (1978). *On human nature*. Harvard Univ. Press, Cambridge, Mass.

Wilz, V. J. (1970). The disinhibition interpretation of the 'displacement' activities during courtship in the three-spined stickleback. *Anim. Behav. 18*, 682–7.

Wit, J. de and Hartup, W. W. (1974). *Determinants and Origins of Aggressive Behavior*. Morton, The Hague.

Wrangham, R. (1979). On the evolution of ape social systems. *Social Sci. Information 18*, 335–68.

Wrangham, R. W. (1980). An ecological model of female-bonded primate groups. *Behaviour 75*, 262–300.

Wright, S. (1969). *Evolution and the genetics of populations, vol. 2, The Theory of gene frequencies*. University of Chicago Press, Chicago.

Wynne-Edwards, V. C. (1962). *Animal Dispersion in Relation to Social Behaviour*. Oliver and Boyd, Edinburgh.

Young, W. C. (1969). Psychobiology of sexual behaviour in the guinea pig. *Adv. Study Behav. 2*, 1–111.

Zach, R. (1979). Shell dropping: decision-making and optimal foraging in north-western crows. *Behav. 68*, 106–17.

Zahavi, A. (1977). The testing of a bond. *Anim. Behav. 25*, 246–7.

Zannier-Tanner, E. (1965). Vergleichende Verhaltensuntersuchungen über das Hinlegen und Aufstehen bei Huftieren. *Z. Tierpsychol. 22*, 696–723.

General Index

314   *General Index*

Index of Names